Free All Along

Also Edited by Catherine Ellis and Stephen Drury Smith

*After the Fall: New Yorkers Remember September
2001 and the Years That Followed*
(with Mary Marshall Clark and Peter Bearman)

*Say it Loud: Great Speeches on Civil Rights and
African American Identity*

Say it Plain: A Century of Great African American Speeches

Free All Along

The Robert Penn Warren Civil Rights Interviews

Edited by
Stephen Drury Smith *and*
Catherine Ellis

THE
NEW
PRESS

NEW YORK
LONDON

Requests for permission to reproduce selections from this book should be mailed to:
Permissions Department, The New Press, 120 Wall Street,
31st floor, New York, NY 10005.

Published in the United States by The New Press, New York, 2019
Distributed by Two Rivers Distribution

ISBN 978-1-59558-818-0 (hc)
ISBN 978-1-59558-982-8 (ebook)
CIP data is available

The New Press publishes books that promote and enrich public
discussion and understanding of the issues vital to our democracy and to
a more equitable world. These books are made possible by the enthusiasm
of our readers; the support of a committed group of donors, large and
small; the collaboration of our many partners in the independent media
and the not-for-profit sector; booksellers, who often hand-sell New Press
books; librarians; and above all by our authors.

www.thenewpress.com

Composition by dix!
This book was set in Adobe Garamond

Printed in the United States of America

2   4   6   8   10   9   7   5   3   1

Contents

Introduction

In 1964, the celebrated Southern writer Robert Penn Warren set out on a fact-finding mission with a reel-to-reel tape recorder. His aim was to interview leaders of what some were calling "the Negro Revolution." Warren wanted to find out what their goals were and how they planned to achieve them. He was on assignment for *Look*, a popular national magazine. But the project would also result in an unusual, 450-page meditation on American race relations called *Who Speaks for the Negro?*

The book was published in 1965. Some critics praised it as a valuable window into the African American experience and the freedom movement. Others thought it poorly organized and unrevealing. *Who Speaks for the Negro?* was out of print for decades until Yale University Press reissued the book on its fiftieth anniversary.

Warren was greatly disappointed by the relatively poor sales. Albert Erskine at Random House explained the problem in a letter:

"The real trouble, of course, is the absolute glut of reading material on the subject and the feeling of many people that they have read all they intend to about it."

Warren interviewed nearly four dozen civil rights activists, leaders, and writers for *Who Speaks?* He retained the original recordings and their typed transcriptions, which are now held by the libraries of Yale University and the University of Kentucky. Vanderbilt University has digitized the interviews and created a comprehensive website with transcripts and archival material. A selection of these revealing, wide-ranging conversations is edited and presented here.

In *Who Speaks?* Warren wove together interview excerpts with his own impressions of the speakers and larger observations about the movement. In this edited anthology the focus is on the interviews themselves, framed by some biographical and historical context. They are arranged chronologically. This anthology also features two interviews—with Andrew Young and Septima Clark—left out of Warren's book.

Free All Along draws its title from Warren's interview with the writer Ralph Ellison. It offers the opportunity to hear directly from a range of history-making African Americans at a critical time in the civil rights movement. A major contribution in their own right to our understanding of the black freedom struggle, these remarkable long-form interviews also have pressing relevance today.

When Warren hit the road in the early months of 1964, the civil rights movement was convulsing American society, especially in the Jim Crow South. Over the previous decade, activists had launched boycotts, protest marches, lunch counter sit-ins, voter registration drives, rallies, and mass meetings, all to demand equal rights and equal protection under the law for black Americans. In many communities, whites responded with rage and lethal violence. In 1961,

African American and white Freedom Riders challenged segregation on interstate buses. In Alabama and Mississippi, they were attacked and jailed, and one of their buses was torched. In 1962,
white rioters tried to block an African American student named
James Meredith from entering the University of Mississippi. In
1963, four black girls were murdered in the bombing of Birmingham's Sixteenth Street Baptist Church, National Association for the
Advancement of Colored People (NAACP) organizer Medgar Evers
was murdered outside his home in Jackson, Mississippi, and activist
Fannie Lou Hamer was badly beaten by police in a Winona, Mississippi jail. Also in 1963, Martin Luther King delivered his "I Have a
Dream" speech at the March on Washington for Jobs and Freedom,
and President John F. Kennedy sent Congress his proposed civil
rights legislation. These critical events were the backdrop to Warren's journey of investigation.

Look published Warren's lengthy article "The Negro Now" in
March 1965. *Who Speaks for the Negro?* was published by Random
House two months later. At the time, Warren had long been regarded as one of the nation's foremost authors and poets. His best-
known novel, *All the King's Men*, won the 1947 Pulitzer Prize. It
was made into a movie that won the 1949 Academy Award for best
picture. Warren won the Pulitzer Prize in poetry in 1958 and again
in 1979. He is the only person to have won the prize for both fiction and poetry.

Robert Penn Warren was born in Guthrie, Kentucky, in 1905,
the son of a businessman and a schoolteacher. He grew up on a to-
bacco farm, where his grandfathers—both of whom had fought for
the Confederacy—told stories of the Civil War. Warren attended
Vanderbilt University in Nashville, Tennessee, where he met other
Southern writers who would go on to form a literary group called
the Agrarians. In 1930, they produced a collection of essays, *I'll*

Take My Stand, proclaiming the virtues of agrarian life over modern industrialization. Warren's contribution was an essay called "Briar Patch," which historian David W. Blight describes as an "ambivalent" and "poorly argued" defense of segregation in which Warren contended that rural life best suited the "temperament and capacity" of Southern blacks. Warren's attitudes about race, however, became increasingly progressive over the decades; literary scholar David A. Davis says Warren came to condemn segregation as dangerous and damaging to both blacks and whites. But as commentators worked to understand Warren's conceptions of race—in both his fiction and his journalism—many inevitably cited "Briar Patch." In Blight's words, the essay "haunted Warren for the rest of his life."

Warren left the South to study at the University of California–Berkeley, Yale, and Oxford, where he was a Rhodes scholar. He taught at several colleges and universities, finally landing back at Yale, where he was on the faculty from 1951 to 1973. He died in 1989 in Stratton, Vermont.

Much of Warren's fiction, poetry, and journalism concentrated on race and the relationship between whites and African Americans, particularly in the South. Following the 1954 U.S. Supreme Court's *Brown v. Board of Education* decision, which struck down school segregation laws, Warren set out on a reporting trip through Kentucky, Tennessee, Mississippi, Louisiana, and Arkansas. He asked blacks and whites he met along the way what they thought the South would look like in the wake of *Brown*. The result was a short collection of observations published in 1956 as *Segregation: The Inner Conflict in the South*. Blight calls the collection a "prototype" for what Warren would attempt with the later book.

Warren's interview subjects ranged from senior civil rights leaders to young student activists. Most were men. He met them in their offices, homes, and occasionally at a restaurant or tavern. The conversations were relatively informal, and frequently interrupted by the need to change reels on the tape recorder. Warren asked most of his subjects a similar set of questions, drawn from the writings of Gunnar Myrdal, W.E.B. Du Bois, and James Baldwin. He especially homed in on Du Bois's idea that African Americans possessed a double consciousness, a kind of split psyche. In *The Souls of Black Folk*, Du Bois wrote: "One ever feels his two-ness—an American, a Negro."

Warren also questioned his interviewees about Kenneth B. Clark's critique of the philosophy of nonviolent protest held by Martin Luther King Jr. and others. An influential African American psychologist, Clark did not oppose nonviolence per se, but he said that calling for a nonviolent response to racism and segregation could be unrealistic and unhealthy, given the hostility and danger black people faced in a viciously oppressive society. Warren also quizzed his subjects on the idea proposed by sociologist and economist Gunnar Myrdal, in *The American Dilemma*, that racial reconciliation after the demise of slavery would have been more successful had slaveholders been compensated for their lost property.

Warren used both short excerpts and whole sections of his transcribed interviews to construct *Who Speaks for the Negro?* He organized the work in six chapters, some based on geographic location and some on theme. In the third chapter, "The Big Brass," he chronicles his extensive interviews with eight major leaders of the civil rights struggle, including Malcolm X and Roy Wilkins. Warren's subjects seemed to answer his questions conscientiously, though some were clearly more guarded than others. Critics and historians have singled out the interviews with two fellow writers—James Baldwin and Ralph Ellison—as especially candid and powerful.

Who Speaks for the Negro? drew mixed reviews. The *Atlantic Monthly* described the study as "vivid, searching, and compassionate." The *Charlotte News Review* said, "His searching look at the Negro movement becomes a searching look at the white man and his world—and, by inevitable extension, a searching look at Robert Penn Warren." Albert Murray, a prominent African American writer and critic, said in the *New Leader* that Warren's book, although flawed, was nevertheless "the very best inside report on the Negro civil rights movement by anyone so far." Historian August Meier, however, was scathing and dismissive. "For knowledgeable readers, it will seem a poorly organized, impressionist rehash of what we already know," Meier wrote in *Dissent*. "I found it boring."

In an introduction to the 2014 edition, David W. Blight described the book, especially the final chapter, as a writer's "bluntly honest suggestion to his country, whites and blacks alike, about how to face their history, their current crisis, and themselves." In Blight's words, the book is "no mere oral history; it is a personal testament."

A Note about Transcripts

The edited interviews in *Free All Along* are based on electronic versions of the original typescripts produced for Robert Penn Warren, generously provided by the Robert Penn Warren Center at Vanderbilt University. Warren's interviews were conducted to provide material for a book, not to leave behind recordings that would sound good on the radio or in a podcast. So his questions and the interviewees' answers could be concise or rambling, like any spirited conversation. The dialogue is often interrupted when Warren changes a reel of tape, which happens frequently, since the reels for his portable recorder were small. The original transcripts may contain unintentional errors, especially from recordings that were hard to hear.

We have edited the transcripts with an eye toward clear and engaging reading. We have cut or condensed digressions, repetitions, and tangents that don't support the core elements of a given interview. We have also tried to be faithful to the spirit and substance of the conversations. The back-and-forth is at times lively and sympathetic, at times awkward or guarded. When necessary, we have added a few words [in brackets] to provide names or facts that clarify what's being said. In some cases, Warren's questions are paraphrased for economy of words. But the order of the questions is intact, and we have made no intentional alterations in meaning, tenor, or content of the conversations.

We encourage readers to visit the *Who Speaks for the Negro?* archive at Vanderbilt's website. There are a number of interviews we didn't have room for in this anthology. But foremost it is fascinating to sample the conversations and hear what Warren and his interlocutors sound like.

—Stephen Smith and Kate Ellis

Free All Along

Joe Carter

February 8, 1964

New Orleans, Louisiana

Reverend Joseph Carter was a fifty-five-year-old farmer in 1963 when he defied a crowd of angry whites to become the first African American in more than half a century to register to vote in Louisiana's West Feliciana Parish.

A Baptist clergyman, Carter was aided by organizers of the Congress for Racial Equality (CORE) to challenge the long-standing practice of local officials preventing black people from voting. Carter had been trying unsuccessfully to register for years. When he heard that CORE was holding voter registration clinics in a nearby parish, he asked organizers Rudy Lombard and Ronnie Moore to hold one in West Feliciana. The parish is about thirty-five miles north of Baton Rouge.

In his interview with Warren, Carter recalls a day in August 1963 when he and a fellow pastor went on their own to the courthouse in St. Francisville (the seat of West Feliciana Parish) to try to register. The CORE organizers had offered to go along, but Carter declined their company. He wanted someone local, the Reverend Rudolph Davis, to go with him. At the courthouse, Sherriff W.C. Percy confronted Carter in a hallway and arrested him. Carter was held in the local jail for thirteen hours and was finally released on a $200 bond. Carter's wife, Wilmeda, *encouraged him to drop the effort, fearing he would be injured or killed by the local Ku Klux Klan.*

CORE then began holding weekly registration clinics in the parish. Black people outnumbered whites in West Feliciana two to one. In October, Carter and forty-two other prospective black voters arrived at the courthouse to find a group of local whites blocking the front entrance. So Carter and the others slipped in through a side door, which three officials from the U.S. Department of Justice then guarded. The group had been taught how to take the voter eligibility tests that were said to be required only of African Americans. The parish registrar delayed serving the group until the end of the day. Only four managed to take the test; Carter was the only one to pass. Carter and some of the others were later threatened by local whites, but Carter told Ebony *magazine, "A man is not a first-class citizen, a number one citizen, unless he is a voter."*

Warren chose Carter's interview as the first he would feature in Who Speaks for the Negro? *In an introduction to the 2014 edition of the book, historian David W. Blight says Carter's account helped Warren develop "a profound vision of the sacred significance of the right to vote for people who had never known it."*

JOE CARTER: Well, I met the CORE [organizers]—Rudy Lombard and Ronnie Moore. I met them on a Thursday in August concerning the registering, and I told them that I had tried and that I couldn't get my neighbors to go with me.

I knew that I was a citizen of the United States and not only our own little parish. I was fifty-five years old and I had never done anything to go to jail, to be disenfranchised, but [because of] the state or the parish laws I did not get to register. I could hear over the radio and on the television, they wanted every citizen to vote. Well, after [the CORE organizers] explained to me the vote, I wanted to do it. And I was glad to lead the people here out of their ignorance and enlighten them about how to go about it. So, I made an agreement with them how I would go down and ask the registrar, but I tell them that I didn't just want to go by myself. I would like to have somebody to go with me. Well, at that time there was only just me and one with them from the West Feliciana Parish, where we have another minister, Reverend Washington. He said, "Well, Reverend Davis, he wants to register."

So, Reverend Davis sent me word that we would go to ask to register—he made arrangements for nine o'clock. So, we went down to the registrar's office. Rudy and Danny wanted to go with us. I told them, no, I would rather to go by myself, you know, without having strangers with us. And they says, "Well, if you-all go down and have any trouble, let us know."

When we went in the courthouse we didn't see nobody, we didn't hear nobody. Well, they didn't have any signs, you know, "Registrar's Office." Well, we seen the sheriff's office, we seen the jury room, and we seen the circuit [court] office. We had to inquire, where was the registrar's office?

Well, there was a white man there. We said, "White folks, can you tell us where the registrar is, please?"

He said, "In there." Well, it was two doors—he didn't tell us [which] door. So, we turned around and Reverend Davis went to the assessor's office and asked him. He just say, "Up there."

Well, we went on up and by time we got to the registrar's door, just before we got to the door, the registrar walked out the door and pulled it behind him and stood in front of the door. Said, "Good mornin,' boys, what can I do for you-all?"

So, Reverend Davis said, "Well, we come to see if we could register to vote."

He said, "Well, you got to bring something. You got to show something. You got to carry something."

Reverend Davis turns, he says, "I really don't know what you mean by that. You tell me what you mean, probably I can produce what it takes."

He said, "Well, you got to go back home and get your two registered voters out of the ward where you live."

At that time, the high sheriff had come down the hall, so Reverend Davis said, "Well, the high sheriff knows me. And not only that, all of you here knows me."

He says, "Yes, I know they call you Rudolph Davis, but I couldn't swear to it."

As I turned, [the sheriff] said, "Here boy, here boy, you boy."

Well, I was looking at the registrar you see, and I turned around and I said, "You speakin' to me?"

He said, "Yeah, you come here." So, I turned round and went on back to him. And he walked off down the hall, like he was going back to the sheriff's office. He had a pencil and a card in his hand.

He said, "What's your name?"

I said, "Reverend Joe Carter."

He said, "What's the matter with you fellows? You not satisfied?"

I said, "Not exactly."

He said, "Well, if you ain't, from now on you will be, you hear?"

I said, "Yes, sir."

He said, "Go on back where you come from." I turned to go back.

He said, "I ought to lock you up." Well, I didn't say anything. I just kept walking. I didn't make him any answer.

Then he hollered to the deputy, "Grab him, Dan, don't you hear him raisin' his voice at me? Consider you're under arrest."

Well, I turned my face to him, you know. And then he searched me—started at my heels and come on up searching me. Said, "Take him out there and put handcuffs on him. Lock him up."

Well, I had never been to the jail. [A deputy said,] "Who's been talking to you?"

I said, "Nobody been talking to me. Don't you know we got radios and television and I read the papers?" I said to him, "The *Journal* says it wants all citizens to register and vote."

So, we're going on into the jail and they put me in the cell. They come back about ten minutes later, this young white man come back and unlocked the jail cell and told me to come out. I went on down the hall where the deputy sheriff took my fingerprints first and then stood me over aside the wall and he take my picture. Then he put me on the scales, took my weight, took my height, and asked me how old I was. So, I told him I was fifty-five, three months and five days old today. After that, he asked me did I have any children. I told them I had two daughters, they both live here. And, I had to give my oldest daughter's house number. My baby girl had just moved and I hadn't been there to the new house and I couldn't give them the number.

They take me on back [to the cell]. Then, the high sheriff, he come in the hall, and said, "Put him under that shower. He's musty. Stinks." I didn't say anything. So, they give me the [prisoner] uniform and I went in and start pullin' off clothes.

He says, "Who been talking to you?"

I said, "Nobody."

He said, "You ain't going to tell me, huh?"

I said, "Well, I ain't got nothin' to tell you." I put that coverall on and went on in [the cell].

About nine-thirty or a quarter to ten that night, they came back. Somebody had got [bail] money from somewhere. So, I went home where I had a bunch of people there, waitin' for me.

My wife said, "Joe, you oughtn't have went down there." She said, "Now, if you go back down, I'm going to leave you."

I said, "Well, you can get your clothes and start now, because I'm going back. I'm on my way back tomorrow."

Well, we heard from the neighbors—they said, "Don't go back, don't go back tomorrow."

Well, I was the first man who made the attempt to register, so told them I was going to be the first man to go back.

Clarie Collins Harvey

February 9, 1964

Jackson, Mississippi

Clarie Collins Harvey was a prosperous businesswoman and active civil rights organizer based in Jackson, Mississippi. In 1961, she founded Womanpower Unlimited, which, as she explained to Robert Penn Warren, started from her desire to deliver warm clothes to Freedom Riders unexpectedly jailed in the city. Freedom Riders were African American and white activists traveling together on bus trips through the South to challenge segregation in public transportation. When the riders were arrested in Jackson, Harvey organized local church congregations to donate goods for their care. Then she tapped into a network of women outside Mississippi, who began sending the Freedom Riders everything from bedding to magazines. The work of Womanpower Unlimited, an interracial, interfaith organization, expanded to include organizing rallies, voter registration drives, and business boycotts.

Harvey said in a 1981 interview that Womanpower Unlimited was a bare-bones but highly effective operation. "We had no overhead," she said. "What funds came in went directly where they were needed. We received and paid no salaries. The women cooked [for] hours and nobody got a penny for anything. We were truly volunteers." Womanpower Unlimited fed activists hot meals when they got out of the notorious

Parchman Penitentiary, as well as during major demonstrations. While few women rose to prominence in a movement dominated by men, hundreds of women in Harvey's organization offered core support to movement organizers and activists, unencumbered by "bureaucratic inefficiency and territorial infighting," as historian John Dittmer writes.

The challenge for Harvey was doing all this work while running her family's funeral business. Her morning would begin with planning calls to Womanpower volunteers and then move into a full day at the office arranging and directing funeral services. At night, Harvey said, "there were mass meetings, the rallies, and . . . more planning." She typically put in eighteen- and twenty-hour days.

When Medgar Evers, Mississippi field secretary for the NAACP, was gunned down by a white supremacist, Harvey's two worlds came together. She had met with Evers shortly before his death to discuss organizing tactics. She then served as his mortician. Thousands of mourners came to view Evers's body in her funeral home before it was transported to Arlington National Cemetery.

Clarie Collins was born in Meridian, Mississippi, in 1916 to ambitious, highly educated parents. Her mother was the first African American librarian in Mississippi, and her father, originally a mathematics professor, founded a successful mortuary business. Collins earned her undergraduate degree at Spelman College and a master's degree at Columbia University. When her father died in 1939, Collins returned to Jackson to run Collins Funeral Home and Insurance Company with her mother.

Harvey was a longtime leader in the Methodist church and from a young age traveled abroad to advance ecumenical work and international peace. In the last thirty years of her life, she was appointed to an array of university boards and government advisory committees and won national and international recognition for her work as a business pioneer, community organizer, and Christian leader.

Robert Penn Warren saw Harvey speak at a strategy session of the

Council of Federated Organizations (COFO). More than one hundred organizers had gathered to discuss the voter registration drive planned for the summer of 1964. In Who Speaks for the Negro? *Warren says Harvey is "a woman of education and experience of the world," and describes her as "tall, very handsome [and] fashionably dressed." They met at her house for the conversation he recorded, and he starts by asking how her interest in the civil rights "drive" began.*

CLARIE COLLINS HARVEY: It goes back to the sort of family background that is mine. On my father's side, my grandfather tells that he and his brothers would not be beaten during slavery time. When they had some infraction, the master was angry with them, they would go hide out in the woods and stay until his temper cooled. Then they would come back. But they were such good workers on the place that he would give them some minor punishment. This was right here in Mississippi. Now, on my mother's side of the family, my people were independent merchants, dating back to my great-great-grandfather, who evidently must have been a slave. And, then, after slavery, had set up a little business where he was a peanut vendor and would sell peanuts at the trains as they came into the station there.

ROBERT PENN WARREN: After the Civil War, after the emancipation.

CCH: After the emancipation, in Meridian, Mississippi. Then his son, who was my great-grandfather, through hard work—my mother tells of him working so hard that when he would come in from the fields, you could hear the sweat sloshing in his boots—he worked so hard that he got enough land in Lauderville County to have a plantation and to have many people working for him, living as sharecroppers on the plantation. And then his daughter, who was my grandmother, married an Alabama man. Instead of taking

their share of the family property, acreage, they were given money
to set up a business in Meridian, Mississippi. And I have in my files
downstairs their contract for going into the grocery business, which
was signed back in 1900, where my great-grandfather, my grandfather, and my granduncle all go in this grocery business. Now this
business was operated for about forty years, until my grandfather
got too old and he retired and came and lived here.

Then shifting back to my father's family again, my father was
one of founders of the NAACP here in Jackson, Mississippi. He
and a Mr. [A.J.] Noel and Mr. [John W.] Dixon. For two or three
years only three people would meet, those three men. And then,
finally, when they were just able to get more people interested and
working with it, they started a youth council.

RPW: What year was that, when it was founded, roughly?

CCH: It was in the 1920s.

RPW: Pretty early then.

CCH: That's right. And then along probably in the '30s they
started the first youth council, and I was a member of the first
youth council, along with the daughters of the other two men. And
the daughter of one of the men became Gladys Noel Bates. As an
adult, [she] filed the first suit for the equalization of teachers' salaries in the state of Mississippi. So here, again, is an explanation of
why I'm involved in the civil rights movement—it's family background, tradition, the type of stock from which I come, that makes
me interested in this sort of thing.

One of my daily burdens is my own immediate staff in the office. My secretary, whom I inherited from my mother, has been
with us twenty-five years. She is the sort of person that believes that
everything white is right, and is definitely not for the movement
at all. And then, also, my husband's sister, who comes from the
Northern background that he comes from. She falls right in the

same pattern of this secretary who grew up here in Mississippi, and worked for whites, and learned to feel that they were superior to Negroes. Here are two people who react negatively to Martin Luther King, and against what we are trying to do in the movement. I say this is a daily burden that I have to bear because I don't feel like I can communicate with them. I try to keep posted on the bulletin board all the things that are going on in the movement, and whenever there's an opportunity we do discuss these things. But they are two people who feel that Dr. King isn't doing too much: "I wish Martin Luther King would just go on home and tend to his business." They feel he's in it for personal gain or merit.

RPW: How widespread do you think that notion is?

CCH: I don't think it's very widespread. But I think it's unfortunate that you have people who have a great influence on other people holding that point of view, and not really realizing what the movement is about.

Harvey turns the conversation back to the question of whether violence is a tactic the movement should embrace.

CCH: There is the feeling now, listening to people talk, that they have been patient too long, and that the Justice Department is not doing anything about their grievances. Therefore, they feel that they must take things in their own hands. Here you have the possibility of violence erupting from the Negro against the white group.

RPW: Taking things in their own hands, what would that mean?

CCH: Well, it would mean a fight. It would mean mob violence. It would mean physical action with knives, guns, and what have you. Now what this would solve—it would solve nothing. It will compound the problem. But they just feel that this stuff is so built up. They go down to register [to vote] and the registrar disappears. So they stay there all day and then somebody comes in, "Well, we got to close up now. You have to come back tomorrow." You see, all these harassments and frustrations are just at the explosion point on a lot of people. It's a very real thing now in Mississippi, and may get entirely away from all the nonviolent [action] Martin Luther King is preaching.

Warren asks about Harvey's support of the Freedom Riders, activists from the North and South who challenged racial segregation on Southern bus lines by riding in racially mixed groups. Some were attacked and many were arrested.

CCH: I noticed that some of the girls did not have sweaters. It was very cool, although it was mid-May [of 1961]. Our minister, Reverend E.A. Mays of the Central Methodist Church, was kind enough to take one of my sweaters back to the jail and give it to the young lady. So this planted a seed within me—the need that the [Freedom Riders] were going to have if they remained in our community when they had not come prepared to stay. And the other factor that came out very clearly was that these people had never intended to be arrested in the first place. They were sort of captured coming from Alabama to Mississippi. They were escorted by the police on the buses and they made no stops to use restrooms. So when they got to Jackson, all of them had this tremendous physical urge, and they drove up to the Trailways bus station, and the door to the Negro waiting room had "out of order" on it. So they were funneled by this line of police who were standing there into the white restroom, and they were arrested. They hadn't planned any of this but were forced into it, and to their arrest.

So the idea came to me to call some of the churches and ask if they would make contributions to help provide for the physical needs of the Freedom Riders, and to send me two women from each church. So, by Sunday afternoon, we had twelve women and at least $75 in hand. And from that small beginning we were able to get two hundred women to work across the summer, providing for the needs of these persons. Monies came to us from local groups and from individuals, as well as from people across the country. The sort of thing we did was to send them clothes and toilet articles and writing paper and that sort of thing. We could not go ourselves, as women. We had to send it by ministers or by a lawyer. We went on some occasions and we were asked, "Well, are you a licensed minister?"

"No."

"Well, then you can't go in."

And then, of course, they sent many of the Freedom Riders over to Parchman [penitentiary]. While they were at Parchman, we could do nothing for them. We sent things to them, but the things were not given them. When they [got out] we would meet them at the jail and take them to our homes and churches to feed them and get them cleaned up.

And many of the Freedom Riders said that their sanity was maintained while they were under torturous conditions, in this tremendous heat, and with the brutal treatment they were receiving up in Parchman, because they knew that back in Jackson, Mississippi, there were women who were concerned and interested and who represented something of the mind of the community. They felt that their efforts were not being wasted.

RPW: You think that many people here were waked up by that change?

CCH: Yes, I think that the presence of the Freedom Riders did more for Jackson's Negro community than anything that I know has happened in my years of living here. Because we had been very disunited. We had no sense of unity at all on social issues as Negroes. Particularly for our young people who got jailed with some of the

Freedom Riders—some of them heard of Yale University for the first time because they were cellmates with somebody who had studied at Yale. They heard of universities and colleges that they had never heard of before. They heard of professions that were open that they had never even heard of before—and found out that Negroes did go into them. It gave them an ideal, and a cause, and a hope, and an exposure that they hadn't had. So that besides unifying the community, it did tremendous good for our young people in giving them goals.

RPW: I hadn't thought of that aspect of it.

CCH: Yes. This was tremendous. It also brought courage. We began to look at ourselves and say: Well, you know, maybe we ought not to be just so satisfied living as we are. Maybe there is another way of life that's possible right here. Maybe we don't have to send our children to Los Angeles and to New York and Chicago and Detroit for jobs when they get educated. Maybe they can get their jobs right here if we do certain things for ourselves within our community. As long as we have the people who are going to help open our eyes and make opportunities that are right here, and who are willing to help us—well, why not stay here and do something about it?

RPW: James Baldwin writes in his last book . . .

CCH: Is this *The Fire Next Time?*

RPW: Yes. That the Southern [white] mob does not represent the majority will of the South. He says that this is based on the testimony of those best qualified to observe—those people being the actual embattled fighters on the Southern front. Would that seem to make sense to you?

CCH: I think that makes sense. I think, though, that the mob is the one that gets the publicity. I think that the real tragedy in the South is the people of goodwill who remain silent, who let the mob take over and exert the pressures and get the publicity.

RPW: Baldwin goes on to say that the mob fills a moral vacuum. The other forces can't find any way of expression.

CCH: Yes, the other forces are not courageous enough to find a way of expression. I feel that they could, if they would.

RPW: Is it a problem of organization, too? Fighting a focused organization?

CCH: A lot of the problem is probably of leadership. I think the lack of leadership has been great in the white group, as well as the Negro group, because so many of our best people have been siphoned off—white and Negro—to other areas, because they haven't been able to find the job opportunities and the economic security that they needed within the community. You have thousands moving away every year, white and Negro, some of your best minds.

RPW: Yes, Mississippi has been sort of the seed bag of manpower for the country for a long time.

CCH: Yes. These people that have left would have given us the sort of leadership that we needed to keep the mob in its proper place. Of course, they say this is why the Citizens Council was organized—to prevent mob violence and to get moderate control, but it hasn't worked out this way.

RPW: The old question that we hear over and over again, in one form or another: Can there be a solution for "the Negro problem" without a solution for "the poor white problem," in the South?

CCH: I would think not. I think the two have to go hand in hand. I don't think you can help one without helping the other, and I don't think you *should* help one without helping the other. One of the major problems in the South that has affected both groups is economics, and it's reflected in poor education for whites, as well as poor education for Negroes. And if this problem of economics is helped, then it should spread across the board, and this will mean a tremendous amount to our state. Meeting basic economic needs is really fundamental.

This question of the poor whites and the poor Negroes getting rapport and a working relationship, I think it can be done. Because I don't really feel that they have great antipathy for each other. They have been used by the power structure, pitted against each other, and they really don't have deep-seated resentments against each other. [They] could work together if given an opportunity to do so, and certainly if they felt they were going to better themselves, and better themselves by a cooperative working relationship.

I had an experience the other day, sitting in the bus station in Hammond. I was sitting in what was formerly the white side of the station, and I was the only Negro sitting in there. All the other Negroes were sitting where they had been accustomed to sitting before the law changed. I had eaten breakfast and took a seat, one seat removed from a white lady sitting there. And she leaned over to me and said, "Are you an insurance lady?" And I realized that I had one of my business briefcases, and that's why she asked. We began to talk. And she was definitely poor white. She didn't have any resentment because I was there and she didn't mind the other people staring because we were talking. And she was talking about some of her personal problems, why she had to go to Baton Rouge, and I think this is pretty typical of a private person.

RPW: The other notion: the South cannot change until the North changes. This is said over and over again by Baldwin, by many sociologists, that it is a national problem, not a sectional one.

CCH: I think the problem is an international problem, for that matter. The problem of race and the problem of minorities and the problem of using people. Colonialism is another face on the same type of problem. But I don't think that you could say that the South won't change until the North changed. My reason for remaining in the South and working and struggling is because I am hoping the South will point the way, because the problem is so serious and intense here. I hope we can point the way for the whole nation.

And it's interesting noticing how peoples in other countries—Africa, particularly—are gaining respect for us in America because of the stand we are taking in the civil rights struggle. For example, when I was in Ghana in 1962, I was there for the World Without the Bomb Peace Conference. And a judge in the supreme court there—a Ghanaian woman—said to me, "My dear, your American whites are so childish."

And I said, "What do you mean?"

She said, "They lean over backwards being nice to us here and yet we read about when they go home, they kick you in the teeth." She said, "How do you think that the mother feels when they are nice to the mother and they mistreat the child?"

Now this was a different idea to me altogether, because the Africans that I had known who had come over here to study looked down on me, and other Negroes, because we have been slaves. They never seemed to want to identify with us socially. But here's this whole new respect for us, looking upon us as the children of the Mother Africa, because we are now asserting ourselves and really reminding the people in America that there are certain rights under the Constitution that were guaranteed to us.

RPW: Speaking of Mother Africa, many years ago in reading Du Bois, I came across a discussion of what I think he calls the split in psyche of the American Negro. He says, on one hand there's the pull toward a mystical view of blackness, toward the African heritage, toward the community feeling and loyalties based on that inheritance. This being one impulse. The other impulse is toward entering the Western, European-American cultural tradition and, in the process perhaps, eventually, losing all identity. This division of loyalty.

CCH: Well, I think the experiences of my husband and I might be illustrative of the type of thing Du Bois was talking about. Now, my feeling in Africa was one of complete identification, a feeling of going home and that I really had found my roots. My husband had none of that at all. Africa was just like going to South America, or India, or some other place to him. Europe. So, now, right here within my own family is maybe an illustration of the sort of thing you're talking about.

RPW: Well, how would your feeling for Africa, this sense of home, relate to your activity toward integrated, free society here, which possibly means a loss of identity as a Negro? How do those feelings square?

CCH: I can say this: it being a feeling of home did not mean that I wanted to return there to remain. It just made me feel that I had finally touched base, and that I had put my feet down solid on what my roots were. But, it's from this point that I would want to move forward, and this would mean integration. My feeling about mankind is that we all, no matter what race, are children of God. And that He wants us all to have abundant life, whatever the abundant life means for you, whatever it means for me, based on what our individual personalities are, our backgrounds, our roots and so forth. I want to work for that wherever I am.

I think the split in the psyche comes when a person wants to move away from what his past was, and does not have respect for it, and doesn't admire it. Therefore, he's trying to be absorbed by another thing. It's not that with me. It's recognizing what my past is, as a member of a Negro minority, with relationships and roots in Africa, but it's also working with all of the races so that everybody gets their place in the sun.

RPW: Do you see any change for [white] Southerners to keep their Southernness, their sense of loyalty to a personal heritage, and lose the Negro prejudice? Is the Negro prejudice a necessary part of the Southern heritage, or is it an accidental part of the Southern heritage?

CCH: Yes, I think I understand what you are saying. You're saying if they are going to hold on to what they believe is their Southern tradition and so forth, isn't the matter of prejudice and race a natural part of that? I would say that there hasn't always been race prejudice as a part of the Southern tradition. It's just been a failure to recognize that this servant, this slave who has become a servant, is a part of a people and not a part of a thing. And is not a thing which they own individually and which they love like they do their dog, or their cat, or their horse. But that he is a part of a race that has history and tradition and so forth, and therefore, he is to be respected as an individual. I think this is a growth process that a person has to go through.

Warren asks about a criticism made by some civil rights leaders that middle-class and affluent black people do not contribute as much money to the movement as they could afford to.

CCH: There are several reasons. One major reason is that the struggle has been so hard for so many Negroes. When they individually get into a financial, economically secure place, they want the results of their efforts for themselves. This means the split-level house, the Cadillac car—and I have a Cadillac car, but I have it because we have a funeral business and the public demands it—this means the fur stole. This means all the status symbols and all the things that I couldn't have. All the things I saw the white lady wearing when I was a maid in her home. All the things that Mr. Bob gave his wife when I was gardening in his yard. And I said, whenever I was able to do it, I was going to do it for my wife, too. So it's getting this taste of something when they've had nothing.

It's a short-term thing. They lose sight of the fact that when they individually have "arrived"—according to American materialistic standards—they still have not arrived unless all the other people have arrived, white and Negro too, who are deprived. The only way that you help all of them is by sharing what you have rather than pouring it on yourself.

RPW: A comparison sometimes is made between the Negro communities, on this basis, and Jewish communities. That's the common comparison.

CCH: Yes, and the Jewish do it differently, don't they? They help themselves more. Is that it?

RPW: That's the idea—give more. Not only to Jewish philanthropies, but to general philanthropies, in relation to their income.

CCH: Yes, but [isn't] the economic average [in the] Jewish group higher than the economic average in the Negro group?

RPW: Yes, he does not feel as excluded as a Negro. Even if he was poor on the day of arrival at Ellis Island, he had more hope.

CCH: That's right. He had more opportunity. But the Negro has been right down there in the dirt, working in the dirt and sweating in it. So that when he gets his nose above it, he thinks of himself first. I'm very critical of my friends who can think only of themselves. I think this thing has got to be broad-based if we are to get far.

RPW: How much lack of communication, lack of rapport and sense of responsibility is there on the part of the educated, middle-upper-class Negroes, as compared with the masses of Negroes—the bottom of the heap? How much of a split is there?

CCH: I think the gap is closing there. I think you're getting more intelligent, middle-class Negroes who are interested in the total struggle of the Negro than ten years ago, five years ago. I think your most courageous people, though, are the people that are down on the bottom of the heap, in the Negro group. Because the hardest group to move are the teachers who have economic security. They skirt, you know—go around. And in Womanpower Unlimited, we have a few that come and work but they don't know whether they're going to have their jobs next year [by being active in the movement]. But they are at the point now where they don't care. They believe enough in what's happening to do it. So I think the gap is closing. It's not closing fast enough for me. But I hope—our hope is in our masses.

RPW: I'll read a quotation from [author] Roi Ottley in *New World A-Coming*: "Many [Negroes] look with alarm on a world where they must compete with whites and thus lose their unique situation, or status. They prefer, as one Negro observer remarks, the overvaluation of their achievements and its position behind the walls of segregation to a democratic order that would result in economic and social devaluation for themselves at that time." He follows, though, by saying this: "Nevertheless, this group, whatever its shortcomings, has provided a great economic and cultural progress, and constitutes the leavening group in the general population."

CCH: I'd agree with that.

RPW: Is that changing, in your observation?

CCH: I hope it's changing. I think the younger Negroes are more ready to compete across lines with anybody, anywhere. And I think the very fact that my friend's children are going to prep school in the East indicates that they are preparing their children for the total society, where they must compete anywhere.

RPW: There's a protection in segregation that's no longer important to the "privileged Negro"? He doesn't want to be protected, have his benefits only inside the walls of segregation, or his status? He's ready to compete?

CCH: A large percentage of them are. It's something to give up segregation. I mean, there are advantages to it, definitely. Take my business, the funeral business, for example. One of the reasons that we have been able to do as well as we have in the funeral business is because we can only serve Negroes. And Negroes weren't going to the white funeral homes, so that didn't siphon off people to the other community. But with [desegregation] coming, who knows? Maybe you can just choose your funeral home.

RPW: I've been told that the fact that the Hilton has opened up in New Orleans means that many Negro caterers are being very badly hit. They have actually organized and made a protest to the Negro community for patronizing the nonsegregated restaurant facilities.

CCH: These are the things of which you must be aware when you fight to open these doors. You've got to pay the price for them being opened and it means a loss of some things to you that you've enjoyed. And this is the thing that our [white] mayor hammers on quite a bit. He tells the Negro teachers: "If you get these integrated schools, look at all the jobs that you have now. All the money that you get and you won't be getting this anymore." But the thing that we're working for is the step beyond that, where everybody will have a place. So many of them are teaching now because there was nothing else for them to do, and they would be much better qualified doing something else. We're looking for the time where there will be integrated schools at every level, students and faculty, in the high schools and the junior high schools all across town. And not that just Negroes would be knocked out of jobs and just white people employed.

RPW: The president of the Negro Business Association in St. Louis, a few years ago, wrote an article in the St. Louis paper saying that to encourage integration would be the death of Negro business. Do you find that attitude around here?

CCH: Not yet, because we're too far away from that. St. Louis is a border city and that would be more true there. But I know that it will happen for some businesses. The thing I say to our staff here is we want to be so qualified that we can serve anybody who comes, at any time. Because we don't want to operate a Negro business. We want to operate a business that will serve anybody that wants to come. Yes, some people are going to be lost in the shuffle, individually and business-wise. It's just natural. And you've got to face up to this as a reality. If you've got the stuff, you'll make the grade.

The conversation eventually turns to the experience of black people who migrated to Northern cities in search of opportunity.

CCH: I was thinking of the Negro cults in the North, which have posed as churches but have been able to suck up whole masses of people because of the frustration of the people there. I think of the Black Muslim movement, and so forth. The Negro went North with such tremendous hopes. He thought the kingdom had come on earth and that he would find it there. He didn't expect it here [in the South], but when he went North and didn't find it, and found that a lot of times it was a lot worse than here—that it required more money to operate and he was having to live in an apartment infested with rats and so forth—it became much worse for him. Here, at least, maybe he lived in a shack, but he could get out in the sunshine and have a little garden and have fresh vegetables and so forth. So the frustration was so much greater, you see. The pace was so great, see. He came from a slow-moving, Southern society. And then he had to jump, you know, and so he would change.

Aaron Henry

February 10, 1964

Clarksdale, Mississippi

Aaron Henry was one of the most active and widely recognized leaders of the civil rights movement in Mississippi. In his first speech as the newly appointed state president of the NAACP, in 1959, Henry called for a "new militancy" in the push for racial equality. According to historian John Dittmer, Henry told his audience, "Our actions will probably result in many of us being guests in the jails of the state. We will make these jails temples of freedom." Henry had plenty of opportunities to worship in those "temples" during his years in the movement. He was jailed more than thirty times as he led voter registration drives, the launch of a new political party, and boycotts of white-owned businesses.

Aaron Henry was born in 1922 in the Mississippi Delta. His parents were sharecroppers in Coahoma County; Henry picked cotton as a boy and hated it. He attended high school in Clarksdale, Mississippi. After serving in World War II, Henry earned a degree in pharmacy from Xavier University in New Orleans, returning to Clarksdale to open his own pharmacy. It was the only black-owned drugstore in the area and became, as Henry said, "the gathering place and the hub for political and civil rights planning for three decades."

Though a longtime NAACP member, Henry didn't hesitate to work with a range of civil rights groups. In 1962 he formed a coalition with several of those groups in Mississippi—the Council of Federated Organizations (COFO)—and was appointed president. In 1963, COFO launched a "freedom vote," a mock gubernatorial election to prove that African Americans would vote if given the opportunity. Some eighty thousand black Mississippians symbolically voted for Aaron Henry as governor, along with his running mate Ed King, a white chaplain from Tougaloo College.

The freedom vote helped set the stage for Freedom Summer the following year, which included a statewide campaign to register Mississippi's black population, and the creation of the Mississippi Freedom Democratic Party (MFDP). The MFDP challenged the legitimacy of the state's all-white Democratic Party. In August 1964, MFDP delegates, including Henry, arrived at the Democratic National Convention in Atlantic City intent on unseating the official Mississippi delegation. Their bid failed but Henry remained resolute. He felt that MFDP organizers "learned a great deal about the way things work up in the world of high-level politics—heartbreak and all." In 1979, Henry was elected to Mississippi's House of Representatives, an office he held until 1996.

Robert Penn Warren met with Aaron Henry in the back bedroom of the pharmacist's Clarksdale home. It was nighttime and a guard was on duty near the front door with a gun nearby. Henry's home had been firebombed and strafed with bullets. His close friend Medgar Evers, field secretary for the NAACP, had been killed by a white supremacist eight months earlier.

ROBERT PENN WARREN: As a starter, I wonder if you could tell me how you first got interested in the NAACP, and in the civil rights movement.

AARON HENRY: It goes back to a point before I could even

remember, myself. One of the earliest experiences that I remember was the traumatic experience of being separated from a lad that I had known since birth, when it came time to go to school. And we were living in the rural [area]. I was born in this county. And his parents and my parents were the best of friends. Randolph and I became inseparable. And to have to go to one school and he to another at the age of six or seven was one of the early crises of my life. And I just never forgot about it.

RPW: This is a white boy, you mean?

AH: Yes, Randolph was a white boy. And I understand from my mother and from his mother that as children, as babies, they would leave him with my mother at times and me with him and his mother at times. And we both nursed at each other's mother's breasts, as children. And when it came time to go to school, we all looked forward to it. And the great experience that we anticipated was so negated by the question of racial prejudice and racial bias that separated two kids who loved each other dearly. And since that time I can't remember a time that I was not concerned about the race question, and determined to do what I could about it.

RPW: And you have been with it a long time, I understand.

AH: Yes, I became a member of the NAACP as a high school student. The senior class of 1941, in Coahoma County here, were encouraged to take out membership in the NAACP. And after high school, going into the service, there was an immediate need for NAACP philosophy with regard to the many instances of racial bigotry and racial prejudice we ran into in the service. Coming out of the service into college, on the campus of Xavier University, there was a strong civil rights movement. Participating in the National Students Association gave additional opportunity with organizations that were concerned about the rights of mankind.

RPW: This is after the war?

AH: This is after the war, yes sir. And upon coming home from college in '50, we did not have an organized NAACP in the community. In 1952, we organized the NAACP here and I became its president, and have remained president of the local branch ever since.

RPW: I know you've been very prominent in it. In fact, so prominent that I've heard that the bullet that Medgar Evers got might have gotten you, by a toss-up.

AH: Well, I've heard that, too. And we get it from what we consider usually reliable sources within the news media. I'm not anxious to die but I'm not afraid of it. One thing that the death of Medgar accomplished for me: it freed me from any fear of it. I know that I can never give any more to the cause than Medgar Evers gave. And he was the best friend I had. And I'm willing to give as much.

RPW: This was a deep, personal friendship then?

AH: Yes sir, it goes back to around '50. We both got out of school about the same time. We came out and began working in the freedom movement together.

RPW: There have been threats and small acts of violence against you, haven't there here?

AH: Well, yes. Our house was bombed and set afire and shot into. And the store's been bombed.

RPW: The store's had the windows knocked out, too, hasn't it?

AH: Yes sir, the windows were knocked out pretty frequently.

RPW: Was it one case of shooting into the house, or more?

AH: Two. These things happen usually late at night. And some wild, careen of cars come through and they shoot at random. Perhaps not aiming, but just shooting. A bullet could cause serious difficulty.

RPW: Well, bombing isn't quite that casual though.

AH: No. The time that they bombed the house we were all

asleep. The concussion awoke us. And of course the incendiary set the house afire. And we were able to get the fire out, however, before any serious damage was done to any of the people, any members of the family or any of the visitors who happened be here at that time.

RPW: Do you think that was just a bomb to frighten you, to intimidate you, or do you think it was meant to destroy the house?

AH: I think it was meant to destroy us.

Warren asks about criticisms of the NAACP by other civil rights organizations and leaders.

AH: I take this position: that it's important that we keep our eyes on the target, which is freedom, and also on the enemy, those who are in opposition to all Americans or all citizens obtaining citizenship in America. To some degree it's a kind of jealousy that some might hold because of the prominence that the NAACP has in the civil rights field. Sometimes we're criticized for moving slower than others would have us move. But when we look at the fact that, regardless of who else gets in jail, it's always the grand old NAACP that, number one, puts up the bond money to get him out of jail, and number two, furnishes the legal talents to get him out of the difficulty with which they are involved.

RPW: There is an argument that one encounters that dependence on legal action, the insistence on the legality of the process, has inhibited the achievement of civil rights, because it carries no threat with it.

AH: Oh, no, no. I can't agree with that at all. The mere fact that the NAACP has been involved in legal action, it has served as an apparatus to determine actually what the law is, what the law says. Without which there would be no precedent, without which there would be no direct action, knowing what the final legal outcome is going to be. Now, I don't mind violating many of the Mississippi statutes. But those that I violate I know are in contrast to the law on the federal level. And I would not want to become involved in violation of the laws of this state that would be upheld by the Constitution of the United States. The legalistic approach that the NAACP has taken has clarified this for us. Therefore, we can, without hesitation, become involved in direct action, because we know the First Amendment to the Constitution gives us the right to protest. But the good old NAACP has established this right in our own mind. Consequently, when we violate this law, we are not violating what we consider an actual law, but a practice within Mississippi that we want to get rid of.

RPW: I've heard it argued, too, with the legalistic approach keeps the image of a law-abiding society as what would come out of the period of protest.

AH: I think that's important. We do want to be law-abiding citizens. The legal image of this nation that has been identified by the work of NAACP lawyers, and others, really brings the possibility of creation of the direct action movement. The Constitution of the United States stands for the equality of mankind. This country, itself, was built on acts of protest—the Boston Tea Party and various other activities that were responsible for the birth of this nation. Were it the official position of our country to deny the right to Negroes to be full and free citizens of this country, I doubt very seriously if the protests that we are waging, of a nonviolent nature, would continue to be waged in this restrained, dignified manner. Because without the hope, without the knowing that the United States sanctions what we're doing, then we would be in open rebellion against the country. Therefore, the restraints that we are now able to impose upon those who participate would not be possible if the victories that we seek were not so assured.

Warren asks Henry about Kenneth Clark's critique of Martin Luther King and nonviolent civil action as a source of potential pathology and instability in the psychology of black people.

AH: Dr. King's philosophy is built on an understanding of Christianity. I certainly agree that following through on an ethic of Christianity is not, shall we say, common sense. It's not a kind of reaction that one would normally be expected to understand.

Dr. King's philosophy—which is the philosophy of many of the others of us—is that Jesus Christ forgave his oppressors. And if we are to be true followers of Christianity, then we, too, must be able to forgive those that oppress us. But King is very careful in identifying what he calls love. The word that he uses is *agape*. And when we rise to love on the *agape* level, we love men not because we like them, not because they like us, not because there's something physically attractive about them, but we love them because God loves them. Because the Redeemer of this world caused them to be created. And we know that He loves everything He created. Therefore, it is up to us to imitate the leader of the Christian faith, as hard as it might be, and as difficult as it might be. We know that freedom is not easy, that without some suffering, there will be no freedom. And I'll go along with King all the way in this redemptive kind of love that espouses a love of mankind, because God himself made him and He loves him.

RPW: I've heard it said by admirers of Dr. King that only by this is there basis for a future society. That you can win every lawsuit, and seize every right, if necessary by force, and then have no society when you got through without this human recognition across the lines of race.

AH: I don't think that we can win our freedom by using the same apparatuses that have been used in Asia and Africa. In Ghana and Nigeria, in other countries of Africa, when the Negro has emerged to freedom, he has driven out the white oppressor. And the land has been left to the blacks. But here in America, when we gain the freedom that we know we're going to get, our white brother and our black brother are going to be still right here. Neither's going to drive the other out. Therefore, there has to be this symbiotic kind of response and respect for one another.

Warren describes a kind of informal sociology experiment conducted in New Haven, Connecticut. It involved a picture of a man brandishing a knife. Warren says the knife carrier is "invariably," and wrongly, identified as black.

AH: I think that the stereotype here is answered in jest by [comedian] Dick Gregory. Dick has brought quite a bit of the humor and, to some degree, the solution to the problem in his banter and humor. Dick said that Negroes usually were depicted as carriers of knives because "the white people won't sell us no guns." But I see about as many white fellows with knives as Negroes. I think that, in our own community, a Negro would come nearer being arrested for bearing a knife than would a white man.

RPW: Certainly that's true.

AH: Therefore, we get more publicity about having knives than the whites do. Many of the things that a Negro gets arrested for, the white man is either chastised for doing the same thing and sent home, or nothing is said at all to him about it.

RPW: But in New Haven, a significant number of Negroes have accepted this white man's stereotype of the Negro, and put the knife into the Negro's hand.

AH: Mississippi is not a mutation in America. The bigotry that exists in Mississippi is perhaps more overt than exists in New Haven. But this question of racial prejudice, frankly the question of white supremacy, is present throughout the Western world, in American and European culture. Wherever Western culture is involved you have a system of white supremacy. Show me a Negro in the legislature of England, France, Italy. Wherever you have Western culture there is always white supremacy.

RPW: Undoubtedly true. Of course, there are no Negroes in England—no significant number—nor in Italy.

AH: Well, they say that there are some in Russia. I have no feeling of kindness toward communism at all, and I haven't seen *Pravda* espousing the Negro cause to the point that you see Negroes in the presidium either. So, this white supremacy is not at all confined to Mississippi. It's nationwide and to some extent worldwide.

RPW: James Baldwin said that the Southern mob—[the crowd] you meet on the streets of Jackson, or Little Rock, or New Orleans, Birmingham—does not represent the will of the Southern majority.

AH: I think that's true. Many of the people in the South are not permitted, because of real or imagined fears, to espouse the goodness they really feel in their hearts. Political opportunism causes the expressions of racial bigotry to the point that many people feel that they can't win an elected position unless they espouse the cause of racial hatred. And when you study the history of [Southern segregationist politicians such as James O.] Eastland and [James K.] Vardaman and [Theodore G.] Bilbo, you will find that, in many instances, these men sired Negro children by Negro women. Which gives you to understand that they really didn't hate the Negro. But the fact that Negroes are not registered to vote in any appreciable number gives rise to the political necessity of espousing racial hatred if the politician intends to win at the ballot box.

Now, once the Negro acquires the right to vote, you're going to have a whole lot of white people talking about how good we were to Negroes, even back then. And how we felt about Negroes even then but were afraid to say it. Now, we go back to our feelings of Christianity here. If they will really begin, right now, to act right, they'd be surprised how fast and how quickly we forgive. But the white man is afraid that his deeds are going to follow him. And he feels that once the Negro gets in power, the Negro is going to remember all of the dirty deeds that he's gotten from the white community. Therefore, he continues to prolong the day, as long as he possibly can, that he will have to suffer for his crimes. In other words, this old eye for an eye, a tooth for a tooth, and a man reaping what he sows.

But when we do get suffrage, get the right to vote, it is our determination to really show America how democracy can really work. And how the freedoms that we seek for ourselves will be definitely shared with everybody else. Because we realize that freedom is a peculiar kind of a commodity. You can only keep it by giving it away. The only way that a man can be free is to give freedoms to all of the other people that he comes in contact with. And this is a general feeling among the leadership of the Negro community. None of us have the vengeance and the hatred to carry.

RPW: This is the general feeling, you say? You don't think it's confined to persons approaching middle age or older? It would apply to the young, too?

AH: It applies, very much, to the young. The question of being sure that all people enjoy the rights and privileges of the American citizen is perhaps more imbued in the minds and hearts of the young than in the old.

RPW: Even when they are not Christians?

AH: Sure. Even when they're not Christians. I don't think that it takes a Christian to feel this kind of responsibility. It takes a person that has experienced difficulty. I think that the greatest ally that the Negro gained during his whole crisis was the white enlisted man that served in World War II and in the Korean War. This white man went to the army never having experienced any kind of segregation or discrimination in his community. And here he goes into the army, he finds that the PX system is so arranged that what comes in is placed in the officer's PX, and they get what they want. And then it's sent down to [the lower ranks]. And the quarters on the base where the officers live is so much better than the quarters where he lives. And he got to see what segregation and discrimination means. He realized that, when it was doled out to him, he didn't like it. And he began to have a greater appreciation for the fight that the Negro is making, trying to get rid of these same oppressions. And look at the broad spectrum of white support that the Negro has in his cause for freedom—you will find a great majority of it comes from veterans of World War II.

RPW: Many of whom I've been told had their first chance to know a Negro, personally, in the army.

AH: That's true. They only knew him as a servant, in some servile occupation, before.

RPW: Or had never seen one at all.

AH: They only knew about what they had read about them, or what they had heard about them, and usually this was in derogatory terms.

RPW: You're a businessman. What do you find in Mississippi, or in other places you know, of Negro anti-Semitism?

AH: If this is anti-Semitism, I'd like it to be defined as such. In the fight for human dignity, we have never underestimated our opposition, but we have overestimated our support. We felt that, naturally, we would have the Jewish people on our side. We thought, naturally, we would have labor on our side. Because the enemies of all three are usually found in the same group. Here, we don't have the Jews supporting us.

RPW: In Mississippi?

AH: No.

RPW: But you do elsewhere?

AH: Yeah, elsewhere. And it was this image of Jews, as we knew them on the national level, that caused us to feel that we could count on the Jews in Mississippi. Here, in our hometown, we have absolutely no support from the Jewish community. Frankly, some of our greatest oppressors are found in the Jewish community, which saddens me. And if that is anti-Semitism, then we have learned it reluctantly.

RPW: Do you think that the Mississippi Jews, for instance, are slightly more vulnerable than Gentiles to social pressure? That's why they react this way?

AH: I would think so. They know that once the white man clubs or clobbers the Negro into submission, that he's probably next. And it's to his advantage not to have become involved in the problems of other oppressed people. But it would be hard, for me, not to become involved in the problems of a person who was being oppressed.

RPW: Do you notice any difference in attitudes of white people under thirty and over thirty? Is the younger generation changing its attitude on the race question?

AH: I'm sorry, I can't. That's a thing that I would like to believe. But when I observed the riot at the University of Mississippi last year, I observed boys who had fuzz under their chins and girls who still wore too much lipstick—in other words, kids between fourteen and eighteen years old. These kids, from the day that they were born, many of them had heard only that the Supreme Court decision of 1954 was not the law of the land. It need not be obeyed. And here they're facing on their own college campus the presence of the Negro, which goes against all they have been taught. They begin to throw the bottles and the bricks and the racial epithets and the curses. Which said, to a lot of people, that the sociological and the psychological utterance that we had taken too long to be a truism—that the younger generation will straighten this thing out, if only given a chance—did not follow the lines of the [saying].

RPW: Depressing thought.

AH: Yeah, it is a depressing thought. I would like to say that we can count on the younger white to be much more tolerant than the older white. But then you realize that the greater amount of the violence—the bricks that are thrown, the people who are knocked off stools in sit-ins, the kids that bombed our house—were between nineteen and twenty-two.

RPW: You identified them, did you?

AH: They were captured the same night. And we understand that each one had about $500 in his pocket.

RPW: Paid to do it?

AH: We think so.

RPW: I've heard it said that the riot set development here back ten years. The whole generation in college that now runs Mississippi with this in their ears.

AH: I don't think that at all. The riot has really propelled us into what can become a new era. I say that because, prior to the riot, our contact with the campus of University of Mississippi was next to nothing. Since the riot, almost weekly, sometimes daily, there are students and faculty persons who come by just to exchange ideas and views on particular issues. These students and faculty members would not have dared be seen in the company of the president of the NAACP prior to the riots. The riots actually freed them.

RPW: Well, that would seem to prove that there's something to be said for the younger generation then.

AH: Except that many of the people who take this opportunity are not necessarily young people. It's a mixture of old and young.

RPW: How much contact, in terms of the civil rights movement, do you find between the more prosperous middle-class, as it were, upper-class Negroes, and the masses of the Negroes? Is there more communication now, in recent years, than there was, or less?

AH: There's more. The reason is because of the involvement of the younger Negroes, the teenagers who are the sons and daughters of this older, middle-class black bourgeois Negro. And once momma's red-haired boy is in jail, and has been slapped around by the police, regardless of what he's there for, she becomes enraged and becomes more amenable to the civil rights struggle than before. And one thing that the white policemen have not been able to do, they have not been able to differentiate between the child of the Negro lady that has set the image of stereotype in a community, and the Negro that is now striving for freedom. And because of that nondistinction, the Negroes now take the position, from a cliché, that if we hadn't been in a bed together we wouldn't be in this jam today. Which says that we're all Negroes. We're in the same strawberry patch, the same jar of jam. So, therefore, we might as well act like it and try to work together to get out of it. The overt activities of the white community have done more to unite the Negro community than any other thing.

RPW: That leads me to another notion. Where does [movement] leadership come from? What social bracket?

AH: It's not indigenous to any strata. You'll find the leadership personnel will range from persons who can't read or write to people with PhDs. And the person who can't read and write will have just as much persuasion over the group that he is involved with.

RPW: Natural force and natural intelligence.

AH: Yes sir.

RPW: But there's no real danger, then, of a break between leadership and the masses?

AH: No sir. I don't think so at all. What really happens is, the leadership finds out which way the mass wants to go, or what the mass want to do, and then gets in front and leads it. But the fellow who lives on the plantation, who digs the ditch, who makes a dollar a day, and sometimes nothing, is just as much concerned—and many times more concerned—with becoming free than the man who is maybe a little better off. Take a minister in a pulpit. He is no more a leader to the PhD than he is to the little child in catechism; each one follows him. So I think that the position of the church in Negro life, where we have this democratic kind of society, has had, and will have, great bearing on the surge toward freedom of the Negro community.

RPW: What church do you belong to?

AH: I'm Methodist. And we're moving too slow. We've got segregation within the Methodist church that we've got to get rid of.

RPW: Are you making headway?

AH: Yes. We have come to the point where there is much discussion. This will be one of the main topics that'll be discussed at the annual convention this year. And there has been some relaxing of the barriers. But it's going to have to be relaxed much more than that.

RPW: Are you finding any significant support from white Southerners in this?

AH: Yes, the white ministers—well, the white ministers with which I'm in contact—are quite concerned about ridding the church of the jurisdictional system. Thus, giving them a church doctrine, or a legal basis, to preach the brotherhood of man.

RPW: It's sometimes said, and I have a quotation here from a Negro sociologist and historian to this effect: "The Negro's plight in the South will be lightened substantially only when the plight of the poor white is lightened, when these two can no longer be pitted against each other in hatred and contempt."

AH: That's pretty much a true statement. The power structure of Mississippi, for too long, has manipulated the Negro against the poor white and the poor white against the Negro. It is told to the Negro, every time there's a crime committed by white men against a Negro, that was a redneck that did it. "It wasn't us. Oh no, we don't do that. It's the rednecks."

And they have told the white, illiterate, poor man that every crime, particularly a sex crime, is committed by a Negro upon a white woman. And, of course, they do this because sex is the thing that the most limited mind can comprehend. And that's the scarecrow that they use. "You've got to keep these Negroes in their place, or they're going to take all your women."

Now, to me, that's a serious indictment on the part of the white male toward his white woman. To feel that the only thing that is keeping her from embracing every Negro she sees is because the white man keeps his foot on the Negro's neck. Frankly, if I were a white woman, I would be completely insulted by this line of reasoning. And this thing about Negro men seeking, insatiably, the association of white women—now most Negro men that I know wish to God that our white brothers were satisfied with their own women as we are with ours. You can hardly come into any Negro neighborhood at night without seeing some car with a white man circling, trying to find some Negro lady to have pleasure with. If she wants him and he wants her, that's two people's business.

RPW: It's a private affair.

AH: A private affair. They want to get married, that's their own private affair. I take quite a dim view on the [laws] of my state that negate the possibility of holy matrimony between the races. But there's nothing about adultery and fornication. And they use these types of expressions about the Negro to the white, and about the white to the Negro, that keeps us apart.

Now, the best thing in the world that could happen to Mississippi would be somewhat of a wedding of the Negro and the poor whites. A populist movement that would break the stranglehold that the power structure of the white community now has over both the Negro and the poor white. And there are only two divisions between the poor folks in our state: there's the poor white folks and poor colored folks. And I think the sooner we realize that, the better off each of us is going to be.

RPW: Do you see any economic competition between the Negro laborer and the poor, white laborer, in a state which is poor and doesn't have enough jobs to go around?

AH: Yes. The pay scale that is now used is a threat to everybody. It is a prostitution of the labors of the white people, in that the white employer says to the white worker: "If you don't agree to work for this dollar and a quarter an hour, I'm going to hire a nigger for seventy-five cents." The power structure is only content to be sure that what the white man gets is better than what the Negro gets. I think that when employment is based on ability, without regard to race, creed, or color, that this, in itself, will create a situation where industrial personnel will be willing to come into our area, and with it perhaps create many more jobs than there are now.

RPW: The race situation has prevented industrialization? New plants?

AH: That's my feeling, sir. And when we break this stranglehold on race there will be many more jobs. Perhaps enough jobs to go around.

RPW: Is it noticeable in Mississippi that some Negro business-men, and others who have more or less privileged positions, actually oppose the civil rights movement? This is true in some localities.

AH: I don't see how. If a Negro says he opposed the civil rights bill, there are either two things present: he's either a liar or he's a fool. He might say that he opposed the civil rights bill because he is speaking the language that someone who can do him a favor would want to hear. And he enhances himself, possibly. But to be against the civil rights bill is to be against yourself. And it's hardly conceiv-able that a rational, truthful man could take a position against the civil rights bill.

RPW: In a St. Louis newspaper, the president of a Negro business association wrote an article saying that integration would set back Negro business in St. Louis by a generation.

AH: I presume what he was getting at was that the Negro busi-nessman in St. Louis does not run his business in competition with the American market. It's no good to be the best Negro business-man. You've got to aim at being the best businessman in town in order to gain the clientele that is out there.

RPW: Open competition, in the long run, would benefit the Negro.

AH: Yes sirree, I do believe it.

RPW: There're always casualties.

AH: In any sociological change there're going to be casualties. In the American way, the person who builds the best mousetrap is going to get the business. And I think that Negro people have got to be prepared to take their chances on the open market, and conduct their businesses as a business should be conducted, and not rely upon any advantage that race might give them.

Warren asks Henry about the recent verdict in the trial of Byron De La Beckwith, a white supremacist who was acquitted by an all-white jury for the 1963 murder of state NAACP leader Medgar Evers.

AH: I'm pretty much a skeptic but I accept the verdict in the Byron De La Beckwith trial as the second act of a well-written drama, with the actors playing their parts superbly. I think that the decision of a hung jury was made before the trial started. The third act of the drama will show Beckwith a free man. The first act was the election of the jury.

RPW: Do you mind explaining that?

AH: [The lawyers] took a lot of time in securing twelve members of the jury. I think that it could have been done in five minutes and been over with.

RPW: It's never that way though.

AH: (laughs) Well, no, it's never that way. But I'm saying that the stage that has been set for the Byron De La Beckwith trial attempts to erase some of the mud from the name of Mississippi. And, to my mind, all the time they took selecting the jury was a part of the act. There never has been a white man in Mississippi given a penalty in a capital crime against a Negro. And there have been situations, perhaps, where the web of guilt was wound much tighter.

Warren asks Henry about the suggestion by Gunnar Myrdal, a famous Swedish sociologist and economist, that if white slave owners had been compensated for their lost human property during Reconstruction, the violent and repressive Southern reaction to emancipation might have been mitigated.

AH: I take the position that if the white community had accorded my grandma and my grandpa, at the time they were freed from slavery, recognition for the labor that they had given free, that they could have lived like millionaires forever, because of this exploitation.

The big thing that was wrong with the way the slaves were freed was none of us possessed the land. And I'd like to go back to Moses, who promised the children land if you follow me. And, of course, from the land comes all things that are conducive to life. And there was no place called the promised land as an area, but it was simply that they were promised land. After the Civil War, the Negro slaves were not even promised land. The Russians, when they freed their slaves, there was land reform. England, when it freed its slaves, there was this land reform activity. The American Negro was the only group that was freed from slavery with no possessions whatsoever. And because of this situation, the progress of the American Negro has been slower than the Negroes in other communities. I have seen the plantation system grow. And we have seen that, as Negroes began to buy and acquire land after the Civil War, that it was not too long before the [white] man who owned the land in the first place had connived and somehow secured all of the land back. And the Negro reverted from a slave to a tenant farmer or to a sharecropper. And his lot has not been that much better off.

And right now, 1964, we should give serious thought to a land reform program in the South. Look at the way these mass plantations have come into being. Negro [farms] have been taken for taxes, where Negroes have been charged smaller amounts for taxes than should have been charged over the years. And [the courts] take the position that it's the owner of the land's responsibility to be sure that he's properly taxed. After some fifty or sixty years this great tax debt comes against the land and the Negro can't pay it. And the land is confiscated.

RPW: Is that fairly common?

AH: It's fairly common in the growth of the large plantations in this area.

RPW: I hear now and then—particularly in Mississippi—the notion that only by some sort of threat of violence will real progress take place toward social justice for the Negro.

AH: That all depends on what you mean by threat of violence. You see, any act that the Negro takes toward gaining his rights as a citizen is considered a threat of violence by the white community. If it's going into a church and espousing the right to vote, that provokes the white community to violence. If it's printing a handbill and passing it out in some communities, that's a threat to the tranquillity and peace, and a threat of violence to the particular community. So you would have to define, exactly, what is a threat of violence and whether or not action, guaranteed by the Constitution of the United States—the First Amendment that gives us the right of freedom of assembly and freedom of expression—can be construed as threats of violence.

Warren asks Henry how his wife has been holding up in the face of violent threats against him and his family.

AH: Well, Mrs. Henry has stood this turmoil and difficulty remarkably well. Frankly, without her encouragement and support and understanding, it would be impossible for me to carry on. Because I'm away from home too much, more than any married man likes to be away from home. The telephone calls come almost every day about some kind of violence, or [anonymous callers speaking] vulgarities and obscenities, which no man would really want his wife to have to put up with. But she's able to ask questions, like: "Certainly you must be Christian," and "You wouldn't do that."

When Rebecca, our daughter, answers the phone and the man

says, "Yeah, I just shot your daddy," she just looks at the phone and says, "Aw, fellow, you kidding."

These kinds of expressions on the part of my family are really sustaining to me. And I'm grateful for it. And I don't know whether I would be able to continue in this activity were it not for the fact that I have the complete support, understanding, and love of my family.

RPW: You have friends who come in to keep watch on the house at night, don't you?

AH: Yes. We started this after Medgar was killed. We do take some precautions. And because the psychological well-being of my family is important to me, [as I] continue in the field of civil rights, we have permitted our friends to come in every night. There's someone in the house, or around the house, every night since the death of Medgar.

RPW: Are they armed?

AH: They're armed, yes sir.

RPW: But since that time there's been no further trouble at your house?

AH: No, and I suppose, to some degree, it's due to the fact that after Medgar was killed, I went to the chief of police and revealed to him the source of information that I had about the threats that had been made against my life. And he told me that he'd heard several threats, too. And he asked me if I wouldn't let him take out a [life] insurance policy on me. You see, he and I have been involved in a libel difficulty. At one time, I was arrested on a morals charge.

RPW: Here in Clarksdale?

AH: No, in an adjoining county. The chief of police of my city and the county prosecuting attorney of my county were the only interrogators. And I felt that they had a part in concocting this fabrication, and I told them so. And they reacted by filing a libel suit against me. And the reason that the chief of police was asking for this life insurance policy was in the event that he won the suit, he wanted to be able to collect his money. And, of course, I parried it as if I thought he was kidding (Warren laughs). And then in the next couple of days, he sent an insurance agent over to the store to try to persuade me to let him take out this policy. And if I had submitted to it, I'd probably been dead the next day.

RPW: That's asking for it.

AH: Well, yes (laughs). So I discussed with him the hiring of a guard. I asked him about the city police department supplying us with protection. And he told me that he didn't have the men to spare and he couldn't do it. So we hired a guard. And the next couple of nights he came down to the house and then arrested my guard and took my gun.

RPW: The chief of police of Clarksdale?

AH: Of Clarksdale, yes. But that only set off a furor in the community. Many people donated more guns than we'd ever had before. And there have been no more confiscations of the weapons that we use. But every person that serves as guard of the house is now armed. And [the police chief] can come and take the gun whenever he gets ready. There'll be plenty more that will be available to us.

RPW: What hour of the night does the guard come on?

AH: He comes on around eleven. And he's here all night long. Many of them come much earlier and spend the evening looking at TV. Some of them come before I get here in the evening and go to bed and take a nap. Then get up when I'm ready to go to bed.

Warren reads a quote about the lengthy and gradual nature of fundamental social change. He asks Henry to interpret the phrase "Freedom Now," which had been adopted by civil rights activists.

AH: Well, I interpret it this way: the freedoms that Negroes have been seeking go back to the year of 1863 [the year of emancipation]. And we have been patient. We have tried to take into consideration that this will not be an overnight accomplishment. But we think that, after a hundred years of trying, it's time for freedom now. We don't think that this is any abrupt request.

RPW: Well, assuming that it is overdue, the social process still remains. So suppose every legal bar were removed tomorrow morning. The big civil rights bill passed, with teeth. All the legal restrictions [on black equality] removed. The process would not be complete.

AH: No.

RPW: What becomes of "Freedom Now" in this situation?

AH: Well, you see, the law will not make you love me, but it'll stop you from lynching me. And that's what we've got to be concerned with. The law, itself, is one of the greatest forces in social change that we can possibly have. And I think that my white brother owes me a deep debt of gratitude when I permit him to give me my rights piecemeal. They're mine, *now*. He's lucky that I don't grab them all right now. When I work for you for ten dollars a week, Saturday come I want my ten dollars. Don't come talking about I got two dollars now and eight dollars later. And that's what the struggle and the cry for "Freedom Now" is all about. We've been laboring nearly four hundred years and we want our payday. That's it.

Robert P. Moses

February 11, 1964

Jackson, Mississippi

Robert Moses, an intrepid and soft-spoken civil rights organizer from Harlem, worked some of the most dangerous terrain in the Jim Crow South: the vast plantation territory of the Mississippi Delta. Moses played a key role in organizing the 1964 Freedom Summer campaign, recruiting hundreds of student volunteers from Northern colleges to help conduct an ambitious black voter registration drive in Mississippi. Moses was also deeply involved in the Mississippi Freedom Democratic Party's (MFDP) challenge to the all-white Mississippi state delegation at the 1964 Democratic National Convention. Moses went by the nickname "Bob," and in a movement brimming with charismatic leaders and powerful orators, he was a self-effacing, grassroots activist who sought to empower and learn from the everyday people with whom he worked.

In the summer of 1960, Moses signed on to travel the South as an organizer for the Student Nonviolent Coordinating Committee (SNCC). In Cleveland, Mississippi, he met and was influenced by Amzie Moore, head of the local NAACP. Moore encouraged Moses to enlist college students to come to Mississippi and help the voting rights movement. The following summer, Moses completed his teaching contract in New

York and returned to Mississippi to devote himself to SNCC and the movement full-time.

Moses launched a voter registration drive with local activists in McComb, Mississippi, in July 1961. An intensely violent white back-lash soon followed. Moses and his colleagues were jailed. White men beat up Moses in a town square. A local organizer working with Moses was murdered. Still, Moses and the movement went on.

Veteran activist Tom Hayden said a key to Moses's success as an organizer was his hunger to learn from local people. "Bob listened," Hayden wrote in The Nation. *"When people asked him what to do, he asked them what they thought. At mass meetings, he usually sat in the back. In group discussions, he mostly spoke last. He slept on floors, wore sharecroppers' overalls, shared the risks, took the blows, went to jail, dug in deeply." Local black people in the small Mississippi towns where Moses worked were especially appreciative of his approach.*

Historian Clayborne Carson says that when SNCC executive sec-retary James Forman wanted to centralize the group's leadership in "action-oriented liberals" mainly from the North, Moses resisted. He wanted SNCC to help develop leadership in local communities, then step aside to let them run things themselves. Moses's selfless devotion to the civil rights struggle—and to the leadership potential in ordinary people—resulted in what Carson calls an "unwanted personal follow-ing," especially among white student activists.

Moses was also central to the founding of the Mississippi Freedom Democratic Party. The mainstream Democratic Party in Mississippi was made up of white segregationists who favored the Republican Barry Goldwater over Democratic incumbent Lyndon Johnson in the 1964 presidential election. At the Democratic National Convention, the MFDP demanded—but failed—to be recognized as delegates to the convention. Historian John Dittmer says the MFDP's defeat at the convention left Moses "embittered and disillusioned with the nation's white leadership."

In the months that followed, Moses spent less time in Mississippi. He left the South the following year, and eventually moved his family to Tanzania. He taught there for seven years before returning to the United States.

In later years, Moses did graduate work in the philosophy of mathematics. He used the proceeds from a 1982 MacArthur Fellowship to start the Algebra Project, which grew into a national campaign to improve and promote the teaching of math in underserved communities.

Robert Penn Warren met with Moses near SNCC headquarters for their interview. Warren was struck by Moses's "extraordinary calmness." He described him as a man with a "preternaturally serious expression on his . . . face, the seriousness emphasized by his horn-rimmed glasses." He asked first about Moses's upbringing.

ROBERT PENN WARREN: Where were you born?

ROBERT MOSES: In New York City, in Harlem, and I went to the schools in Harlem until high school. Then I went to Stuyvesant High School, downtown.

RPW: What accounted for that school shift?

RM: We took a citywide exam, and that was an opportunity to get a fairly good high school education.

RPW: What was the ratio of Negroes to whites in the Stuyvesant school at a given time?

RM: I think I was usually the only Negro in my class. I graduated from Stuyvesant in '52, and then I went to Hamilton College in New York State. I graduated from there in '56, and went on right to graduate school to study philosophy at Harvard. I picked up an MA at the end of my first year, and then we had family problems—my mother died in the next year, and my father was hospitalized—and I dropped out. Then I got a job teaching at Horace Mann in '58, stayed there three years, and then came down here.

RPW: Were you ambitious academically when you went to Harvard?

RM: Well, I wanted to get the doctorate. I liked philosophy, so I wanted to study.

RPW: How did you make the shift to active participation in civil rights?

RM: I wasn't active at all in any kind of civil rights organization while I was teaching, until 1960, when the sit-ins broke out. That attracted my attention. It seemed to me there was something different—something new. [I experienced] a continual buildup and frustration, back as early as high school, and then in college and graduate school, and then in teaching, of confronting at every point the fact that, as a Negro, you couldn't really be accepted as an individual, at any level of the society in which you happened to penetrate.

RPW: Do you think you would still have had this as a personal experience—not as an observed thing, but as a personal experience—if you had continued your work at Harvard and taken your doctorate as planned?

RM: I don't know if I would have. The fact was always that at any given moment in whatever experience you were in, it always cropped up, and gradually I got the feeling that no matter what I did that it would always be there, that at that time it was impossible to be accepted fully as an individual, even though there were a lot of things that were much better and much different than, say, from my father's time.

RPW: Had your father had aspirations and ambitions like your own?

RM: Probably, yes. He was caught in the Depression with two families. At first, his own family hadn't grown up—his father became sick—and then he got married. He had finished high school, but he hadn't gone to college. There was no money, there was no money for anyone, and then he got a job working in the national armory. We had long, long talks as we were growing up—talks which I can see now were really about the question of opportunity, and the question of discrimination. There were questions generally revolving around whether or not he was satisfied in life, and whether his purposes were frustrated. Anyway, he decided to put most of his energies into his family. There were three of us, and he wanted to see us all through school and college. Most of his sacrifice went in that direction.

RPW: It sounds as though you were very close to him.

RM: Yes.

RPW: When did you make the actual step to leave teaching and to move into this [civil rights] world?

RM: In the summer of 1960 I decided to come down [South] and see what it was like. I went down to Atlanta to work with SCLC [Southern Christian Leadership Conference], and Dr. King, but they were in the process of reorganization and changing executives, so there was no place to fit in.

Warren asks Moses about Kenneth Clark's critique of Martin Luther King's program of nonviolent activism and the supposed pathology it engenders.

RM: We [in SNCC] don't agree with King's philosophy. The majority of [students] are not sympathetic to the idea that they have to somehow love the white people that they are struggling against. There are a few within the group, say, who have a very religious orientation, who preach this, and there is constant dialogue and discussion at meetings about nonviolence and the meaning of nonviolence.

RPW: But nonviolence for SNCC is practical nonviolence, is that it?

RM: Well, most of the members in SNCC are tactical. It's a question of being able to have a method of attacking, rather than to always be on the defensive, and having to wait until something happens to you, and then try and do something about it. But instead, you just go right out and do something about it—be able to launch an attack.

RPW: What about the effect that King has had at moments of crisis where violence seemed imminent—general violence, as in Birmingham—the effect that he has been able to exert on people who are not avowed followers of his?

RM: Well, there's no question that he has a great deal of influence with masses of people. I certainly don't think that effect is in the direction of love. I think the effect is in the direction of practical steps, that whatever you believe, you simply can't afford to have a general breakdown of law and order.

RPW: This is a matter, then, of a tactical nonviolence and a looking forward to the society to be created, is that it?

RM: I think that is a strong argument. In the end, everybody has to live together, and the local people—Negroes—understand this very well. They're the first to tell you this. They put it in terms of when [Northern civil rights workers] are gone, we'll still be here, and we have to live with the people here. In Mississippi, the idea has been to send in workers in communities where they stay and live and work, so that there isn't this moving in for a brief time and moving out again. So the concept has been to work with students and to prepare them to take a year off from school—and some of them have taken longer—and go and really live in these communities, and work and stay there.

RPW: The attitude you report from the local people—when you are gone we have to live here—that might have either of two meanings. One, we have to pick up the pieces and bear the burden of reprisal. The other one being some vision of a society which was lawful in itself.

RM: In the end, Negroes and whites are going to have to share the land. The less overlay of bitterness that you have, or the less marks of violence that you have to overcome, the more chance of [cooperation]. You're constantly trying to find different ways in which you can get real change, but still not leave such a legacy that it's impossible to have some reconciliation.

RPW: Do you see the possibility, after you experience it in the South, for cooperation between the poor white and the Negro?

RM: I just don't know. We've had some contact with some whites and what seems different now is that most of the poor whites have moved into cities, and they've gotten jobs in industry, on the basis of Negroes not being able to get these jobs. And it seemed to me that they would want to hold on to them. I just don't see that kind of breakthrough at this point.

RPW: Nobody is going to resign a job to give it to somebody else.

RM: This is the problem right now in the North. In these construction industries, where the people are laying down in the streets and asking, literally asking people to give up their jobs, move over and make room for us. Nobody is going to do that. That kind of struggle has to be taken into a wider struggle in which everybody demands more jobs for everybody. You get these people together and work to say that everybody has to have jobs.

RPW: Back to your personal experiences, have you been the object of violence? In Mississippi?

RM: It happened when I first came down in 1961. What happened was, [in the] summer of 1960, I came down and then made a little trip through the South. In Mississippi I found a person—Amzie Moore—who wanted to work on [voter] registration in the Delta.

RPW: Up in Cleveland [Mississippi]?

RM: In Cleveland. Amzie and I sat down in 1960 and plotted out a voter registration drive for the Delta. And I went back North to teach for a year and came back in '61. Well, I couldn't get started in Cleveland, but the farmers from the neighboring county, Amity, came out and we began taking people there [to register to vote].

RPW: The Negro farmers?

RM: The Negro farmers. And once I was attacked on the way to the courthouse. There were two farmers and myself. We were going to register. And [while] walking on the main street in town, three white, young fellows came up and one of them began to pick an argument. They singled me out and began to beat on me, and I had about eight stitches on the top of my head. We went to trial and a couple of days later he was acquitted. This little town, Liberty, a town of maybe a thousand people, has a long and vicious history. In fact, just last week one of the farmers down there [Lewis Allen] was killed.

RPW: [Lewis Allen] had consented to be a witness in another murder trial, hadn't he?

RM: Right. This farmer was killed, which led to Lewis's participation in the trial. He had to testify. He wanted to tell the truth, and he told the truth to the FBI, but the local authorities—he told them what they wanted to hear.

RPW: He told the local authorities what they wanted to hear? But told the FBI the truth?

RM: Yes, and we believe that the FBI leaked it to the local authorities. The deputy sheriff came out, you know, and told Lewis what they had learned. And they had been picking at him ever since. That was in September '61. At one point, the deputy sheriff broke his jaw. And that deputy is now sheriff. And then they killed him.

RPW: How was he killed?

RM: With a shotgun. They laid in wait for him in some bushes. It was in the nighttime, and he was coming back home and he had to get out of the truck to unhook the fence. When he got out they just shot him.

RPW: Has there been any arrest on that?

RM: No arrest. I doubt that there will be.

RPW: Is that your only experience of that sort?

RM: Where I myself was attacked, yes. Except . . . well, no. I forgot. Last year in Greenwood [Mississippi], we were driving along just out of town and some white people had been circling the town. About three or four carloads of white people. One of them followed us out of town. There were three of us in the car, sitting up front. And they opened up [on us] about seven miles out of town. Bullets rained just all through the car. The driver had a bullet in his neck, and he was slumped over into my lap, and we went off the road. I had to grab the wheel and stop the car. And then he almost lost his life. He had a .45 that was lodged just about an inch from his spine. None of the rest of us were hit at all, just shattered with glass. But I think it's interesting because [Byron De La] Beckwith—the fellow who killed Medgar [Evers]—is from Greenwood. And the people who shot us that the police arrested—there were some arrests on that case—they answered to the same general description. They were middle-aged, middle-class white people. Just as Beckwith is. Now, they've never been brought to trial.

RPW: You're recently married, aren't you? What view does your wife take of your hazardous occupation?

RM: Well, that's hard to say because she doesn't—I guess it's—I mean you just go on living.

RPW: You take it day by day?

RM: Yes, otherwise there is no real way to confront that except to, within yourself, try to overcome that fear. That took, for me, quite a while.

RPW: Can you put your philosophy to work on that? Did the Harvard seminar help you any?

RM: Not the Harvard seminar. It went back a little further. When I was in college I read a lot of [Albert] Camus. And I picked it up again. I just finished, while I was in jail this last time, I read through *The Rebel* and *The Plague* again. This was about a week and a half ago. And the main essence of what he said that I feel closest to is that it's important to struggle. That is, in working against some of these forces, it's important to recognize in the struggle certain humanitarian values. It's possible to eke out some corners of love, or some glimpses of happiness, within that.

Warren asks Moses if he thinks local black people in Mississippi ever resent his "superior" education or accomplishments.

RM: No, I don't. When I first came down, it was something that I just very consciously played down. If you establish your relationship with people on another level and they identify with you, then afterwards when they find out something like that they are not resentful. They become proud, or something like that. It can be transformed into a positive thing.

RPW: This is something of the ambivalence that I suppose exists in all societies [and is said] to exist in the Negro society. On the one hand, a kind of jealousy or amusement of that achievement, and on the other hand a kind of identification with the achiever, the Negro achiever. At least, many Negroes have written about this and have talked about it.

RM: Well, of course, when it's a Negro achiever then there's an additional problem of his achieving in the white world. Particularly down here in Mississippi, because it means that he's an Uncle Tom, or that he has to compromise with the white world at some point, or that he isn't free. He can't now participate with us or even do the things that he wants to do, and he becomes a conservative and a person who's trying to hold back the change, trying to hold on to what he has, trying to protect that.

RPW: The sneers one can hear directed at Ralph Bunche or Clarence Mitchell or various other people—certain writers—Ralph Ellison and people like that.

RM: I always think that most of that is due to lack of ability to understand on a more complex level, and to understand all the different facets of society. It's the kind of evaluation which people want to make from a distance and it really becomes an abstraction. They can't really make that kind of evaluation without getting in close and knowing what kind of tension that person lives under in making his decisions.

RPW: Just take Mr. X, who is very able and enjoys a fine reputation, is distinguished in some profession or occupation. Naturally he has some white friends. Now, if he has white friends does that [count] against him?

RM: You have a duty to ask them what are they doing in this

big [social] change—what public life are they pursuing? It doesn't have to be directly in a revolution. But if they're doctors, the time has come for them to prepare themselves so that Negro people get the best medical care. If they're teachers, then the time has come for them to prepare themselves to know what's going on in the educational revolution that the country is going through, and to see that the Negro students that they're teaching now are getting a real education. There's so much that needs to be done. The fight is of such proportions that, it seems to me, we can ask legitimately what commitment has he been making to it? And not just in terms of funding or supporting, but in terms of his own profession, his own skills. How is that being used to help the Negro along and help the whole society?

RPW: How much of a split remains between the black bourgeoisie and the masses? Is that being narrowed, that breach?

RM: It doesn't seem so. The new Negroes coming out of school now, more of them, I think, are aware of identification with the masses. But most of the people who are the old line of bourgeoisie, I don't think that identification is there.

RPW: You can find, actually, resistance to the impulse toward integration. I have read several articles by Negroes, one by the president of the Business League of St. Louis—a Negro business organization—saying integration would set Negro business back twenty-five years.

RM: So, he's got to compete now with the general market, and he's got to produce enough services and goods and so forth so that the Negroes themselves don't have to get the secondhand. Where you find the Negro businessman who is worried about what integration is going to do to his business, he's usually giving the Negro a secondhand deal anyway, higher prices, or worse products or something.

RPW: What about that split that is talked about often—I encountered it first in [W.E.B.] Du Bois many years ago—between
the impulse toward loyalty to Negro-ness, the *mystique noir*, the
notion of an African tradition, or at least of a shared American tradition? This split—for some people it's a very important problem,
it's a deep problem, for others it's not. How do you feel about it?

RM: For myself, personally, the problem has been to find a
broader perspective. I don't feel that it's a problem of identifying
Negro-ness, or this mystique, or anything like that. You know, it's
just historical. If you look back through the family, as far as I can
trace it you get all sorts of elements, and there's no way of saying
[what] belonged to Negro culture. It seems to me that it evaporates.
My family—there are all sorts of things mixed in there. Neither,
however, do you want to integrate into the middle-class white culture, since that seems to be in vital need of some kind of renewal.
I think that in the struggle that we're going through you find a
broader identification, that it leads to identification [with what]
other people are going through. That the struggle doesn't become
just a question of racial struggle; it ventures into other planes: political, the question of humanitarian struggle, and the question of
justice. If you cut it differently like that, then you can get a picture
of yourself as a person caught up historically in these circumstances.
And now your job is to try and work something out. And in working that out, you finally begin to get a concept of yourself as a
person, and that whole question of needing to identify yourself as
[belonging to] Negro culture, or needing to become integrated into
the whole white society, that disappears.

*The conversation moves to how civil rights workers, many from edu-
cated, middle-class families, engage with Southern black farmers and
laborers.*

RM: The students are constantly renewed by the people who come off the land. The farmers, they're unsophisticated, but simply voice, time and time again, the simple truths. They speak from their own lives and their own personal experience. So the students are rooted in that. This is what keeps them from going off on some kind of real tangent, as long as they keep working with the people. The people are really the force of values. At this [organizing] meeting, for instance, that we had on Sunday . . .

RPW: Yes. I was here for a while and I was very much struck by the quality of some of the people speaking from outlying counties, these older people, particularly, these old men.

RM: But, see, there were some in [the civil rights] leadership who were against this kind of meeting. They're for the kind of meeting where you get well-dressed, cleaned-up Negroes who have maybe some semblance of an education. They want these people to be represented. They don't want [ordinary folk]. They're embarrassed by them getting up and maybe they don't speak English well. Maybe they grope for the words.

RPW: "Redish" for register, for instance.

RM: Right. And [some leaders] were complaining about the fact that just anybody can get up and talk. It's that kind of thing that the students are really battling against. That, somehow, people have to be cleaned up and presented before they're ready for the larger society and are presented to white people.

RPW: To take another tack: Why did communism never make any headway with the American Negro? That was a fruitful situation, I would think, both in the North and in the South.

RM: The people I know who are older now [who] were in the [movement] back in the 1930s and early '40s. They say that they just became disillusioned, that the Communists were really not interested so much in the Negro. And the [common] people are not really concerned with the abstract level of politics; they're concerned more with concrete levels of what happens to the individual. Progress is made in winning their allegiance, which means, in a lot of cases, working on compromises. You get bogged down with this, trying to bring one guy along, and you never get up to this level that you're working for. There's a tendency to sacrifice people for platforms.

RPW: Tell me this, why did this movement—and not merely SNCC but the whole Negro revolt—why did it come when it did instead of twenty-five years ago?

RM: My father and some of the people of his generation, they made the point that they had to come along first and prepare young people so that we could do the work that we're doing now. We have, in essence, their support, where they wouldn't have had their parents' support. Now, other people point out the whole question of the move from Africa and the rise of an image in Africa of people being able to control their own destiny.

RPW: You mean, that the American Negro changed his self-image as a reflection of the African situation?

RM: I think that there's no question that that has some . . .

RPW: Some merit. Would there have been enough educated Negroes thirty years ago to mount this vast organizational effort and to spearhead it, to use the cutting edge it has now?

RM: I don't know. Maybe not.

RPW: I was just trying to get you to assess what have been the educational and cultural gains in one generation.

RM: It seems to me that all of this sprung up out of World War II. I've been thinking back on what happened and it seems to me that in the late '40s, when I was in junior high school, part of the move around the country was to begin to provide educational opportunities for Negroes in the North. A conscious move for able students to open up doors which had previously been closed to them. Going to Hamilton [College] was simply a part of that. Special money was available and they were looking for Negro students and it was part of the move to begin to provide some education. The gains of World War II, in terms of the Negro in the North, where they needed people to work [in defense industries]—Negroes were subsumed into a higher standard of living. So that laid the basis for it, too. And also there's the returning to the South, after being in the war and fighting and so forth, and having to come back to the same situation they had left, I think that left a real residue of bitterness.

RPW: What about the change in climate of general opinion, including white opinion—not just a change in Negro attitudes, the Negro situation, but a change in climate, the spiritual climate, the emotional climate, the intellectual climate—over that period of twenty-five to thirty years?

RM: This is really what the [1954] Supreme Court [*Brown*] decision did. It didn't integrate the schools or anything. It gave the Negro the legal basis and the moral basis for fighting to integrate the schools. And so they're carrying on the fight. [Negroes] realized the white people were not going to do it. They weren't going to lead them.

For instance, at Hamilton, the change in [white] attitudes was, "Well, we have to do our part, to try and open up a door or two for the Negro, and let's see what happens." And the difference was, before they weren't really interested in even trying to open up a door to see what would happen. They were apprehensive about getting the wrong person up there and having it fail. And while I was up there, I was glad to have that opportunity, but still deeply bitter about some of the realities of the campus and some of the realities of the white attitude. They were willing to go so far but not any further. Now you're getting a different kind of change. I think everything happens with pressure. It's always the pressure from underneath which forces people to realize that they have to do some kind of changing.

RPW: The conception of the Negro, from 1865 to the present— the white man's picture of the Negro—has changed through pressures of all sorts.

RM: I'm sure it has. Even down here, even in Mississippi. Referring to the sheriff in Canton, he told some of our fellows—they're planning Freedom Day there too at the end of this month—he told them, "Well, you-all are fighting for what you believe is right. And you're going to fight. And we are fighting for what we believe is right. And we're going to fight, also." Now, that seems to me a tremendous change.

RPW: It surprises me, to tell you the truth.

RM: All of a sudden [whites] can realize that these are people. Now, these guys, they're not particularly well educated or anything like that. They're just from the South. Negroes born and raised down here. And here they're saying, okay, you have something that you believe in but we have something we want. And we're going to just fight this thing out. Now that, it seems to me, is a tremendous kind of change.

RPW: The sheriff is not a man of, I suppose, much education or much experience outside this county, as a matter of fact. If he says this, it must reflect something that's happened in the county itself.

RM: Exactly. It's a tremendous movement among the Negro people in organizing. It's a tremendous struggle that's taking place, but part of it is the recognition by the white man that there is a struggle and that Negroes themselves are struggling.

RPW: What about the Freedom Day in Canton? What is the nature of the program?

RM: We're trying to get the National Council of Churches to

get involved with another group of ministers and probably have another picket line downtown.

RPW: Does this involve a boycott?

RM: They're having a boycott. That's already part of the picture.

RPW: How effective has it been?

RM: The boycott, I guess, is fairly effective. But it's just going to be very bitter. There's no question about it.

Warren asks Moses about the concept of the slogan "Freedom Now."

RM: I don't know that that's a concept. It's an emotional expression. It's a feeling. I think it's an attempt to communicate a sense of urgency—how urgent the problem is.

RPW: It's a poetic statement.

RM: Right. And what it's linked up to is the fear that the white person, and the people who run the society, are going to take as much time as you give them. That is, they will always stall for time and will always say it takes time. For instance, it's very interesting to watch [the movement in] Atlanta [where people are] making distinctions between what they call the doves and the hawks. The hawks are the people out asking for instant equality—freedom now. The doves are siding with the elements in the civil rights movement who are ready to work for social change over a period of time.

RPW: Well, that is associated with the question of the brinksmanship of violence, isn't it? That the threat of potential violence can be used for peaceful change? Keep it just at the boiling point but don't let it boil over the pot if you can avoid that.

RM: Well, there's two distinctions. [Leslie] Dunbar of the Southern Regional Council has an image which he uses. He calls it the annealing of the South. He describes a process whereby towns or communities are heated up, and in the process of this heating up

they can be remolded. And then in the cooling-off period this re-
molding takes place, and they go back to a different level or different form. And then they're heated up again to get over another
stage. We are involved in this now because we're planning a huge
summer effort, maybe involving up to a thousand students to work,
this summer, in Mississippi.

RPW: On the registration program?

RM: The registration program. They'll have freedom schools
and community centers and there will be some political activity.
The people are running for Congress and carrying out this freedom
registration and getting ready to challenge the Mississippi Democratic Party.

RPW: You mean really running for Congress?

RM: They're really running. We plan to have some people who
will enter in the primaries—the Democratic primaries—and also
run again as independents in the general elections. And there are
two ways of looking at this. One way is that this is brinksmanship,
and it's purely psychological. You play with this to bring a community or a state or whatever up to this point, and under this threat
you get a change.

RPW: But the threat is not one of violence?

RM: No.

RPW: You may get some, but you're not offering it.

RM: Right. The threat is that the community will . . . there will
be a breakdown. And rather than face such a possibility, [white
opponents] will capitulate and give in. The other feeling is that it's
inevitable. A change doesn't come about unless you really face this
risk. And we [organizers], personally, are facing the same risk. We're
not asking anybody to face a risk that we do not face.

RPW: But you're not proposing the brinksmanship of violence.
You are running the risk of violence by way of reprisal or repression.

RM: That's just a part of the risk that you take. And at every point, what you balance out is the risk against the possibility of change. You tell the people that this is what's open to them, the need for this kind of sacrifice, and that they have to run the risks if they want real change.

RPW: I have heard it said here, in the last few days, that part of the problem of voter registration is the fear of not passing [literacy and poll tests], not the fear of reprisals in many cases. A fear of being incompetent for the tests for registration.

RM: What that fear is, is the fear of being embarrassed, of not knowing the answer and therefore thinking that it's their fault, and being embarrassed.

Warren asks Moses about civil rights demonstrations that spark violence.

RM: Personally, my own philosophy is not geared to capitalizing so much on the kind of outburst in which you get emotional involvement. What's called for is an emotional release about the specific incident, which in itself is a trifling incident, and the emotional release is needed because it's been built up over a series of these incidents. The problem is to capitalize on that emotional energy, to get a chance to get at those people and explain to them the whole situation that they're involved in, and what has to be done to make real change, and then to recruit from within that group their people. That's the time you can get people and start them to working.

RPW: If this resentment and aspiration could be channeled by SNCC and similar organizations, it would be constructive.

RM: Right. The possibility is for it to be constructive and maybe to find solutions. Everybody has been talking about [federal] marshals. I mean, we've protested time and again to the Department of Justice. We felt you need marshals, you need law enforcement agencies down here. Mississippi will not actually enforce any of these [civil and voting rights laws]. And the whole question on voting ties around the problem of creating an atmosphere in which Negroes are not afraid to go downtown. What happened in Hattiesburg, with the picket line thrown up, was the courthouse was neutralized. The presence of the picket line neutralized the courthouse. And the ministers and the people on the picket line, and the police guarding them, had the same effect as if they were marshals. They were there to keep law and order, the police. So this meant that, for the time being, it was safe for Negroes to go down, and they went down. And that seems to me a constructive way out of an impasse. Now, you're not sure what's going to be gained out of that. You're not sure yet whether the white people will settle for this kind of thing, or whether they will arrest everybody on the picket line and return back to the former situation, [where they] put you right back in the past.

Charles Evers

February 12, 1964

Jackson, Mississippi

Charles Evers had a long and varied career both in the civil rights movement and in numerous professions, including disc jockey, insurance agent, funeral director, bootlegger, and numbers runner. Charles Evers was running nightclubs in Chicago when his younger brother, Mississippi NAACP field secretary Medgar Evers, was assassinated by a white supremacist in Jackson in 1963. Charles Evers returned to his home state to take up Medgar's place in the organization.

Charles and Medgar Evers were both born in Decatur, Mississippi. They both served in World War II and graduated from Alcorn Agricultural and Mechanical College. Charles settled in Philadelphia, Mississippi, where he worked in the family's funeral business and ran a taxi company. But Charles eventually ran afoul of local whites by agitating for black voting rights, suffering economic pressure on his business interests and personal threats against him and his family. Charles moved his family to Chicago.

On the early morning of June 12, 1963, Medgar Evers was returning from an NAACP meeting. He was shot to death in front of his home by Byron De La Beckwith, a member of the Mississippi Citizens Council, an organized pro-segregation group. Though evidence pointed to Beckwith, he was acquitted twice by all-white juries in 1964 (Beckwith was eventually convicted of the murder, in 1994).

Charles Evers returned to Mississippi and astonished NAACP officials by declaring he would assume his brother's post as head of the state chapter. Rather than risk an embarrassing spat with the dead man's brother, the NAACP's top national executive, Roger Wilkins, acquiesced. Medgar's widow, Myrlie Evers, worried that her bother-in-law's shady past would tarnish the memory of her husband. While Charles led numerous boycotts and voter registration drives, historian John Dittmer writes that his "flamboyant and domineering" personality alienated younger activists and caused divisions in the Mississippi NAACP that ultimately interfered with the freedom movement in the state.

In 1969, Charles Evers was elected mayor of Fayette, Mississippi. He was the first African American since Reconstruction to be elected to a mayor's office in the state. In 1989, Evers switched political parties and became a Republican.

Robert Penn Warren met Evers at the NAACP office in Jackson, eight months after Medgar Evers's murder. In Who Speaks for the Negro? *Warren wrote that he found Evers to be agitated yet cordial. He also came to feel, as others did, that the stories Charles told about his role in the movement and his early resistance to white supremacists may have been exaggerated.*

ROBERT PENN WARREN: How did you get involved in the movement?

CHARLES EVERS: Actually, I have been involved in the movement since I was a boy. Medgar and I had worked as a team together from boyhood. We organized [NAACP] chapters over in Newton County and over in Lauder County and Shauver County and Western County. And then up in the Delta section when we went out with teams in our early twenties. And then I was in the funeral business over in Philadelphia, Mississippi. I was president of the Negro Voters League and I was trying to get Negroes registered to vote. I had many hardships. Many economic pressures were applied to me in my business, and they forced me out of business in 1957. They broke me. They sued me. I was sued for personal damages. I was parked at an intersection, and a white lady was in the parking lot, and she got in the car and ran into me and tore my car. They sued me for $5,000 and they said I had injured her back. That was confirmed by the courts.

RPW: Was that appealed?

CE: I couldn't get an attorney to represent me. Then I went to St. Louis to a meeting, to the National Funeral Directors' meeting, and while I was there my wife was attending a funeral. She was carrying a woman to the cemetery [in our hearse] with the funeral procession and a white man ran through the funeral procession and tore my [hearse] with the body in it. They sued me again for that and fined me a tremendous sum.

I was the first Negro disc jockey in Mississippi. They got me fired from the radio station in Philadelphia, Mississippi. I had a restaurant downtown in Philadelphia and they closed it up, revoked my license. And then they began to ask the casket companies who were selling me caskets and embalming fluid not to sell me caskets and not let me have fluid. They applied so much pressure to me until I had no choice. I had to give up my business and seek employment. I had never had a job before. I had worked for my father and my uncle in the funeral business and I had been in my own business for years.

Then I began to look for employment. I couldn't find it anywhere in the state. So I told Medgar, "Look, Medgar, I'm going to go away and get a job, and I'll send money. But you stay here and keep carrying the fight on, get our people free, and free ourselves." I said, "Any time you need me I'll be back, whether it's day or night."

And so we agreed. I said, "Now remember the pact that we made when we were boys: that whatever happened to one of us, the other one will carry on until the same thing happens to him."

RPW: This was your agreement as boys?

CE: Yes. I must have been about fifteen, I guess. Medgar must have been around twelve. At that time, the late senator [Theodore] Bilbo was campaigning for reelection. He would come to our home [town] every time there was an election. He would stomp and he would lambaste the Negroes and tell everybody he was going to send them back to Africa.

RPW: Which town is this, now?

CE: Decatur, Mississippi. The county seat of Newton County. We'd always go and listen to him, you know. We were about the only Negroes who would go up and listen. And we'd always sit right in front of him. My dad had always told us that we were as good as anybody, and that regardless of the man's color, God loved us all, that we were all God's children, and we had the rights of anyone else. So we felt that way. It was brought up in us.

We were sitting down in front of [Bilbo] this particular day and he said, "You see these two Negroes down here? If you don't keep them in their place, someday they'll be in Washington trying to represent you, taking my place and the rest of the good white people's place." And I sort of looked up at him and smiled at him. And he said, "He's even got the nerve to grin at me."

I said, "He may be telling the truth."

And Medgar said, "You're right, Charlie. Some day we may be in Washington representing all the people of Mississippi."

And from that day on we decided that was something we could do. And then a few months later, a friend of my dad's was lynched. He was accused of insulting a white woman. They came and got him and dragged him out of his home, hooked him behind a wagon, and dragged him down the streets into a pasture not too far from our home. Hung him to a tree and shot him in two with shotguns, until part of his body fell to the ground. And his clothes laid there in the pasture for weeks and weeks. And we used to go by and see them.

RPW: What year was this, approximately?

CE: Oh, it's hard to say. It must have been 1937, maybe, '38.

RPW: Do you remember his name?

CE: Yes, Mr. Tingle. So it hurt my dad and it hurt us. We asked, "Dad, why did they do it? Why did they do it?"

And he said, "Son, just because he was a Negro."

I said, "Isn't there something we can do? Something that Negroes can do, that the law would do to stop people from doing this?"

Dad said, "The laws, themselves, encourage that type of thing in Mississippi. We're going to have to straighten it out ourselves." And that's one of the most important things that made Medgar and me more determined to become fighters for equality of all men, not just Negroes, but all men.

RPW: Was your father in the funeral business too?

CE: My uncle was in the funeral business. My dad was a lumber contractor and he owned shares in the funeral business, but he never actually was an undertaker. I lived with my father and uncle and worked with my uncle in the funeral business.

That was actually the beginning of our determination that we would really do something. We began to go around and ask our people not to buy newspapers from the white boys who would come around. And there was a furniture company. We tried to get our people not to buy furniture, because the white [sales] people would come in and sit on the side of our parents' bed, and they would call our mothers by their first name. We asked [our parents],

"Why do we have to say 'yes sir' and 'no sir' to the whites? They don't say it to us."

And my dad said, "Well, that's just an old custom, son. It always has been that the Negroes have to respect the white people."

I said, "Dad, why can't they respect us?"

He said, "White people don't feel that we are supposed to be respected. They feel that we're just a piece of property, or a tool or something to be used, that they are our superiors and have no reason to respect us. It's something that we just can't help."

You see, my father was not an educated man. He never finished the sixth grade. But he had a lot of common sense and he had the nerve of a lion. You couldn't frighten him. What gave Medgar and me so much courage was that he never would let white people frighten him. I remember once we were at a commissary—a commissary is a little store where Negroes go and buy their commodities on Saturdays—and we used to have a running account that we would pay every Saturday. This particular Saturday, we went in to pay the account. The store owner, who was named Jimmy Bulware, had a great reputation of beating Negroes if they didn't pay the bill he said they owed. So this Saturday he gave my dad his statement.

Dad said, "Mr. Bulware, this is wrong. I don't owe you this money."

So [Bulware] cursed him and told him he did.

Dad said, "Don't curse me. I don't owe you this money."

Medgar and I were standing beside Dad, and the commissary was jam-packed with people—Negroes mostly, and a few white— so Bulware broke for his cash register drawer underneath the counter. And my dad jumped between him and the cash register and grabbed a bottle.

He said, "If you open that cash register I'm going to bust your brains out."

Medgar and I picked up a bottle, each, and stood at the door.

And my dad said, "Son, don't turn your back on them. Just stand there."

And dad said to him, "If you dare hit one of us, we're all going down." And this white man stood there and trembled. He just shook like a leaf on a tree. He had a gun lying there, right inside, but he was afraid to pick it up. So I knew then that white men are cowards. And they are easy to become excited if you show any type of nerve or any courage at all. They will, quick, turn and run. They'll tuck their tails.

RPW: Would you generalize that all white men are cowards?

CE: No, I wouldn't say all white men are cowards. I would say that the type who live violently are cowards, those who depend on violent means to secure their ends are cowards. As we grew up, we'd watch the cowboy pictures and we'd notice how all the bad white men would always try to sneak and hide and shoot the brave men in the back. Or they would try to stay in the bushes and shoot them as they passed. That helped us understand that Negroes and white, to a certain extent, are the same; that a coward is a coward, regardless of who he is, and most cowards react the same. That has been one of the reasons why we felt that we should not be afraid of the whites. Stand up to them, respect ourselves and respect them too, and demand respect from them. So we did this clean through our boyhood days. As we came into manhood we served in the army, World War II.

RPW: Both of you?

CE: Both of us, yes. We were in many different branches. During World War II the army was segregated. I went overseas with the Thirteenth Engineers, and we served in the Pacific theatre for three years. Medgar was with the military police department in France. He was in the Normandy invasion, and he served there for two and a half years. Then we both came back in 1946. So we were old enough now to register, and we wanted to register to vote. We began to work in our community to try to talk to the people to get them interested in voting. So then we had many hardships. The whites began to threaten our parents, and they began to threaten us.

Bilbo came back and said, "The way to stop these Negroes from voting is to visit them the night before the election."

And sure enough, they came the night before the election of 1946 and told my father that if he don't stop his sons from trying to register, something bad is going to happen to them. In the meantime, Medgar and I were in school down in Lorman and we were coming home for weekends and working with the voter registration and organizing NAACP chapters. Dad told us what [the white people] had said.

And so I said, "Dad, I was involved in New Guinea and I fought in the Philippines, and I wanted to fight here in Mississippi to have the thing that we fought for [back] there. This is our country and I don't care what no white man says. I'm going to stay right here in Mississippi and enjoy it. And if I can fight there for it, I can stay here and fight for it."

Medgar felt the same way. Medgar said, "We're going to register. We don't care what they say."

So that morning we went up to register. Mr. Brand, who at that time was circuit clerk, had known us all our lives. He came up and he said, "Come here, Charles, you and Medgar." He carried us into a room and he talked to us.

He said, "Now, look, son. I don't have no right to tell you not to register and not to vote, but it's going to cause trouble. If I were you I'd just go on back and wait. The time will come when you can register."

I said, "Mr. Brand, we've waited too long already. I want to register now. Not tomorrow, but now." So we registered.

RPW: Both of you?

CE: Both of us. We registered. And the election was coming up, I believe, about two months, three months later. And we got five others to register. We came back to vote, that's when the trouble really came. When we got back to Decatur to vote for the election that fall, they must have had over two-hundred white—I don't want to say hoodlums—with shotguns and overall pants on and rifles. And they blocked the door. Medgar and I pushed the door. First we were going to get our ballots. They tried to stop us from getting the ballots.

Mr. Brand said, "Step aside and let them get the ballots."

So when he gave us our ballots, they blocked the booth. They blocked the door where the polling place was. As I walked up, [a white man] rammed a shotgun in my side and said, "I'll blow you half in two."

And they put a rifle in Medgar's side. And they said, "You damned Evers niggers, you're nothing but trouble, noway."

And I said to him, "You don't have the guts to pull the trigger. In the first place, you're a coward. If you're going to kill me for wanting to register, you keep me right here in the courthouse."

Medgar says, "They aren't going to do anything, Charlie, don't worry about it." And by that time another white man who we had worked for—we had raked his yard and we had played with his sons and my mother once had nursed his wife when she was sick—he walked up and said, "You niggers are going to get in trouble if you don't go on back home."

"Mr. X," I said, "the point of it is we just decided we want to have the same thing you have, that is, our freedom and right to register and vote."

He said, "Well, If you don't get away from here, you're going to wind up getting shot."

I said, "Well, you don't want to shoot me as long as I'm looking at you, but we turn our backs you possibly will."

And by that time a white lady, who we thought quite a bit of, had heard what was going on. She came over and said, "Charles and Medgar, please, they'll kill you."

And so we said, "Okay."

I said, "Look, you've beaten us but you haven't defeated us. We'll be back."

And then they said, "You damned Evers niggers are going to get all the niggers in Decatur killed if you don't stay at home and tend to your own business."

So we didn't say anything. We all got outside on the courthouse square, and I told Medgar, "Look, you and the other two fellows go down one way, and the others will go with me down in a different direction."

So as we were going down the street, here comes about three or four carloads of these whites. We'd always be well armed, so I said, "Listen, if you touch one of us, we're going to leave you right in the street. Now, we're not going to bother you, don't you bother us. But nobody is going to take a whipping from any of you white people, do you understand that? If you're going to kill, I'm going to get one of you first."

So they stood there and they cursed and we kept on walking. And they drove alongside and cursed us all the way down the street.

RPW: Were they armed?

CE: Yes, they were armed. They had shotguns in the car. And they said, "You'd better not be in town when night comes."

So Medgar and I decided we were going back to school, which was Alcorn College. We were going back to school that afternoon. But then we stayed because we thought they might bother our parents. We had a barn out back on our property.

I asked Medgar, "You stay in the barn and I'll get in the garage."

Our other two friends stayed across the street in one of our rent houses, in case they came. By now we had learned, in case people should attack you, the best way is to get them in a crossfire and you can't miss. We felt they were going to come in large numbers and we planned to get them in a crossfire. So we sat up all night waiting for them to come, and they didn't come. Medgar and I got in the car the next morning and drove back uptown and went into the courthouse and caught them unaware because they thought we were gone. We went into the circuit clerk's office and asked them, why do they feel the way they do about us?

He said, "Charles, I told you before that it's just not time yet."

And I said, "Well, when do you think the time will come?"

And he said, "I don't know, it's going to take time."

And then we said thank you, turned, and walked on out.

RPW: What kind of a man is the circuit court clerk?

CE: I must say he was a fairly decent man. He actually didn't ever show any resentment for us. He never showed where he was for us, either. He seems to have been the type of person who wanted to advise against any possible trouble or possible violence. He was not a violent man.

RPW: Do you think he had some sense of the injustice of the situation, some regret about it, or not?

CE: Yes, I do. I think he was a man who knew they were wrong, but the position he held, he knew that he would be crucified had he spoken out. We had worked for him a long time and we knew him and he knew us. He knew my father, he knew my mother, and he knew all of us. And I feel that he was a fair man. There were many there who were fair. But these people who were so bitter against us were the ignorant whites who had nothing to offer. And their own way of proving that they were somebody was to try to keep the

Negro depressed and deprived of his rights as a citizen and as an individual.

RPW: But there never was an attempt by the other white people in the neighborhood to interfere with this [intimidation], to stop this?

CE: No. You see, in Mississippi, the white men who differ with the extremists are in much more danger than the Negro, because reprisals that will come to them are much severer than would come to us. That's why so many good white people in Mississippi are afraid to speak out, and there are many.

RPW: James Baldwin says in print that he's convinced by the testimony of Southern Negroes that a Southern mob does not represent the will of the white majority but fills, as he says, a moral vacuum.

CE: Partly, I agree. I won't say it's the majority. But I will say that I don't think that the mob represents all the whites of the state. I can't say that it doesn't represent the majority. Evidently, it is the majority because they seem to be too solid on it. A person having lived in Mississippi, it would be hard for them to judge on whether or not that's the case. I've lived here all my life, with the exception of the four or five years I was away trying to save money to come back to Mississippi. I can't say that Mr. Baldwin is altogether right. I would say that there are a large number of whites who do not approve of this type of thing, but I can't say that they're the majority. I think I would be exaggerating to say that the majority of the whites in Mississippi feel that this thing that we are fighting for, and dying for, is right.

RPW: I don't want to interrupt your narrative. Go ahead and tell me more of this straightahead story, will you?

CE: I think we left off when we tried to register and vote.

RPW: That's right. You came back the next morning to the courthouse.

CE: Yes, we came back from there. Then we went and got in our car and [went] back to [college]. We had many calls, many letters from home, from our Negro friends, asking us, please, don't come back to Decatur because they're going to kill us. And Medgar and I felt—until his assassination—that if we must go, then we must. We took a chance in France, we took a chance in New Guinea, we took a chance in Manila, we took a chance in going to Japan, to fight for democracy, to fight for the things that this country was established for.

I said, "If I have got to come back to Mississippi"—the two of us felt this way—"and be denied these things, then my fighting and my sacrifices, all the years I sacrificed in the army, have been in vain."

If I had the nerve and the courage to go and face people I've never seen before and never heard of and never even spoken to, well, the least we could do is stay here and face people who we grew up with, and who we knew, we had served, who have served us, who we have worked beside, who we have played beside. If I don't have the nerve to stand up to them and tell them what I want, then we must be a phony all the way. So we felt that we must let Mississippi know—and I still feel and Medgar felt—that this is our state. And we went and fought for this country. And all we want out of it is an equal opportunity, no more and no less.

When we [graduated], I went in and took over the funeral parlor which we had in Philadelphia, Mississippi. Medgar then went into Mound Bayou and headed up an insurance company. At that time the [company] president was Dr. T.R.M. Howard, whom we looked on more or less as a father and as a counsel to us because he was one of the few men who seemed to have understood what Medgar and I wanted. He was one of the few Negroes in Mississippi at that time who was willing to stand by us and push us and urge us on.

RPW: Most Negroes were willing to stand aside?

CE: Well, they weren't willing, they were afraid. I wouldn't dare say that no Negro—including the Uncles Toms, as we called them—didn't want the same thing that Medgar and I wanted. But many of them didn't have the courage and the guts to be willing to stand up for it.

RPW: All this hopelessness, too.

CE: Yes. They always felt that it was a hopeless and a useless fate, that the white man was in charge, he always remained in charge. That this was his country and he would control it. Well, we were trying to get our people to see what I'm still trying to get them to see—what Medgar died trying to get them to see—that this is not any one person's country, this a country of all the people, and you have to let the world know that you are willing to pay the supreme sacrifice, as all other great Americans did, to make it a better place to live. And one of the greatest ways to do that is through political participation. Register and vote. Education, self-denial, self-respect, respect for others, and demanding respect from them.

RPW: How much progress do you think has been made in that way in the last fifteen years?

CE: A tremendous amount. More than we had ever dreamed would come. I think there are many instances where it was brought about by the two wars that we had. You see, the Negro in Mississippi has always been denied communication, association with other people. A person's intelligence is no greater than his exposure. We in Mississippi, most of us have been brought up on farms, and we've worked in these kitchens and in these backyards and on these plantations for nothing. And that's all we ever got. My father, he lived sixty-eight years and he left Mississippi once. He went to Chicago to visit my sister on her dying bed. So he knew nothing but Mississippi. And there are thousands, should I say, of Negroes who have never been out of Mississippi, who have never been fifty miles from where they were born.

So, until World War II came, we thought that the whole world was just like Mississippi. We had no ambitions; we had no outlook on the world or life. And the war threw all of us into the army with men from all over the world and all over the country, and we listened to them talk and saw how free they were. When I went into the army I had finished high school, and [I met] a boy who hadn't even finished eighth grade. He was much more abreast, much more learned than I was. He could discuss things that I hadn't even heard of. I knew then that there must be a better place, that Mississippi had deprived us of all of the things that others are getting throughout this country.

RPW: The same thing is true, to a substantial degree, of the white boy growing up, too, isn't it?

CE: Right. The whites of Mississippi are in the same predicament we are. And our basic trouble is ignorance. And the only thing that the poor whites know, and the poor Negroes know, is what these politicians get up and holler on the radio and newspapers and television. Therefore, there's not a line of communication between the Negroes and whites. And they don't know what the Negro wants, other than this politician who is in there for his own personal gain, just saying that all Negroes want to do is to come down and marry your daughter and destroy your homes. He never says that all the Negroes want is an equal education, to learn to be a first-class citizen. He never says that Negroes want to be able to participate in political affairs. He never says that the Negro wants to equip himself in education to where he would be able to serve in any capacity where he's needed. He never says that Negroes want to be lawyers and doctors. He never says that Negroes want to be dignitaries, to go out and represent our state or our country. But all he's sure of is that the Negroes want to become intimate with your daughter. And no man approves of anyone who wants to come into his life through his daughter.

RPW: Do you think the nonviolence technique has been the key to success so far?

CE: I do. The only way that we have is through nonviolence,

there's no other way. Violence will never accomplish anything in our fight.

RPW: You know, of course, that there are people—Negroes—who disagree with you, that the time for violence is probably coming.

CE: Yes. Here's what I feel. I don't believe in violence, but I believe in self-preservation, and protecting yourself. I said that Medgar and I always tried to protect ourselves. Now, that doesn't mean that we are violent. I wouldn't ask any Negro to be driving along in his car and let a bunch of white hoodlums ride beside him and start beating him, or come into his home and drag his son or his daughter out, or his wife out, and beat them. We don't consider when we protect our people in that respect as violence. Violence is to arm ourselves and start shooting people on the streets, start—as they do us—beating them up as whites have done to us all these years, taking them by their hand and by their feet, dragging them and hanging them in a tree and shooting them in two like they did Mr. Tingle, many years ago. That's the type of violence we don't believe in. But I don't want nobody to ever think I don't believe in protecting myself or protecting my own or my family.

RPW: Let me ask about the trial of [Byron De La] Beckwith. How did the verdict strike you? Now, I have run across the notion that it was rigged. What do you think?

CE: I feel that—and I guess maybe I'm a little liberal in my thinking—that there was someone on this jury who wanted justice done. And I feel that the prosecutor did everything in his power, along with his aides, and the Jackson police department, to bring about justice. Because they felt a crime had been committed, and I feel that somewhere there's been a change of heart among men in Mississippi, some men. And I feel that they did the very best they could.

RPW: It was an honest job?

CE: I actually believe that. Maybe I'm wrong. You say it was rigged. Well, if it was rigged, it was the first time in the history of Mississippi that they even thought enough of a Negro to even rig a trial.

RPW: Even to try and impress the outside world.

CE: Even to try and impress the outside world. So I feel that it won't bring Medgar back, and Medgar wouldn't want it any other way. He wouldn't want me to feel any different.

Evers describes his brother's funeral service at Arlington National Cemetery.

CE: Senator Bilbo said once, in Decatur, on the courthouse square, that someday if you don't stop these Negroes and keep them in their place, they'll be in Washington trying to represent you. That's when we were just boys. And the funny thing about it, when Medgar's body was carried to Washington, after he was assassinated, it didn't bother me too much. I had never broken down until we got to Washington. As I sat in the limousine waiting for them to bring his body out of the church in Washington, and put him into the hearse, and as we began to ride to the cemetery, it all came back so clear: that many years ago Bilbo predicted this, and now, here we are, representing all our people, in Washington. And that was the time I broke down. It just seemed so real and the prediction had come true, although he didn't mean it in that sense. The point of it was, we were there, and we were representing all of the people—not Negroes, but all of the people of Mississippi. Because the tragedy that happened to him affected everyone, white and black, Indians, Chinese, Japanese, and all. Because they know, too, that until all of us are free, and we are free from this type of intimidation, that none of us are free.

Ralph Ellison

February 25, 1964

New York, New York

Ralph Ellison was one of the most influential and widely acclaimed American authors of the twentieth century, and for one book: Invisible Man. *With publication of this debut novel in 1952 Ellison became the first African American to win the National Book Award. The modernist novel tracks the odyssey of a nameless black protagonist who journeys to New York from the South and slowly forges an identity in the face of ubiquitous racism. Robert Penn Warren described the novel as "the most powerful artistic representation we have of the Negro under . . . dehumanizing conditions" and "a statement of the human triumph over those conditions." In Ellison's National Book Award acceptance speech he said, "Despite my personal failures, there must be possible fiction which, leaving sociology and case histories to the scientists, can arrive at the truth about the human condition, here and now, with all the bright magic of the fairy tale."*

Over his lifetime, Ellison won a slew of other awards, including the Presidential Medal of Freedom and induction into the American Academy of Arts and Letters. He had a long teaching career at well-known colleges and universities, including New York University, where he held an endowed professorship. Ellison sat on numerous arts commissions and advisory boards, including the Newport Jazz Festival and the National Council on the Arts, and he delivered lectures at institutions such as the Library of Congress. Despite the ongoing public recognition of Ellison's genius, and occasional publication of his nonfiction essays, one question loomed: when would he publish his next novel? Ellison spent decades working on a successor to Invisible Man *but died before completing it. As critic Mark Greif writes, "The thing that made Ellison's life truly complicated after* Invisible Man *was his steady promise of a spectacular second novel, begun in the mid-1950s, which he worked on . . . for forty years." After his death, Ellison's literary executor John Callahan gave final shape to a novel Ellison had been laboring over. It was called* Juneteenth *and published in 1999.*

Born in 1914 in Oklahoma City, Ralph Waldo Ellison was named after the poet Ralph Waldo Emerson, whom his father hoped he would emulate. Ellison's father loved literature and often read to his two sons. The elder Ellison delivered coal and ice for a living, and was lifting an ice block one day when a shard broke off, fatally impaling him. Ralph Ellison was only three years old when his father died. Ellison's mother worked as a maid and a janitor to support her two boys, and encouraged them to be ambitious. She died when Ellison was a young man.

As a boy, Ralph Ellison was a promising cornet player. He majored in music at the Tuskegee Institute, intent on becoming a composer. He also devoured books in the school's library. He later said that he didn't give up music, but "became interested in writing through incessant reading." Ellison traveled to Harlem in the summer of 1936 to earn money for college expenses, and never returned. He spent his first night in Harlem at a YMCA. The next morning he stumbled upon the writers Alain Locke and Langston Hughes in the lobby. They, along with Richard Wright, mentored Ellison and soon he was publishing reviews and essays. For a time he had a job as a researcher and writer for the New York Federal Writers Program, part of President Franklin D.

Roosevelt's Works Progress Administration. Ellison served as a cook in the merchant marine during World War II, then returned home sick. "Part of my illness was due," Ellison said, "to the fact that I had not been able to write a novel for which I'd received a Rosenwald Fellowship the previous winter." When Invisible Man *was published it was an immediate hit. It remained a bestseller for months and, over time, sold millions of copies.*

In his introduction to the 2014 reissue of Who Speaks? *historian David W. Blight says that Robert Penn Warren "seems to have met an ideological and imaginative soul mate" in Ralph Ellison. Warren recorded their conversation in Ellison's home at the northern tip of Manhattan, facing the Hudson River. He described Ellison as calm and wryly funny. He said Ellison had a way of breathing out through his teeth that reflected his "humorous, ironical recognition of the little traps and blind alleys of the world, and of the self."*

ROBERT PENN WARREN: You say that many Southerners have been imprisoned by the feeling of a necessity of loyalty, of a necessity of being Southern, and that is clearly true. Now, there's a remark often made about Negroes, that they are frequently imprisoned in the race problem, in focusing on the race problem. I am concerned with a kind of parallelism here between these two things. Do you mind, if you have anything to say on that topic, exploring that a little bit?

RALPH ELLISON: The parallel is very much there, very much a reality. We know that there is an area in Southern experience where whites and Negroes achieve a sort of human communication, and even social intercourse, which is not always possible or always present in the North. I mean, that's the human side. But at certain moments a reality, which is political and social and ideological, asserts itself, and so the human relationship breaks up and people fall into these abstract roles. A great loss of human energy goes into maintaining our roles. In fact, much of the imaginative energy, much of the psychic energy of the South among both whites and blacks, has gone into this particular, negative art form, if I may speak of it that way.

RPW: Just the strain of maintaining this stance?

RE: I think so. Because in the end, when the barriers are down, there are human assertions to be made in terms of one's own taste and one's own affirmations of one's self, one's own way of life, and this is a big problem for Negroes. There is much about Negro life which Negroes like. Just as we like certain kinds of Negro food. The dieticians might not care for it, but it satisfies our taste and it expresses a culture and it expresses us, and that's good enough. And one of our problems now is going to be to affirm those things when you're no longer kept within a Jim Crow community. Do you think that there is some form of life which is more enriching? Do you think that there is going to be a way of enjoying yourself which is absolutely better than this? It's a matter of finding a human core after the fighting has stopped.

This holds for whites. It certainly shows up in the white Southerners, the mountain people, who turn up in Chicago. They have a real problem there. They feel they are alienated, their customs and mores are in conflict with those of the big city just as ours were, and still are, as we come to the North. The problem is finally to affirm without being contentious about it.

RPW: To affirm in a simply pluralistic society, without . . .

RE: Yes, without any value judgments, negative or positive, being placed upon it. I watch other people enjoying themselves, I watch their customs and I think it one of my great privileges as an American, as a human being living in this particular time in the world's history, to be able to project myself into various backgrounds, into various cultural patterns, not because I want to cease being a Negro, not because I think that these are automatically ways of conducting oneself or extending oneself, but because it is a privilege, it's one of the great glories of being an American. You can be somebody else while still being yourself. And one of the advantages of being a Negro, if we'll ever recognize it, is that we can do this and we have always done it. We have always had the freedom to choose or to select, to reject and to affirm, that which we have taken from any and everybody.

RPW: In a paradoxical way it's a bit more fluid than anyone else, the situation of anyone else.

RE: That's right. It's been more fluid and we had no particular investments, once we left the Negro community and left being snobbish behind. If anything, within the world beyond the restrictions of social movement and political movement and economic opportunity, we probably have more freedom than anybody.

RPW: I know some people, Ralph—white people or Negroes—who would say what you are saying is the current apology for a segregated society. Of course it's not. I know that. I know it's not. Some Negroes say the challenge of segregation made me develop whatever force I have, and are called apologists for segregation. How do you answer such a charge?

RE: Well, there's no answer to such a charge beyond this, is that if I am . . .

RPW: If a damned fool is a damned fool, you can't change him.

RE: You can't change him. If one thinks that by asserting reality, by recognizing what my life is like, by recognizing what my possibilities are like—and by the way I'm not, for one minute, pretending that the restrictions of Negro life do not exist—but I'm on the other hand trying to talk about how Negroes have achieved a very rich humanity under these conditions. Now, if recognizing this makes me an Uncle Tom, then heaven help all of us.

I know, in the first place, that there has been the necessity for

Negroes to find other ways of asserting their humanity than in terms of political or military force. We were outnumbered, we still are. This did not cow us, as a lot of people like to pretend. It imposed a discipline upon us. And we see that discipline now bearing fruit in the freedom marches, and the willingness of little children and old ladies to take chances, to walk against violence. This is an expression not of people who are suddenly freed of something, but of people who have been free all along.

RPW: How do you relate this, Ralph, either positively or negatively, to the notion that the Negro movement is a discovery of identity?

RE: I don't think it's a discovery of identity. I think it's an assertion of identity. And it's an assertion of a pluralistic identity. The assertion, in political terms, is that of the old American tradition. It's revealing the identity of people who have been here for a hell of a long time.

My notion of American Negro life is that it has developed beyond any restrictions imposed upon it, historically, politically, socially, economically. Because human life cannot be reduced to these factors, no matter how much these factors can be used to organize action, to prevent action. Negroes have been Americans since before there was a United States. And if we're going to talk at all about what we are, this has to be recognized. And if we're going to say this, then the identity of Negroes is bound up intricately, irrevocably, with the identities of white Americans. This is especially true in the South.

RPW: It is, indeed.

RE: There's no Southerner who hasn't been touched by the presence of Negroes. There's no Negro who hasn't been touched by the presence of white Southerners. And, of course, this extends beyond. The moment you start touching culture you touch music. You touch popular culture, you touch movies, you touch the whole damned structure, and the Negro is right in there helping to shape it.

RPW: Now, what about another notion, that the tradition of slavery and the disorganized quality of much Negro life after emancipation, meant the loss of role for the man? Patriarchy was the rule; the man, you know, bossed the family. How does your line of thought relate to that so-called fact?

RE: Well, I'm willing to recognize or to agree with the findings of the sociologists, the historians, that the Negro woman has been a very, very strong force in the Negro family. I'm also willing to say that the disorganizing effects of slavery, and of the lack of opportunities for the Negro male, has made for a modification of the Negro family structure. But I am not willing to go as far as the sociologists go, who would set up a rigid norm, you see, for the Negro family or for the—usually what they're talking about—the white Protestant family, and say that this is the only type of family which is positive. I know that some of the most tyrannical heads of families are Negro men. I also know that some of the most patriarchal and benign heads of families are Negro men. This, too, is true. I guess I'm one of the few . . . let's see, my father's father was a slave.

RPW: That close?

RE: That close, you see. Now, what are they talking about? My grandfather Alfred Ellison was known as a stern father. He was a man who was respected in South Carolina. And I guess if the old-timers are still there, black or white, they will talk about Uncle Alfred, because he was a man of character who had insisted upon certain things. In fact, he insisted so hard that my father ran off when he was a teenager to join the American army.

On the other hand, now, my father died when I was three years old and my mother stood in for us. I was never made to feel neglected. I felt sometimes ashamed that we didn't have a father. But I knew my father, I knew him very well. My mother sacrificed and worked to keep the unit of the family. That is part of the strength which she had gotten. She did not come out of a broken family. She knew her father. She was part of a big family with a Negro man at the head of it. So much of this seems to be abstracted from the continuity of life when you put it in a historical perspective.

RPW: I have observed that, time after time, in talking with Negroes I've interviewed in this series of things, a very strong reference to a father or a father-presence, a strong, driving personality.

RE: Yes. Well, that is true, I admit. The other things to be said—and this is the other side of the disorganization which did exist—you always had all these respectable men in the community who always went through the ritual of being concerned for the orphans and the widow women. And these women had a special status. The men did try to look out for them. Some of these were uneducated men; some of them were professionals. That was a part, at least, of Oklahoma City, the Negro community there. The first two boys who were signed up to go on the first encampment that the Negro community got together for the boys were Herbert and Ralph Ellison, my little brother and me. Because they were doing this for the community, and they looked out for those people who . . .

RPW: Because you were orphans?

RE: We were orphaned. And they respected my father. They knew what he was like and they knew what my mother was like.

RPW: Let me cut into some matters of American history, some American figures for a moment. Could you give a sort of character sketch, an estimate, of Thomas Jefferson?

RE: Well, Thomas Jefferson was a most sophisticated man of his times, an idealist given over to, I guess, a great concern with human possibility, drawing upon all the thought of European political philosophers, who set out with his colleagues to build a better way of life in this country. He was limited by the realities of his time, by the system of government and the necessities of production, which included slaves, and a number of other things. He was a politician. We tend to forget this too about him.

RPW: If he hadn't been he would have been in another line of work.

RE: He would have been in another line of work, and it's part of the fate of the politician to be involved—very deeply involved—in moral compromise. There's a lot being said about Jefferson's theories of Negro humanity and so on—

RPW: That's one of the things I'm getting at: what weight do you give to that, or what perspective do you put it in?

RE: Well, I put it in the perspective of history, of human history, and exactly that. I don't care whether he liked Negroes or not—I mean, that isn't important. What is important, it seems to me, is that he helped set up the Constitution. As long as I have the Constitution, I have the possibility of asserting myself and not depending upon any paternalistic ideas which Jefferson might have held or might not have held. You cannot demand too much of any human being. He moves out of his own historical circumstances, he moves in terms of his own personal life, he moves out of a complex of motives and ideals and frustrations and cowardices and heroisms which is faced by anyone who is lucky enough to get in a position of making important policy. But one thing is certain. His concept of human possibility was broad; in fact, it was noble. If he couldn't quite see some of my own people mixed in this, included in this, that's too bad. But the fact of it is that his efforts—and I think I'll probably live to see the day when the University of Virginia [founded by Jefferson] will be an instrument, an institution which helps extend the possibility of Negroes within Virginia. All you can ask is that a man do what he sees to be done as well as he can. I think that Jefferson did this.

Ezell A. Blair Jr., Stokely Carmichael, Lucy Thornton, and Jean Wheeler

March 4, 1964

Washington, DC

Robert Penn Warren met Ezell Blair at a conference on nonviolence at Howard University. Some months later, Blair arranged a group discussion for Warren at Blair's basement apartment in Washington, DC. Four young people were included, all students at Howard University who had been working in the civil rights movement.

Stokely Carmichael was born in Trinidad in 1941. He immigrated to the United States at the age of eleven and lived with his parents in New York City. Carmichael studied philosophy at Howard University. As a college freshman, Carmichael took part in his first Freedom Ride and was arrested in Jackson, Mississippi. He spent forty-nine days in the notorious state penitentiary known as Parchman Farm.

After graduating from Howard in 1964, Carmichael went on to become a leading organizer for the Student Nonviolent Coordinating Committee (SNCC) in Mississippi. He was initially a disciple of Dr. Martin Luther King Jr., but after experiencing the brutality of white supremacists in the South, he grew increasingly militant. When

*Carmichael was arrested in 1966 during a protest march in Missis-
sippi, he declared it was time to stop chanting "freedom" and demand
"black power" instead. The slogan quickly spread. Later, Carmichael
had a brief association with the Black Panthers, but soon left the group.
In 1969, Carmichael moved to the West African nation of Guinea,
where he took the name Kwame Ture and spent much of the rest of his
life.*

*Ezell Blair Jr. was one of four black college freshmen who staged a
historic sit-in at a whites-only lunch counter at the Woolworth's five-
and-dime store in his native Greensboro, North Carolina. On a Monday in February 1960, the Greensboro Four, as they came to be known,
sat down and politely ordered coffee at the lunch counter. A store man-
ager asked them to leave. The next day, twenty-nine other well-dressed
men and women from the Agricultural and Technical College of North
Carolina took turns asking for, and being refused, service. The protest
grew. By the weekend, some 1,400 protesters picketed the Greensboro
Woolworth's. The sit-in movement quickly spread to other restaurants
and towns throughout the South. The Greensboro Four acted on their
own initiative, not at the behest of any civil rights organization. A local
white businessman who supported the NAACP and gave money to the
Agricultural and Technical College encouraged their protest plans.*

*Blair was attending Howard University Law School when he and
his peers met with Warren. Blair later studied vocal performance at
the New England Conservatory of Music and worked as a teacher and
counselor in Massachusetts. In 1968, he joined the Islamic Center of
New England and changed his name to Jibreel Khazan.*

*Howard law student Lucy Thornton was born in West Point, Vir-
ginia, in 1939. Her mother ran a local seafood restaurant and was
active in the NAACP. Thornton grew up going to segregated public
schools. When she was twelve, the school board declared that African American students would be bused to an all-black school twenty*

minutes away, and that their local school would be closed. Black towns-people—including Thornton's mother—created their own makeshift school but were arrested for violating state law. Thornton began attending the county school but each autumn tried to register at the white school. She was rejected each time. The experience got her interested in becoming a lawyer.

After high school, Thornton attended the historically black Hampton Institute, where she encouraged fellow students to boycott local businesses that mistreated black customers. In 1961, she and fourteen other young African Americans were arrested for refusing to sit in the balcony of a segregated Virginia movie theater. After graduating from Howard Law School, Thornton practiced law for nearly fifty years. She was an early proponent of civil rights for transgender people.

Jean Wheeler was an activist from Detroit. Just months after the interview with Warren, which took place in the late winter of 1964, Wheeler volunteered to work on a SNCC voter registration drive in some of Mississippi's most dangerous territory: the town of Philadelphia and surrounding Neshoba County. In June of that year, civil rights workers James Chaney, Andrew Goodman, and Michael Schwerner disappeared. Though the men were widely thought to have been killed, Wheeler remained committed to helping the local SNCC campaign.

Wheeler and other SNCC workers set up shop in Philadelphia on the top floor of a two-story building. They strung barbed wire across the narrow stair to slow potential attackers. The men slept in the building, while Wheeler roomed with a woman down the street out of respect for community standards. Wheeler wedged a chair under the doorknob each night—there were no locks on the doors. "I went to sleep terrified and each morning woke up grateful that I was alive," Wheeler wrote. On August 4, the bodies of Chaney, Goodman, and Schwerner were discovered in an earthen dam. They had been murdered by white supremacists.

After her civil rights years, Wheeler became a pediatric psychiatrist and a published author.

ROBERT PENN WARREN: Mr. Blair, you were in the first sit-ins in Greensboro, weren't you?

EZELL A. BLAIR: Yes, I was.

RPW: Can you tell us something about the origins of those sit-ins? How were they arranged and planned beforehand?

EAB: The sit-ins originated, the idea originated with my roommate Joseph McNeil. We were all freshmen at A&T College [North Carolina Agricultural and Technical State University]. And one day, Joseph McNeil came into the room and he had a disturbed look on his face. I asked him what was wrong with him. And he told me he had just come from, I think, the Greyhound bus station in Greensboro. He asked to get served there at the lunch counter and he was refused. So I said, "Well, you know how things are. You know how segregation is. It's been here all the time. Nothing we can do about it."

RPW: Was he from the South or was he from the North?

EAB: He was from the South. He was from Wilmington, North Carolina. And I asked him, "Well, what can we do?"

And he said, "Well, we ought to have something like a boycott."

And I said, "A boycott?"

And he said, "Yes, we should go in and sit down at the lunch counter [and] ask for service. And if they refuse us, then we continue to sit there, and if we're thrown in jail, we go to jail. And then we ask the people not to buy in the place." And he named Woolworth.

RPW: And then what happened?

EAB: Well, we told our friends David Richmond, who's from Greensboro, and Franklin McCain, who's from Washington, and they liked the idea. So in the ensuing weeks we talked of our plans, things about the rights of man, and how we felt about being Negro, and the rights we felt should be ours. And finally, on January 31, 1960, the night before [the sit-in], Joe came into the room and asked us, were we ready to go? At first, I thought he was kidding. So, Frank, who was the largest guy in the group, said, "Are you guys chicken or something?"

And we said, "No, we aren't chicken."

And he said, "Well, we're going tomorrow down to Woolworth to sit in."

And I said, "Okay, we're going." Like that.

We told a local merchant there who worked with the NAACP. He always liked to [support] revolutionary ideas, but most of the conservatives in the NAACP at the time didn't like him because they said he was too much of a radical. So when we told him what we were going to do, he decided he would help us. He said he would give us money to buy articles downtown at Woolworth. He said he would contact reporters and the police department and everything like that. So the scene was set. We went downtown and we purchased articles at the merchandise counter at Woolworth, and then we proceeded toward the lunch counter, and we sat down, and we asked for service. So that's how the idea started.

RPW: Did this have any relation to the old March on Washington movement? Had you all read about that?

EAB: Well, no, we hadn't. We had not read about any of the previous movements.

RPW: Of course, that was a long time ago. That was back in '41.

EAB: I asked Joe where'd he get the idea from and he told me he got the idea from a boycott which took place in Wilmington in 1959, when he was a senior at high school there. He said they had a talent show and it was sponsored by a local soda pop firm. The prizes were all given to the whites and the Negroes didn't receive any prizes there at all. And the [Negroes] protested it by not buying sodas from the soda pop firm, and the firm reviewed its policies. They decided they would give the talent show over again and they gave out prizes to Negroes after that. So this is where Joe said he got the idea from. I didn't hear of any previous movement. Of course, the only one that we knew about was Martin Luther King's movement in Montgomery.

RPW: CORE [Congress of Racial Equality] was the organization that came in to back you up, wasn't it?

EAB: I think it was on the second day of our demonstration we called for the NAACP, but CORE came down first. Dr. [George] Simkins, who was president of the NAACP at the time, called in . . .

RPW: The local president.

EAB: The local president of the NAACP at the time called in CORE [field director] Gordon Carey. And Mr. Carey came down and he offered his assistance to our Student Executive Committee for Justice. This was a student group, which spearheaded the movement. We told any outside organizations coming in—because towns-folk might say that the movement was being taken over by outside people—we thanked him very much for his aid but we declined to take it. The next day, Herbert Wright, who was the youth secretary of the NAACP, came down, but he couldn't offer too much assistance. He only gave us moral support. So we passed up both.

RPW: Some of the reports on that are a little different from this account. Because some of them said that CORE came in immediately and was accepted. But you know because you were there.

EAB: I was there and we thanked [Gordon Carey] very much, but we told him, "We appreciate your aid but we would like for it to remain a student movement at the time. And if we need your help, we will call." And he went on to Durham, I believe, the next day.

RPW: Now, this is a rather important point. Some of the printed accounts say—unless my memory tricks me—that the appeal was made by your group to Mr. Simkins, is that right?

EAB: Yes, that's true. Dr. Simkins.

RPW: And Dr. Simkins, instead of going to the [national office of the] NAACP, as might have been expected, called in CORE, because he assumed that the NAACP would be too legalistic and not militant enough.

EAB: This is, to a certain extent, true. I think the Greensboro chapter of the NAACP was sort of blacklisted by national [organizers] after Dr. Simkins did this. When we left the Woolworth store on February 1, 1960, we were asked by a reporter from the *Greensboro Record*, "Were we sent there by the NAACP?" And we told the reporter, "No." Although some of us had been members of the NAACP when we were in high school, at the time none of us were members of the NAACP.

RPW: But you had repudiated both organizations as far as their help was concerned.

EAB: Yes, this is true. We wanted to sort of destroy the old idea that Negroes have to be told everything to do by the NAACP or CORE. It wasn't that we had disrespect for the groups, because we respected them very much, but it was just the idea that college students coming downtown, sitting in at [a lunch counter], couldn't do these things unless they were told to do it by somebody else.

RPW: The sit-in, itself, was not motivated by a notion, a criticism of the NAACP's previous role. Is that right?

EAB: Well, partially yes and partially no. When we talked about doing something to remove segregation in Greensboro, we mentioned the fact that the legal method, which had been used by groups like the NAACP, while it was a good method and a lasting method to be put on the books and so forth, was not a good method when it came to the immediate removal of discrimination. And we wanted to have a personal involvement in removing discrimination, which we felt the NAACP wouldn't go along with. And if they did, then the national office would take about two or three months before it gave us approval. By that time the idea would be lost, as many ideas of this nature were probably lost beforehand.

No, we didn't take a disrespectful attitude toward the NAACP. Oh, we realized that it has been the forerunner of the civil rights movement for a long time. And we respect the organization very much for what it has done. But we felt that it was time for new action to be taken in the South.

RPW: Here's a remark attributed to Mr. [Roy] Wilkins: "CORE furnished the noise but the NAACP pays the bills." That there's only one organization that can handle a long, sustained fight.

EAB: Well, I really don't think Mr. Wilkins is sincere about what he said because I think as a result of groups like SNCC, or SCLC, CORE—and other groups working in the South—the NAACP is getting many of its funds to fight the legal battles. Not taking anything away from NAACP. I think it's doing a very good job and will continue to do so. But the movement since 1960 has switched from a legal, courtroom battle to a battle between men, in regard to segregation. This is the basis of the present movement now.

RPW: But you don't mean to imply, do you, that a matter of direct action, nonviolent direct action, should supplant the continued effort to set up the legal framework and the legal philosophy that underlie the direct action?

EAB: No. While it is good to establish laws on the books, one of the main problems we have now is that we have many laws on the books in regard to segregation and discrimination in the schools and so forth, [but] we are having a problem of getting people to accept these laws. This is where direct, nonviolent action comes into play. These laws say no discrimination. So we are seeking equality.

RPW: The use of the direct action, then, is a way of implementing the law and of supplanting the law?

EAB: I think you can't separate the two. You need both, but I'm in disagreement with those who feel that the legal method is the only answer. And I am disagreeing with those who feel that the nonviolent method is the only answer. The conflict comes in where one group feels that the other group is of no use to the movement.

RPW: Let's change the subject a bit. Mr. Blair, how would you describe this so-called New Negro? How would you distinguish this character from previous characters? Or do you believe in this definition?

EAB: I don't think there is any such thing as a "New Negro." I think more people now are adopting the idea of a direct action. And more members of the Negro race, as well as many whites, now want to know more about the history of the Negro. And this new idea of militancy is being adopted by more people in mass numbers. There have been many people before us, such as [W.E.B.] Du Bois, and [Paul] Robeson and Walter White and Roy Wilkins, James Weldon Johnson, and so forth, who have been what they call "radical Negroes," or "New Negroes." But they were only small in number.

Now, since 1960, and since King's movement in Montgomery, there are mass numbers who are accepting these ideas, that we must do something, personally, to remove segregation. And so I think while the idea of the New Negro is still with us, in many respects the idea is not a new one; it's something that's existed all the time.

Warren asks how involved Southern black people have become in the civil rights movement and its leadership, especially in groups like SNCC and CORE.

EAB: From my observation, [the movement] has been primarily composed of college students and high school students who want to do something about eradicating segregation. The majority of CORE members are college students and high school students. The NAACP is made mostly of professional people, and so is the Urban League. But I feel that the movement, since 1960, has become mostly college students. And, especially since 1963, the movement has become one in which we have adults involved—people old enough to register to vote, people who have jobs, people who are seeking all these things that we've been talking about: better employment, less police brutality, and so forth.

RPW: Two things, like the registration drives and the boycotts, including the bus boycott, have moved toward a mass base, is that it?

EAB: That's right, yes.

STOKELY CARMICHAEL: I'm not sure. If we start with the Montgomery movement—that had mass movement in that everybody was a part of it—but that was a passive action. They just didn't take the bus. Wasn't anything that was going on in the street. Now, I would say the first mass movement that resembled the new wave, ever since 1960, would have to be Albany, Georgia. We had seven hundred people arrested from the town. And we got the demonstrations against segregation [in public] facilities and all the [people] of that town walking up and down the streets. Since then, we've had Cambridge, [Maryland]; we've had Danville, [Virginia]; we've had Birmingham; we've had Greenwood and Jackson, Mississippi. It has become, since then, a mass movement. Now, there are a few professional agitators—I don't have qualms about using the word "agitators" at all—who do agitate. But once a movement gets going, in most cases, it's aimed at a mass movement. You go back to '61, the Freedom Rides, for example—when we were arrested, we just went into jail. But now a number of SNCC people came and decided to start agitation in Jackson to get Jackson's people to go to jail, and they got fifty people from Jackson, Mississippi, to go to jail. That was a big step up. And from then started the whole thing about mass movements in jail.

Warren asks the students about W.E.B. Du Bois's idea of a split psyche in black Americans, where there are competing impulses to identify with an African heritage or with mainstream American society.

LUCY THORNTON: Yes, my first reaction, of course, would be thinking of Socrates: "Know thyself." You would think that the problem or the dilemma that Mr. Du Bois speaks of is one which is very common to Negro Americans today, because we do face the problem of amalgamation into the whole of American life. And I think that we, as black people, have an obligation to know ourselves. Know ourselves as black men. Be proud of what we are and contribute to America, what we could actually offer to this culture. I believe there is something unique which the black man can offer to this melting pot, insofar that there is still a melting pot.

SC: Professor [Melville] Herskovits, in this book *The Myth of the Negro Past,* tried to show that Negroes in America had some connection with African ritualists in the African culture. Professor [E. Franklin] Frazier clearly answered him and showed him that he was just all wrong on that issue.

RPW: That the Negro is totally of the American culture.

SC: Totally of the American culture. And that makes the Negro a unique specimen in America, because he is the only one who is totally American. And, I forgot the name of the psychologist out of the University of Chicago who contends—he's Jewish and he was in one of these camps in Germany—and he wrote a book, but I forgot the name of it also, in which he showed that the people who were oppressed usually take on all the mannerisms of the oppressors. This, for instance, would be a classic example of Frazier's black bourgeoisie. When the oppressed people take on all the characteristics of the oppressed, they exaggerate.

As far as the movement has developed thus far, it's not a revolution. It's not even a reform. Negroes have been trying to get into the established system as it is now. "Let us get into your job, let us get into your restaurant, let us get into the housing neighborhoods, let's get into your schools. We just want to get into it." That's the way it's been so far, and that's a fact.

RPW: There are some people—James Baldwin among them— who will say, in part at least, that the Negro is prepared to offer a fundamental criticism of middle-class American values.

SC: Baldwin is right and he's not right. The Negro whom he speaks about is not the Negro who the white press allows to speak. The Negro who speaks [to the press] is the one who says, "Yes, I am wearing a tie and a suit. I'm clean. I've been to a college in the South, and I'm a college professor in the South, or I'm a Negro lawyer or a Negro doctor. And my accent is clear. My English is superb, and I have a Cadillac, and what else can you expect of me?"

That's not the Negro that Baldwin is talking about. The Negro that Baldwin is talking about is the one who's down on the bottom with nothing to offer. In that sense, then we really have integration, because [when] we talk about integration, we talk about bringing two things together. You know, I have my chitlins, I have my wine on Friday night, I'll come in your house, you eat some of my fried chicken, and I'll eat some of your *à la carte* whatever-it-is. But as far as it's seen now, it's just the Negroes fighting to get into something. It's like you're giving up everything. You're giving up your jazz. You're giving up your soul music, your Ray Charles—as we say, the nitty gritty—to get into this.

RPW: Now, we spoke earlier today, you and I, of [Professor E.U.] Essien-Udom on black nationalism. He makes the point—if I remember the book correctly—that even the separatists and the black nationalists like the Black Muslims are actually, perhaps unconsciously, moving toward a full acceptance of American middle-class values. That this provides a conduit, a backstairs ladder to the achievement of middle-class values, even though they are not specified by that group.

SC: I think that's a fair diagnosis because Negroes in America have not been presented any other alternative, you see. I prefer to say the Italians were having trouble and the Italians were having some home culture to fall back on. We have no home culture to fall back on. None at all. We have a subculture within a main culture. And the main culture suppressed us. But I bet you if you went South and asked a Negro girl or a Negro boy to draw a picture of a man on the board, they would inevitably draw the picture of a white man or a white woman, with features of a white man or a white woman. Recently, for instance, they did a psychology test where they had Negro dolls and white dolls. And they would have Negro girls come and pick which doll was prettiest. And inevitably they picked the white doll.

EAB: Many of us in the movement now are going through these experiences—whether we should adopt the full values of white, middle-class society or whether we should develop within ourselves, and through this thing that we call the movement, an image of what we'd like to think of as being ourselves. Being accepted as Negro and not as white. I know many times I have confronted this problem of whether I should adopt the values of a middle-class American society or whether I could be myself, the Negro. I don't think all the white, middle-class values are good for Negroes at this point.

RPW: Or for white people.

EAB: Or the white people. I don't think that we should accept these values because, while this is a capitalist society we live in, Negroes, who are in many instances on the bottom of the income bracket, could not think of wearing a hundred-dollar suit down the street every day, or driving a Cadillac. We just don't have the economic ability to do these things. So I don't think integration is the best thing for us. We already have interracial marriage. You can look around and see Negroes of many different complexions. I do feel that we, as a group of people, should try to develop more unity among ourselves. And I feel this is one of the things that the civil rights movement is doing. Many young people now are beginning to feel proud to be black. There still is, I should say, a greater sense that the Negro is turning into white. They use straightening combs. They process their hair. They imitate everything American white society does. But I hope to see, [through] this movement, that the Negro will recognize the fact that once and for all they are Negroes. That we're black. And that there are many things that we can contribute to American society, which are good. And that there are already many values and contributions that we have made to American society.

LT: I'm very much aware of the people, even within my own family, who would very strongly say that we're *so* American. And we've gotten this certain amount of acceptance. But the Negro or the black man in this country still has to know and accept and be proud of himself as a black man, and have America accept him as the same. Because the black man can find himself lost in the white man's America. In other words, he can do everything under the sun which would make him an ordinary, A-1 American man. And he thinks that he's been accepted, not only by Negroes, but by the larger society, as just another American. He reached the top of a ladder. He's a great man in everybody's book. But it's gonna come back to him over and over—as much as he wants to abandon the idea—that he's a member of a minority, he's just another black man. When he gets to the top of it all, there's gonna be somebody who's in that majority, white and probably not worth one-ninetieth of what he's worth. He's gonna step on his toes and spit in his face, and say, "Look, you're still black." Yes, he's an American, very much American. Probably more American than the person who just said that to him. But keep in mind you're a black American and you have a place, you know.

Warren remarks that the white, Southern segregationist fears his culture is under attack, that he's being robbed of his identity and his history by those who demand racial equality. He says the poorly educated or unreflective Southerner sees segregation as essential to his sense of self.

sc: The whole statement is very, very ironic because if the white Southerner knew anything about his history, number one, he would know that after Reconstruction there was no official segregation in state law. That Negroes and whites went to school together because the South, at that time, had just received free schools.

rpw: The Civil War generation thought segregation was preposterous.

sc: They certainly did. And it didn't come until Mississippi started instituting the black codes, so that his whole tradition, his whole feelings, were molded by institutions.

rpw: A generation back.

sc: A generation back. So that when he tells me now that you can change the laws but you can't change the people, he evidently doesn't know what he's talking about.

lt: By the way, few Negroes would say they're Southern. There are very few would dare say they're Southerners. And I would agree with Stokely that there had been a time when, in fact, the white man recognized the black man's existence. And now, all of a sudden, he wants them erased from his mind. He thinks this is something that he's forced by law to put up with or something to segregate out of his society, to keep out altogether. I think more and more the new Southerner will realize the black man has a place there in the South. That the black man can, in fact, help to make the South a great South again. In other words, they'll have to recognize that more than just the brawn and the labor of the black man made what they call the "Old South" great. They've got to recognize that this black man can stand side by side with them in education and everything else and make the South what it ought to be today.

The conversation turns to whether black business and community leaders in the South are reluctant to be associated with the civil rights movement because integration might mean the loss of their caste superiority within black communities.

EAB: It's popular now to be in the movement. Like in Greensboro, North Carolina, for instance, there once was a time when Negroes would oppose integration because Negroes, themselves, on the whole, were not in favor of it. Now, since the idea of desegregation has come about through the masses of the Negro community, many of them have jumped on the bandwagon; and they go along with it. And so you see, maybe, this outstanding attorney in the community, or this Negro businessman, supporting desegregation of the lunch counters, or the jobs and so forth. I think that they recognize that desegregation is not a real threat to them. I don't think Negroes are going to go outside the Negro community. As long as we live together, I think we're going to socialize together, I think we're going to pray together, and so on. Having seen a few integrated situations, and having found the Negro still comes back to the [neighborhood] café and so on, they have realized that their interests are not so much in danger as they thought.

JEAN WHEELER: The point I wanted to make is that along with desegregation in public facilities, [there] is getting people registered and getting people voting. I don't know why people always keep talking about desegregation as the focus of the movement. I think that surely is a part of it. But at least on par with that is the effort to develop political strength in the South. And the businesspeople know that when it comes time to find a leader, they are going to be the ones. If only because the things that they represent are the things Negroes in general want to have. Everybody respects a man with education. So these people, I think, can now see gains they couldn't see before for themselves. Because when it comes time to redistrict the town, or when it comes time to send somebody to Congress, it's going to be one of them.

Warren asks the students about Charles Evers's suggestion that white segregationists, having been raised in a culture that respects courage, will recognize and be sympathetic to the bravery of civil rights activists.

EAB: I agree with him on that statement. When we started the sit-in movement in 1960, we met the mayor of Greensboro and representatives associated with Woolworth's stores. They were straightforward when they found out that we weren't going to back down. They told us that we were giving Greensboro a bad name and that this would hurt the city economically. And we told them we weren't going to move. And then the gentleman told us, he said that he respected that. He said, "Look. We're not worried so much about you starting trouble. What we're worrying about is the poor whites starting trouble. The fighting and so forth. We know that you're going to be nonviolent." This was a great shock to me because this was the first time that I had ever come into contact with the middle-class or the upper-class white community admitting that the poor whites would cause trouble.

Warren quotes journalist Carl Rowan, who predicted that all the racial unrest in the South might be merely a dress rehearsal for the upheaval that would occur when the civil rights movement took on prejudice in the North.

EAB: I agree with that. About 51 percent of the Negroes live outside the South nowadays. And most of them live in the North. Most of them who come from the South are not educated. They've gone to the North with the idea of the "glorious North," or the candyland where opportunities are bright. And going there they find out, in many instances, it's worse than the South. And even with Negroes having the right to public accommodations and so forth in the North, they [overlook] the problem of getting equal job employment, of getting decent housing. In reality, there is still segregated housing. And so many of them can't face up to this problem. As a result of this you can expect there to be more racial imbalance and more racial conflict than there is in the South. And you can expect more violence in the North than you can in the South.

When it comes down to it, Negroes are prisoners within their own country. It's really going to be a fight where we have to stand alone. Violence would not work, I don't think. We're outnumbered, number-wise. We're outnumbered, gun-wise. We're outnumbered so far as the law is concerned because in most communities the law, the police, which are supposed to secure the community's peace, are really using it to uphold segregation.

Kenneth B. Clark

March 7 and 15, 1964

New York, New York

Kenneth B. Clark was an influential psychologist and social activist. He devoted his life to researching the impact of racism on children and improving public schools in poor urban communities, especially Harlem. "The most horrible thing about Harlem—about all the ghettos," Clark said, "is the day-to-day destruction of human potential." Clark tried to avert that destruction with the zeal of a missionary, opening a psychiatric clinic in Harlem in the 1940s to serve African American families and, in the 1950s and '60s, developing large-scale programs designed to integrate public schools and equalize learning opportunities for all children. These programs were often scuttled by political machinations well beyond his control and by entrenched racism, but Clark remained a staunch integrationist. He believed the fight for equality would never be achieved through racial separatism, which he said was a blind alley that signaled "the abandonment of hope." Clark struggled to maintain his own sense of hope, but he was convinced that the fight for social justice was "the highest form of life."

Kenneth Clark is best known for an experiment he created in the late 1930s with his wife, Mamie Phipps Clark, which demonstrated the damage of racism and segregation on black children. In the so-called doll

JW: I know the argument very well, that we are outnumbered, that it would be a massacre, and so on. But as soon as you start saying, "We're beat before we're started," then the whole depth of what you're doing has been lessened because you are not willing to take it all the way. I personally am willing to take it all the way. If I get shot then I just have to get shot. As long as you let whoever's pushing you up against the wall know that, you have a much better chance of winning. But I think that as soon as Negroes start saying, "Well, we can't win anyway," they're very close to lost.

EAB: I'm in it all the way. But if violence came and I had no resort but to protect my home and my family, I would. I don't read [the situation] the same way Martin Luther King reads it. I am not a minister, and I don't take the same views that many ministers take, the nonviolent attitude. I think there comes a time when a man has to stand up. And in America, people respect a man who is brave and who will stand up for a cause. Now, if this leads to violence, then I say let it come.

test, the Clarks presented a brown doll and a white doll to young African American children and asked them to identify which of the dolls was a good or bad one, which they preferred, and which they identified with. In repeated studies in the North and South, a majority of the children would choose the white doll. "The results of our studies," Clark said, "were indicative of the dehumanizing, cruel impact of racism in our allegedly democratic society. . . . These children were . . . seeing themselves in terms of the society's definition of their inferior status."

Clark found particularly stark evidence of this when he conducted the experiment with a young African American boy in rural Arkansas. When he asked the child which doll was most like him, the boy pointed to the brown doll and said, "That's a nigger. I'm a nigger." Clark said that he found the boy's response "as disturbing, or more disturbing, than the children in Massachusetts who would refuse to answer the question, or who would cry and run out of the room."

The Clarks' findings were used as evidence by NAACP lawyers in the landmark 1954 Brown v. Board of Education *case, in which the U.S. Supreme Court ruled that segregation in public schools was illegal. In the unanimous opinion, Chief Justice Earl Warren wrote that separating black children from others in school "generates a feeling of inferiority . . . that may affect their hearts and minds in a way unlikely ever to be undone." A 1950 report Clark had written to that effect was footnoted in the decision.*

Kenneth Clark was born in the Panama Canal Zone in 1914 and moved with his mother to New York City when he was a young boy. Clark attended relatively integrated schools in Harlem and earned his bachelor's degree at Howard University in 1935. He married Mamie Phipps, a fellow Howard student, in 1938. In 1940, Clark became the first African American to be awarded a doctorate in psychology by Columbia University. He joined the faculty of City College of New York in 1942 and later became the school's first black full professor.

Clark was a prolific writer and published numerous studies on racism and segregation over his lifetime. He was a frequent contributor to the opinion pages, railing against racial separatism and reminding readers that America had yet to fully enact the 1954 Brown *ruling.*

Clark served on the New York State Board of Regents, was the first black person to be elected president of the American Psychological Association, and was honored with an array of lifetime achievement awards. Despite the accolades, Clark could be despondent. "There are times," he told a journalist in 1982, "when I feel that all I've done with my life is produce documents—reports, memorandums, books—and that as for actually helping produce social change, my life has been one big failure. It's as if I were a physician, and the disease had metastasized." Until his death, in 2005, Clark continued to work on the patient.

When Robert Penn Warren interviewed Clark in 1964 he sensed two sides of the famous psychologist. In Who Speaks? *Warren wrote that Clark was a man of warmth and courtesy, but that sometimes "he seems to withdraw into a world shadowed by a bitterness not easy to define." Perhaps, Warren mused, "This . . . is merely a mark of our common humanity."*

ROBERT PENN WARREN: Years ago I read [W.E.B.] Du Bois. And I was struck by the topic of the split in the Negro psyche. The drive toward the *mystique noir*, toward the African heritage, toward the sense of a Negro culture as one pull, one pole of experience, and one desire for development. [Then] the other, the exact opposite, the moving into the Western, European-American, Judeo-Christian tradition. Being absorbed into that as fully as possible, even with the possible consequence of the loss of his sense of racial identity. These are two separate impulses. Does this strike you, as a psychologist, as a real problem?

KENNETH CLARK: As a psychologist, I'm convinced that Du Bois was correct. The Negro in America is ambivalent in his feelings about his place in the larger society and in his feelings about himself. It would be a little bit of a miracle if he could have adapted to the whole history of cruelty and oppression and come out of this with a positive, unalloyed image of self, or feelings about the society which has oppressed him in the context of a democratic ideology.

One of the things we ought to recognize right away is that Du Bois was one of the first Americans, Negro or white, to recognize the importance of Africa. Du Bois was talking about pan-Africanism, and the fact that Africa was going to be the significant area of the world in the latter part of the twentieth century, as early as the beginning of the twentieth century. He was saying this when other people barely knew what Africa was. When even the average, intelligent American's image of Africa was largely that of a bunch of savages and cannibals.

RPW: Do you see any cultural continuity of the American Negro with Africa?

KC: Personally, I don't. I think of Africa pretty much the way I think of Asia, or Europe, or South America. In terms of any conscious or cultural continuity between the American Negro and Africa, I think one has to be realistic. One has to recognize that [the] American slave trade systematically sought to destroy any such continuity. The Africans were not brought here and given the opportunity to continue any of their prior heritage.

Warren asks Clark about the difficulty of establishing a positive sense of black self-identity in an oppressive society like the United States.

KC: If one looks at the Negro spirituals, one sees attempts and struggles toward some kind of positive identity through protest, through hope, through an anguished desire for a better lot. I can't buy, totally, the feeling that oppression destroys the identity-surge of human beings. I think, for example, if one looks at the Jews, who have gone through much longer periods of oppression, cruelty, and barbarity, you sometimes get the feeling that the Jewish identity has as its nucleus around which everything else clusters the protest against oppression. That the Jew sees himself as someone who exists because he has been oppressed.

RPW: He also had, in a differing degree anyway, a sense of a cultural continuity and knowledge of his history.

KC: In knowledge of his history [there] was a knowledge of the series of oppressions.

RPW: This brings in Malcolm X then, doesn't it? The creation of the past. As opposed to what might be the real past.

KC: I don't know what is the real past, for the American Negro. I think that Malcolm X is an example—or black nationalism of which he is merely one form—is an example of the struggle to create a past. When the [Black] Muslims call themselves "true Muslims," it is because this was the heritage of their forefathers. I'm not sure how much reality they have here. I think this is real in the sense of a wish, real in the sense of satisfying sort of a fantasy.

If one were to be bluntly realistic and logical about this, it would seem to me that the American Negro's past, functionally, begins with the slave trade. This is the only verifiable continuity that he has. Obviously, he has something before that, but in terms of the meaning of his present experience, and existence, [it] is to be understood in terms of seventeenth-century events, catastrophic events. He was uprooted. He was literally snatched away from whatever past he had and had to begin anew here.

RPW: Now, psychologically, what weight do you put on this fact? On the Negro situation, as opposed to that of say the Jew or the Japanese or any other minority group which brings to America a formed tradition and has a glorious past it knows about?

KC: Obviously, that type of advantage provides some stability of self, stability of the group. It provides a rallying point for the individuals who comprise the group. The Negro's rallying point has had to be shared oppression, you see. He has had to build a sense of group, a sense of belongingness out of the common experience in terms of this new culture. Mainly, he was oppressed. And he had the human desire to become free of the oppression. He has translated his desire to be free of oppression as also meaning to be incorporated into this system, without regard to his color, because he sees himself as an integral part of this society. He helped to build it. He contributed as much as any other group who has comprised America, and more than most.

RPW: Can we make out a case for the Negro situation as being, actually, an existential advantage, psychologically?

KC: I don't quite understand what you mean by existential advantage.

RPW: The fact that he is not burdened with a past.

KC: But I think the Negro is burdened by a past, which determines the future which he's seeking to create. He is burdened by a past that begins with disruption, that begins with stark and flagrant cruelty and barbarity. This is the beginning of his past in a sense. And this past continues into about two hundred years of systematic exploitation and cruelty, which is slavery. This is his heritage. And he has been the object of the problems of whites, who have this glorious past. He is the culmination of the meaning of the white culture in civilization in terms of the dehumanization of him. This is his past. This is the past which he is burdened with. And this is the past of the whites, who are so proud of their past, you see. The

Negro becomes the personification of all that is meaningful in the
white man's past, because he is the stark example of the meaning of
the white man's Christianity. This is a complex past. And it's a kind
of past which determines the nature of his present and the kind of
future he is insisting upon. He's insisting upon a future that will
make the white man whole.

RPW: Make the white man what?

KC: Whole (laughs). There is something ironic about this discussion about who has and who doesn't have a past, when, actually,
the present has fused the past of Negro and white. This may be
terribly disturbing to the white. By the way, this image of fusion is
both literal and figurative, because you asked me about my feelings
about Africa. It might be disturbing to the general American public
for a Negro to dare to say that he feels no more identification with
Africa than he feels with Denmark or Ireland. But actually, in terms
of what he is, he is as much Irish or English or Danish, as he is African, because of this more literal fusion . . .

RPW: You mean blood fusion.

KC: Blood fusion that has occurred in America during these past
three hundred years. You have a blood fusion, you have an historical
fusion, you have a psychological fusion. And I suspect—and I certainly haven't worked this out; I wish I had a little time and luxury
in which to try and work it out—but much of the ambivalence
that Du Bois referred to, and which we see so clearly today among
Negroes, may be a reflection of this total fusion that he is.

RPW: Do you see more resistance now to the blood fusion on the
part of Negroes than in the past? Either in actual intermarriage and
in actual interfusion of bloods, licitly or illicitly, and in the emula-
tion of the white physical ideal, that was true, say, a generation ago?

KC: On the ideological level there's probably a greater resistance
on the part of Negroes to mix with whites now than in the past.

But I think we ought to be careful to make a distinction between ideology, in verbal postures, and what actually happens. I would like to know where one can find reliable statistics on incidents of intermarriage over a period of time.

RPW: There is a paradox here, isn't there?

KC: Unquestionably. The American race is best seen in terms of paradox and contradiction and inconsistencies and mess.

Warren cites a 1963 essay in Commentary *magazine by Norman Podhoretz, then a liberal Democrat, describing his fear of black people as a child in Brooklyn, and arguing that America's race dilemma would best be solved by "the wholesale merging of the two races."*

KC: My first reaction was that this was a curiously and scathingly honest piece. The second part of my reaction was that I thought his solution made no sense at all, for a very simple reason. It didn't work in the past; there's no reason to believe that it is going to work in the future. Norman Podhoretz talked about assimilation of whites and Negroes as if this was something that was new. What he apparently didn't understand was that white males have long been exploiting Negro females. This is part of racism. And one has to look long and hard to find any pure-blooded American Negroes. The mixture of the American Negroes is not a reflection of white women bearing children from Negro males. Well, if miscegenation—which is the real word here rather than assimilation—if miscegenation hasn't worked from slavery, if a white male could be as brutal toward his own flesh and blood as he was toward other Negroes, or colored, in America, why does Norman Podhoretz think that legalizing the mixture is going to change the psychological and social situation any?

RPW: Anyway, it is a long postponement of any solution.

KC: Right. What he is asking for will not be a means toward the end, an ethical end, but will be an indication of the fact that the ethical end was obtained by other means. Once you get a meaningful, equal, human form of interracial mixture in America, this would be one of your best indications that the complexities of the problems of racial cruelty have already been resolved.

RPW: Tell what you mean by the word "race"? What is the nature of this concept?

KC: Well, the word "race" is one of those ambiguous terms that man uses. It is one of those terms in which its very ambiguity is the basis of controversy and confusion and conflict. As I see it, race is used in America as a very convenient pretext by which a group of human beings who have power, or believe they have power, seek to arrogate the power onto themselves and restrict the extent of power status for others.

Warren asks Clark about American Communist support for black people in the years leading up to World War II.

KC: Prior to the Hitler-Stalin pact, the Communists were very concerned about racial discrimination and segregation in the United States. And they were busy telling Negroes, "Don't join a segregated army. Fight for your right to be a full American." After the Hitler-Stalin Pact, the Communists changed their tune and their advice to the American Negroes. The Nazis were not so terrible any longer. There were all sorts of justifications. And, of course, there were many Communists who were disillusioned at that time and left the party. But, when Hitler attacked Russia, in spite of the pact, then the Communists were not any longer so concerned with the indignities heaped upon Negroes in a segregated army. They wanted all Negroes to go out and volunteer to fight the fascist, no matter the conditions under which they were required to fight. I mean, the

same people who were trying to seduce me into the party with croc-
odile tears about the humiliation of segregation were now calling
me—and I mean literally the same persons were talking to me now
after Hitler attacked Russia—calling me a black chauvinist because
I was still concerned with segregation. To this day, I am thankful
that whatever it was that made me suspicious of them when they
seemed so much on my side saved me from ever getting involved
with them. Now you could say: "Look, these people were just being
practical. To them, the future of Russia was more important than
how any individual Negro felt about being segregated."

RPW: So you believe in a socialist society as an ideal?

KC: Frankly, Mr. Warren, I don't know what I believe in, now.
I purchase stock on the stock market. I believe in this capitalist
society. I don't believe that it is always just. Or sensitive or efficient.
I don't think it is always as efficient as it could be. I'll be fifty this
year. And at this age, I can't believe in generalized abstract societies.
I believe in the inevitability of struggle. I believe that human beings
will develop the most vital kind of society in which they are free to
struggle toward developing the best that they can arrive at. I don't
believe in fixed societies. And I am clearly aware of the fact that I
am being incoherent now.

Warren asks Clark to reflect on the civil rights slogan "Freedom Now."

KC: "Freedom Now" means a demand. It means an absolute.
It means an insistence. And in the future, of course, it's going to
mean some kind of accommodation. But the greater the accommodation that has to be made, the greater the weakness of the total
social fabric. There're many people who are stating and mouthing
the slogan "Freedom Now" who have a rather simplistic, literalistic view of it, you see. And maybe this, too, has always been true

historically—that the cutting edge of any movement, like John Brown, the cutting edge has to be literalistic in order to assume that role.

RPW: What do you think of [the radical abolitionist] John Brown, by the way?

KC: I think he's a very powerful force in the growth and development of this country, and . . .

RPW: He was a force, clearly. How would you evaluate him morally or psychologically? Or both?

KC: Well, psychologically, the simple designation of John Brown might be too simple. A fanatic, a neurotic, a liberalist, an absolutist. A man who was so totally committed to his commitment that nothing, including reality, stood in his way.

RPW: How do you treat a man like that in ordinary society?

KC: The society can take care of itself with men like that; it always has. See what it did to Christ.

RPW: Do you think Christ and John Brown should be equated?

KC: Oh, unquestionably.

RPW: Equated psychologically?

KC: Of course.

RPW: In their values or simply in their neuroses?

KC: In their values in their neuroses. And of course in their end.

RPW: Christ said, "I am the Prince of Peace." John Brown lived in a dream of bloodshed. That's some difference, isn't it?

KC: Yes, but Christ also ran money changers out of . . .

RPW: Took the scourge out, but this is to be equated with the Harpers Ferry massacre?

KC: All right, don't push me that far.

RPW: We have to, if we are going to talk about it, you know.

KC: Now, look. Christ was clearly a person committed to values other than those which were prevailing at his time. He not only was committed, but the extent and depth and reality of his commitment were expressed by his life. You know, the fact that he lived his commitment. He did not make accommodation to the realities that even some of his disciples did. Christ was atypical. Christ was alienated. Christ had positive values that he was willing to run risk for. And he paid the ultimate price. Christ, Socrates, John Brown—these people are . . .

RPW: Let me ask you a question, specifically. Suppose a man like John Brown, with the same burning eye, came into your office and said, "I'm tired of this fooling around in this here matter. I'm going down to Mississippi and take six or seven strong, determined people with me, and I am going to slaughter the governor and his entire staff in the Capitol. And come out and say, 'Rise and follow me.' " Now this is almost an exact parallel. What would you do about this man, who came to your office and asked you for a hundred dollars to help finance the trip?

KC: First, I wouldn't give him a hundred dollars.

RPW: Well, would you give him fifty?

KC: No, I wouldn't give him anything. I would probably see what I could do to help this man, if it would not inconvenience me too much. I'm frank to say to you that I'm a college professor, you see. I have a vested interest in either/or-ing. I have a vested interest in maintaining issues on a level of discussion rather than action. And anybody who says anything to me about bloodshed is not going to get a sympathetic response from me. I personally recoil against bloodshed because I think it is just another form of human idiocy. The fact still remains that major social changes toward social justice in human history have come, almost always—if not always—through irrational and questionable methods. Apparently rational, reasonable men who are seeking a change in the status quo are generally ineffectual. Changes in the status quo are more likely to come from irrational, unreasonable, questionable men.

RPW: Let's switch the question. How much of the movement today resembles a revolution?

KC: Well, I think the term "revolution" is sort of a catchphrase and has some kind of a dramatic impact, but I don't think it is too helpful in describing the civil rights movement today. Revolution connotes the use of military methods and weapons, which obviously is not possible here. The second thing is maybe even more important: the desire to change the total political, the social, and the economic structure. This is clearly not indicated here. What I think the Negro is asking for is not a change in the total social, political, and economic structure of this system. All he is asking for is *in*. He is asking to be included. He's saying, "Look, I like this system so much, I want to be a part of it."

Warren asks about how that sentiment jibes with James Baldwin's famous question, "Do I really want to be integrated into a burning house?"

KC: I think this is a cry of anguish and despair. Not to be taken too literally. I mean, you just ask yourself the question, "What other choice [do we have]?"

RPW: That is a rational question, but there may be some deep dissatisfaction with American middle-class values involved here.

KC: Well, look. The guys who work for *Time* and *Life*, or on Madison Avenue, have deep dissatisfaction with American middle-class values—

RPW: I don't blame them, to tell you the truth—

KC: But they don't reject it—they still live in Hastings and Great Neck. And they still buy the status cars, large or small, depending upon the particular fashion. I don't want to disparage out of hand these comments, except that again I have to respect your question and give the best possible answer I can.

RPW: It is a real question, though.

KC: Except that it isn't a real question, because there are no choices. You know, there are no alternatives here.

RPW: This is a real question, though.

KC: Baldwin, to me, is one of the most disturbing, irritating, incisive critics of our society at this time, you see. But this doesn't mean that Baldwin has the answers all the time. I mean, Baldwin expresses anguish. Baldwin expresses frustration, concern, you know, and a wish for something better. And he also expresses the feeling that maybe he isn't going to get even the minimum, so therefore forget everything else, in a sense.

I think what Baldwin is expressing is his desires, what he would like human beings to be like, what he would like the society to be like. Maybe what Baldwin has not yet understood and probably never should understand—maybe he should never accept the possibility that there might be a tremendous gap between what he would like and what can be, because this might reduce his potency, his power as a passionate, incisive critic of what is.

Jim Baldwin has no choice other than to be incorporated within this society and this culture pretty much as it is. Now, what I will entertain the possibility of is that if America is capable of including the Negro more into the fabric of its society, this will—on its face—strengthen the society. Not necessarily change it. Not necessarily change its values, but make the existing values (laughs) less liable to internal decay.

James M. Lawson Jr.

March 17, 1964

Memphis, Tennessee

The Reverend James Lawson had a profound influence on the civil rights movement, teaching the doctrine and methods of nonviolent protest to nearly a generation of activists. A pacifist, Lawson was jailed for refusing to fight in the Korean War. He then spent three years as a missionary in India, where he studied anticolonialism and Mohandas Gandhi's teaching on nonviolent revolution. In 1957, while enrolled in Oberlin College's Graduate School of Theology, Lawson met Martin Luther King Jr., who convinced him to move south and join the civil rights movement. King said, "Come now. We don't have a person with your experience in nonviolence."

In 1958 Lawson was appointed the southern field secretary of the Fellowship of Reconciliation, an organization devoted to peace and justice. He moved to Nashville, Tennessee, where he was able to transfer to Vanderbilt University's divinity school. Lawson began conducting workshops on nonviolent direct action and became a leading figure in the Nashville civil rights movement. His classes drew African American students from Vanderbilt and four black colleges in the area, as well as a smattering of whites. A number of Lawson's acolytes went on to be major leaders in the broader movement, including Diane Nash, James Bevel, Marion Barry, and John Lewis.

Lawson's workshops included role-playing exercises where students would be taunted and attacked to learn how to maintain their "poise under duress," as Lawson put it. When a group of students staged a sit-in at the Woolworth's lunch counter in Greensboro, North Carolina, in early 1960, Lawson presided over a well-trained cadre of volunteers eager to follow suit in Nashville. The most dramatic sit-in occurred on February 27, which was dubbed "Big Saturday." Some three hundred students amassed at a handful of downtown stores and sat down at the "whites only" lunch counters. After one group was harassed, beaten, and arrested, another group took its place. Eighty-one students, nearly all of them black, were arrested that day. In the months that followed, an expanding number of Nashville protesters kept up pressure on the city until local businesses began desegregating in the spring. King called the Nashville Movement "the best organized and most disciplined in the Southland." Lawson deserved much of the credit. According to historian Clayborne Carson, "Lawson's intellectual and moral leadership gave the local Nashville Movement a strength of purpose that no other student group could match."

The president of Vanderbilt was not pleased with this leadership, however, and expelled Lawson in March of 1960. Lawson quickly finished his degree at Boston University and returned south to continue his activism. He was a key influence at the founding conference of the Student Nonviolent Coordinating Committee (SNCC) in 1960, convincing delegates to embrace nonviolence as an organizing principle. At a SNCC conference later that year, Lawson spoke for many young activists when he urged anyone who got arrested to forgo bail and remain in jail. Lawson faulted earlier tactics, saying, "Instead of letting the adults scurry around getting bail, we should have insisted they scurry about to end the system which had put us in jail." The practice of "jail not bail" became a crucial tactic of civil rights protesters as the movement expanded. On May 24, 1961, Lawson had an opportunity to use it when he was arrested in Jackson, Mississippi, along with other Freedom Riders challenging segregation on interstate buses.

James Lawson was born in 1928 in Pennsylvania and raised in Ohio. His father was a Methodist minister who carried a .38 pistol when moving about the South. He organized local NAACP chapters along the circuit he traveled. It was Lawson's mother who shaped his views on pacifism. Historian Michael Honey writes that when Lawson was a child, he hit a boy who called him "nigger." When he told his mother she said, "And what good did that do, Jimmy?" Her words stayed with Lawson and over time he resolved to "never hit out at people when I got angry." He vowed to "find other ways to challenge them."

In 1962, Lawson became the minister at Centenary United Methodist Church in Memphis, Tennessee. He helped organize the 1968 sanitation workers strike in Memphis and in March of that year invited King to come down and lead a march. When King delivered his "I've Been to the Mountaintop" speech on April 3, he praised Lawson as one of the "noble men" in the civil rights movement. King said, "He's been going to jail for struggling; he's been kicked out of Vanderbilt University for his struggling; but he's still going on, fighting for the rights of his people." That struggle would get even harder the next day, when King was assassinated.

James Lawson moved to Los Angeles in 1974 to become pastor of Holman United Methodist Church. He maintained a vital role in nonviolent struggles for peace and justice in the United States and abroad. In 2006, Lawson returned to Vanderbilt as a distinguished visiting professor.

Robert Penn Warren asks Lawson to explain the controversial circum-stances that led him to transfer from Vanderbilt University's divinity school to Boston University.

JAMES LAWSON: This began in Nashville in the early part of 1959, when the local affiliate of the Southern Christian Leadership Conference started the process of negotiation in the downtown area. We adopted the downtown because we felt that we wanted to focus the attention of the city on the major problems of segregation, and the need for genuine integration.

We went on through a process of negotiation, and workshops, and training of students and adults, and testing them in the downtown area, testing some of the places that we'd gone to for negotiation. February 13 was the first major sit-in in the downtown area. Then, for about two weeks, we had sit-ins, which were highly successful in a variety of ways—in numbers, in terms of impact, in terms of making a public issue. Negro people responded to this almost immediately. About the twenty-seventh of February we discovered that the merchants had gone down to the mayor and the city police and said, "You've got to stop the sit-in." We in turn went to the city police.

ROBERT PENN WARREN: Was it an organization that did this or was it just simply a few who took it upon themselves?

JL: It was a loosely knit group. Simply people got together out of a mutual concern and a problem, and not any organization as such. Well, we tried to make overtures to the mayor. We had an independent ministers group. The mayor refused to see them. This was a multiracial group, incidentally. The mayor was unavailable to anyone, both from within the movement and also then from the independent groups that tried to see him. We did have interviews with the chief of police, who told us very bluntly that if we demonstrated on the following Saturday there would be arrests, and said that he had been instructed by the mayor to find what laws could be used. He said the legal department was searching for laws and he said the laws that would probably be used would either be trespass or breaching the peace. So we knew arrests were certain to be the case.

Well, that was what happened. On February 28 we had a major sit-in. There were arrests. We had a program expecting either arrests and/or violence, and both occurred. Because, up to this time, the police had been very protective, making certain the crowds kept moving so that there's not too much harassment during demonstrations. This Saturday, suddenly the police disappeared. And, of course, then the crowds formed. And young white men formed into hoodlum groups, and surrounded the people, and went into stores and whatnot. So we saw violence and then the police came to at least two of the stores and arrested people. We were prepared for this and we were also prepared to have them arrest several hundred people. When they discovered that there was no end to the arrests, they stopped arresting after about an hour and a half of this.

This created even further mobilization, both of the movement and in terms of its support. We got the representatives of the various denominations to call all their pastors to make major presentations in every Negro church that next Sunday morning. They also demanded that the mayor come and talk to them. They began to do such things as raise money and get underneath the whole effort. Well, on Monday morning, when the mayor had been unavailable, they simply sent him a telegram Sunday night asking him to show up at a meeting, and this meeting was held at First Baptist Church, and over three hundred Negro ministers of the city were there. They had asked that about three men would question the mayor as to his policy concerning segregation, and as to why violence was permitted, and as to why arrests occurred. At the end of this meeting with the mayor I was asked to give the summary, which I did. The mayor had emphasized that the sit-in was a trespass upon private property. I took the stance that human rights took precedence over any other kind of right, and I quoted Abraham Lincoln and certain Christian principles that were valid here. He had stressed the fact that this was a breaking of the law. I went on to say, rather, that where the law was used simply to oppress people, then it wasn't really a law. It wasn't justice. It wasn't consistent with democratic thought, and certainly was inconsistent with Christian thought. I said the arrests occurred not because the law was an effort to preserve the finest values of our society, but in this instance the law was a gimmick, to intimidate, harass, and if possible halt a legitimate movement of social concern and justice.

RPW: Would you distinguish between the nonviolent obstruction of law and the violent breach of law?

JL: From the nonviolent perspective, when one finds that, in order to continue to act in a just [way], and in a matter of conscience, when he discovers that he's coming up against the law, he does this in a peaceful, creative fashion, always ready to take the consequences of the law. I think he shows his respect for the law, and his recognition that we are a society of law.

RPW: It's a direct recognition of the fact the society is a society of law; it is implicit in the whole process.

JL: Right. And this can be traced, of course, in American history. A favorite illustration of mine is the fact that we got our religious liberty in the state of Virginia out of the civil disobedience of primarily Baptist ministers, who insisted that they had the right to proclaim the gospel, had the right to organize congregations in a colony where you had an established religion. And Patrick Henry proposed this first resolution. It is said that he proposed it after hearing Baptist ministers preach out of the windows of jails where they had been incarcerated for their breaking of Virginia law.

RPW: I didn't want to interrupt the narrative except to get that point.

JL: Of course, the mayor, hearing this whole statement, then immediately said, "This man is calling for a bloodbath in the streets of Nashville." I'm positive that he was simply trying to get himself off of the hook politically, because here he was being confronted by men who had supported him in the election.

RPW: You're talking now about this group of ministers?

JL: This group of ministers, they had supported him. He was considered a moderate. And he knew that, now, they were not simply questioning him, but they were in a sense challenging his behavior, his handling of the whole situation in the city. The newspapers picked up the mayor's comments, and, in particular, the *Nashville Banner* immediately proceeded to editorialize upon the calling for a bloodbath, and this event went on to investigations, although not in any kind of interviewing with me, personally.

RPW: You mean, calling it a bloodbath by the mayor, this was interpreted as an advocacy, in a subtle way, of violence?

JL: Yes, not only that, but it was an opportunity then to say that J.M. Lawson was an outside agitator, sympathetic with the communist design. This kind of line began to appear both editorially and in newspaper articles. The main article described what the mayor had said, leaving out most of what I had said in the statement that was to be an answer to the mayor. Editorially, they said that the sit-in campaign certainly did mean violence, and did mean a bloodbath, and showed a gross disrespect for law and order and for democratic processes.

RPW: What about relations at Vanderbilt Theological School?

JL: Vanderbilt began to receive many phone calls from primarily prominent alumni. And also, I understand, from the mayor and from some other people downtown concerning my presence at the school, asking [the chancellor] how Vanderbilt permitted me to be there. In fact, the *Banner* editorials were saying that I had been using Vanderbilt University as a nefarious base of operation. At this time I was a part-time employee of the Fellowship of Reconciliation, as the Southern staff secretary, working in the field of nonviolence and reconciliation throughout the South. I had been moving in and out of tense places like Birmingham and Little Rock.

The chancellor then began to receive all kinds of pressure questioning my integrity as a student and my motives for being at Vanderbilt. These pressures then were reflected to the dean. In fact, the dean of the divinity school was ordered to get a statement from me denying what the mayor had said about me, and denying that I was all of these things. So, when I first reached the campus on Tuesday, Dr. [Robert] Nelson asked to see me, and I went immediately. And then, later on, the publicity director of the university came in to help form a statement [from me]. I cooperated and we did get a statement written and we issued it. And that, of course, was insufficient. Dr. Nelson informed me that the chancellor wanted me to withdraw from the school, to withdraw or to be expelled. I had said to Dean Nelson that if it seems that the university is being harmed by my presence, I will withdraw. I'll voluntarily withdraw. But it became very clear that there wasn't a question of the embarrassment of the university; it was rather simply the questioning of my motives and of my integrity. So I had definitely decided that I would not withdraw. Thursday morning, the chancellor called a meeting of the divinity school faculty and students at which he publicly announced that I had been expelled from the university.

So I was expelled Thursday afternoon. We were having mass meetings every night, and workshops every day, and of course many planning sessions, trying to keep the movement as creative as possible. But we learned Friday morning that the warrant for my arrest had been issued. And at about two o'clock in the afternoon or so, four captains of the police department came to arrest me on a charge of conspiring to disrupt business.

RPW: Now, a lot of the faculty supported your position, didn't they?

JL: Right. The divinity school faculty said, "If anything happens to you, it would be happening to us." They took the tack, after my expulsion, that they would try to negotiate with the administration for my return to the campus. And this went on for over a month. Finally, they had their admissions committee reconsider my application for admission. I filled out a new application, blanks and all. They did this on the basis of a remark by the chancellor, in one of their sessions, that he thought if I were to return to the campus it would be through the regular channel of being admitted or readmitted. And so they had accepted me as a student. They took this fact to the chancellor, laid my file on the chancellor's desk, and said that Lawson has been readmitted. He requested additional time to consider it. This was in late May, sometime around commencement time. They felt he was delaying in order to get through commencement. The day after the commencement, in fact, he received the committee again and said, "I cannot let Lawson be a student at the university."

Well, immediately the divinity school faculty, almost to a man, resigned. Their negotiations then were taken over by the med school people, and law school, and quite a number of the men in the physical sciences. In fact, a number of the physicists and biologists had been quite active all through here.

RPW: You felt you had the sympathy of the university faculty, in general?

JL: In fact, one of the things that has not been said is that after the divinity school faculty had resigned, then other faculty people took up negotiations, and they did it in this way: they went to the chancellor's office and said, "We have here the resignations of 160 members of your faculty throughout the university," including almost the entirety of the med school. "There are others who are in the process of writing their letters. You must settle the Lawson matter. You cannot have him expelled in this manner."

It was only at this point that the chancellor decided that he had to reconsider the issue. Well, by this time I had already left the city because I went on to Boston University. They had made a very fine offer to me in terms of receiving my full credits and in terms of not making any further residential or academic requirements upon me, other than that I would complete one semester, and they would accept the program that I had done at Oberlin and Vanderbilt, which they did. So my wife and I then left the city and went on to start at Boston U.

RPW: What was the consequence, then, at Vanderbilt?

JL: The chancellor then issued a statement: the resignation of Dean Nelson would be accepted and Lawson could return to the university. I declined the offer primarily because I felt that in dismissing Dean Nelson he was simply substituting one scapegoat for another. I further felt that where people actively identify themselves with the whole effort for change then we in the movement are responsible for identifying ourselves with them, that we are liable for one another, that we have a fundamental responsibility for surrounding one another with concern and affection, with understanding, and with creative support.

Warren asks Lawson about James Baldwin's suggestion that Southern mobs do not reflect the will of the Southern white majority.

JL: Yes, this is basically correct. I've been reading in the field of history of the Negro and America in the nineteenth century. A buffer was created between the slave owner and the non–slave owner, and between the aristocracy trying to reassert itself after the Civil War and the Negro. This buffer goes on now, and Nashville is a perfect example of this.

RPW: Well, let's explain that.

JL: Since 1960, when we began the public phase of our effort in Nashville, I cannot count the numbers of times that violence has been turned on and off. For example, the first sit-in campaign, in the winter and the spring of 1960, we started off with complete police protection because, of course, we always informed the police chief of what we were doing, and where we were going, and what stores we would be at, and the times we'd be there, and all. Oh, we had complete protection for two weeks. Young men came into the downtown area and tried to harass us, and many of these groups were just moved off out of the downtown area by police officers. Managers in stores, in fact, worked to see to it that unnecessary groups of people never stayed around their stores. Then suddenly this stopped. And we had gigantic mobs. Then when it became clear that a settlement had to be made, the demonstrations went on under peaceful circumstances once again.

RPW: This would seem to imply, then, that the mob does act out the will of the majority, or at least the will of the rich and the powerful.

JL: Right, the power structure. In Nashville, this wasn't the only time this happened. This happened in many instances. It happened with the demonstrations, with the campaign at the downtown movie theaters. It happened in demonstrations at grocery stores. It happened in specific restaurant campaigns. On some occasions, the police themselves acted as the mob, where they roughed up people, or hit people, or pushed people around.

I am quite certain that in the Nashville scene it was the mayor himself, and possibly a few of his closer friends, or even persons of influence on him, who allowed the police to be present at one time and then to disappear the next moment. I'm certain that this was not the decision or the will [of the majority] because I can remember, for example, a demonstration on a main downtown street in Nashville where young white men had a chance to do a certain amount of violence and they chased one Negro boy off the street. He was not related to the demonstration. He was a bystander. They, they chased him off the street up into a second-story beauty parlor, where he worked, and there he tried to fight them off with a bottle. They jumped him in the shop. The police charged in. And the next moment they were bringing the Negro boy out to arrest him. And a couple of white women who were standing on the sidewalk watching this yelled at the police, "You're arresting the wrong one!" There were many [times] white people spontaneously expressed the fact that they did not approve of this permitting of the mob, and then trying to pretend that this was the result simply of a group of people peacefully coming in to demonstrate. It was very obviously the turning on of a faucet or the turning off of a faucet.

My contention is that it is the power structure that either permits or refuses to permit the mob to form. Now, let me give you another illustration of this. Here in Memphis, Commissioner of Fire and Police Claude Armour made it clear, very early, that there would be no mob action in Memphis. And he briefed his police and organized his department in that way. So that in Memphis, in spite of the fact that from time to time you would have a far more difficult element than in Nashville, there has been no significant violence in the city.

RPW: I have a quotation here from Dr. Kenneth Clark on the matter of nonviolence I would like to read to you. "On the surface, King's philosophy appears to reflect health and stability while the black nationalists betray pathology and instability. A deeper analysis, however, might reveal that there is also an unrealistic, if not pathological, basis in King's doctrine. The natural reaction to injustice is bitterness and resentment. The form that such bitterness takes need not be overtly violent, but the corrosion of the human spirit seems inevitable. It would seem, therefore, that any demand that the victims of oppression be required to love those who oppress them places an additional and probably intolerable psychological burden upon them."

JL: If Dr. Clark is defining the nonviolent approach simply as passivity, or of trying to ignore either one's own feelings and personal hatred and hostility, or ignore the presence of violence and injustice—if he's defining nonviolence in that way, then I would quite agree with him. But if he's willing to accept Dr. King's definition of nonviolence, namely that of creative Christian love that comes from the inside of a person, that, in a sense, heals a person inwardly and enables him then to really be a free man. If he defines it in these terms, as we define it, then I think his statement is quite false. He is ignoring the fact that, out of this real definition of the nonviolent approach, we see all the time not only the healing up of anger and fear and guilt on the part of both Negro and white people, but we see remarkable instances of courage, genuine courage.

RPW: Talking about nonviolence, it is sometimes said that the responsibility, in a kind of a deeply ironical way, must be on the Negro, to practice this.

JL: I would tend to agree that, in spite of what has gone on in our history, the Negro does have a responsibility for trying to help his nation come to a noble expression of its ideals.

RPW: That's stating the matter more generally, yes.

JL: Yes, and I think that the only way this can be done is by cleaving to those very ideals. In other words, we talk about the Judeo-Christian tradition that has certainly sustained many of our principles, and have been written even into our form of law. Well, my thesis is that we must be nonviolent primarily because this is the only way that is consonant with this idealistic tradition. The way of love and peace and truth is the only way to achieve these things in society. So at least from that point, I do believe that it is the Negro's responsibility to be nonviolent. From his early appropriation of the Christian faith in the United States, [the Negro's] theology has been very consistent with the nonviolent approach. In the Negro spiritual, as an example, we never find a word of hatred expressed for anyone. Where you, in turn, find a great sympathy with the suffering of Jesus, and the sense that somehow the suffering of the Negro, which is an innocent suffering, is clearly identifiable with Jesus. This whole motive is very significant in terms of the way in which Martin Luther King Jr. has found a ripe audience.

RPW: How much do you think nonviolence is communicable to the masses, black or white?

JL: A tremendous amount of it. I've held workshops in almost every state in the South—workshops on nonviolence, to all kinds of groups, from sophisticated, integrated college groups to very unsophisticated people in the Delta of Mississippi. And I don't vary in terms of the ideas; I vary in terms of terminology. Some of the most exciting experiences I've had in teaching and in training have been in the Delta of Mississippi, where I primarily spoke in biblical terms, and used biblical illustrations, and biblical stories and myths, to illustrate and document the whole idea of Christian nonviolence. I found people who were functionally illiterate exceedingly responsive and aware of this. I've had people say to me, "Reverend Lawson, I have always felt that the only way to change what we have to put up with is through Christian love, and through what Christ talked about."

RPW: Do you think that enough thought has been given to the actual vision of what society would be [with passage of the] civil rights bill? What vision do you have of society if you've accomplished [the goals] of civil rights?

JL: Well, in the first instance, we have not given enough time to defining what it is we want, and then to spell this definition out in terms of the actual kinds of programs which are possible to achieve it. Most of us, and in particular in the emerging nonviolent movement, recognize this failure. It's not a failure of lack of interest; rather a failure in time. We're too involved in the growth of the movement to really get involved in the kind of study necessary to working out this vision.

RPW: What about the notion that it shouldn't be a white man's job, at all, to mix into these things? The repudiation of the [white] liberal is very widespread.

JL: This is widespread primarily among the Northern Negroes, let's say the radical elements. Those of us in the nonviolent movement recognize that in order to achieve the kind of society we want, we must have allies. The Negro is only 10 percent of America. We have got to have people from labor. We've got to have people from the political structures of America. We've got to have people from the churches who are going to want to have an America that reflects a pure kind of democratic society. This cannot be done by the Negro [alone]. We all have to do it together. And so those of us in the nonviolent movement repudiate any effort to say that the white man has no role to play. On the contrary, many of us work assiduously in order to help white people assume their rightful roles.

Andrew Young

March 17, 1964

Atlanta, Georgia

Andrew Young joined the Southern Christian Leadership Conference (SCLC) in 1961 and became one of Martin Luther King Jr.'s most trusted aides. Young helped shepherd the SCLC through major civil rights campaigns it mounted both North and South, and was sometimes jailed alongside King for civil disobedience. He served as a strategist, negotiator, and media spokesperson for the SCLC, and in 1964 was appointed executive director. He held that position until 1970, two years after King's assassination.

In a 1985 interview for the television series Eyes on the Prize, *Young said that one didn't really run the SCLC so much as ride herd on a team of wild horses. "I kind of kept them all on the same road," he said. In fractious debates among SCLC staff—gifted activists who could be arrogant and headstrong—King counted on Young to prevail with reason and a cool head. According to Young, King also chided him for these traits. "You would reason your way out of segregation," King told him, "but it takes more than just reason to get this country straight. You need some folks . . . who are crazy enough to take on anything and anybody and not count the cost."*

Young's willingness to "count the cost" made him indispensable during major public actions. Recalling King's historic march in 1965 from Selma to Montgomery, Young said, "There was absolutely nothing romantic about it." Some three hundred people participated in the march, and they walked ten to fifteen miles a day. "I was running back and forth . . . trying to keep the march together and solving problems from one end to the other," Young said. "I figure anytime they marched ten miles, I did closer to forty."

In his interview with Robert Penn Warren, Young mentions the notorious police chief of Albany, Georgia, Laurie Pritchett, who locked up hundreds of activists campaigning to desegregate that city in 1961. King got arrested and jailed in Albany three times between December of that year and the following summer. After reaching a stalemate, King agreed to leave Albany without a single concession from city leaders, a depressing defeat. He and his staff learned crucial lessons from that failure, however, which strengthened future campaigns in cities such as Birmingham, Alabama, and St. Augustine, Florida.

One lesson Young gleaned was the need for patience. In the early days of his activism, he thought it might take five years to bring about racial equality, an idea he later called naïve. "It turned out that it's a lifetime struggle," he said, "and you move from one phase to the other." People who can't adjust to each new phase will wind up frustrated, he said.

Andrew Young was born in New Orleans in 1932 and raised in a well-to-do family. His father was a dentist, his mother a schoolteacher. Young was athletic and academically precocious, earning a BS in biology at Howard University when he was only nineteen. Against his father's wishes, Young chose to become a minister and was ordained in the United Church of Christ. He was working for the National Council of Churches in New York City when he felt the call to move South and join the civil rights movement. "I didn't know what that meant, or how it would work out," Young said, "but I knew that's where I was supposed to be."

Young would be forever changed by the years he worked with King. In his memoir, An Easy Burden, *Young says King gave him "purpose and sustenance." King left his mark on him, Young writes, "both in indelible memories and in the spiritual and practical lessons of our trials and triumphs." Young left the SCLC in 1970 to pursue a career in politics. He broke the color line in 1972 when he was elected to Congress in Georgia, the first black person to represent the state since Reconstruction. He served in the U.S. House of Representatives for three terms, then became the first African American ambassador to the United Nations, under President Jimmy Carter. In the 1980s, he served two terms as mayor of Atlanta but failed in his bid for governor of Georgia in 1990. Young remained active in public life, however; in 1994, he was tapped to run President Clinton's Southern Africa Development Fund, and in 2003 he founded the consulting group Good-Works International.*

ROBERT PENN WARREN: Do you remember how or when your present views and attitudes toward active participation in civil rights and racial matters began, Mr. Young?

ANDREW YOUNG: I grew up in New Orleans. My father was a dentist. But we lived in a neighborhood where there were very few Negro families. The neighborhood was largely white. Yet my folks were the only professional people in the neighborhood. It was a lower-income neighborhood where my father had a dental office. And I think, very early in life, I ran into both the problems of race and class.

RPW: Were his patients partly white and partly Negro?

AY: They were largely Negro, but at times close to a fifth of his practice was white. And financially, we were a little bit better off than the whites in the neighborhood. And they were prejudiced against us because of race. My parents had certain class notions against them, and against the Negroes who moved into the neighborhood. So almost from the time that I was able to get out into the streets by myself, say at six or seven years old, I was caught in this kind of dilemma. I decided then that people were people and that these external categories of economics and race were of little or no significance. I was almost always getting spanked by my parents for playing with the wrong kids. At the same time, the white children in the neighborhood were being spanked by their parents for playing with us. Negro parents in the South try to compensate for segregation by giving their children all the things that they wanted to have. So we had basketball goals, swings, wading pools, all of this kind of thing. And in our yard we always had the football and the baseball. My younger brother and I insisted on choosing our own friends. And if it came time to have lunch and there weren't too many people there—especially since many of the kids knew that both parents were working and they didn't have any arrangements for lunch—we would insist on mother fixing lunch for everybody that was there.

I began to realize as I got a little older that my parents got their education as a result of somebody else's missionary activity and concern. They went to what was then Straight College in New Orleans. And they talked very affectionately about the people from New England that came down and provided an education for them. And it always seemed to me that the middle-class, Negro community in New Orleans derived its status from somebody else's sacrifice and was doing too little itself. For instance, most of their friends were professional people: doctors, lawyers, all of them doing quite well, beginning to enjoy the affluent life, and they seemed to have no concern for the masses of people in New Orleans. I remember an incident when the Flint-Goodrich Hospital needed some money. Now, most of the [black] doctors and several of the dentists worked there and made most of their money there, and yet they depended almost solely on Northern contributions.

RPW: I understand by reading and by conversation that there is still a great lag between Negro wealth and Negro philanthropy—Negro gifts to other forms of good works, including civil rights.

AY: This is very true. These people, for instance, still would give very little, if anything, to any civil rights organization. They would probably, just in the matter of obligation, take out a small membership in the NAACP, and give ten dollars, twenty dollars a year. Whereas many of them are in the thirty-, forty-, fifty-thousand-dollar-a-year income bracket. So this was in the Negro community that I began to get sensitive. Now part of this was because my parents didn't let me really come in contact with the harshness of segregation in New Orleans. They did everything possible to protect me from any kind of harmful incidents. So I didn't get any bitter experiences in childhood that many Negroes get. Still, it was all around you.

RPW: Some people [say] that segregation actually worked as spur, a stimulus to achievement. This is no argument for segregation, but . . .

AY: I don't think that this was the case for me at all. In fact, I always resisted this. I always wanted to be myself. And my folks used to try to tell me, "You're a Negro and you can't be just as good as the white person; you've got to be better." This was supposed to be an incentive to study. And, yet, I never studied (laughs). I did a lot of reading on my own, but not in terms of achievement or grades.

My folks tried to mold me into their professional pattern and I rebelled against the black, bourgeois value system. After I got through Howard University I finally began to shape some value structure of my own, and choose a direction. It first came out as a desire to work in Africa in some way. And yet I went South to pastor a little church in Alabama, met my wife, and she was concerned about staying in the South. This was my first experience in the rural South. Her mother had taught in a one-room schoolhouse most of her life. And her mother was one of these exceptionally brilliant women that was completely self-educated. I remember we went to Europe and her mother—[from] just a small town, three thousand [people], an Alabama, one-room schoolteacher—sat down and, without looking at a note or a book or anything, looked at our itinerary and just listed off the places that we should be sure to see. Which museums, where certain art objects were. Somehow she acquired a dedication to education. And my wife picked this up. So it was her desire to work in the South, and this is where I began to switch, in terms of working here.

Warren raises W.E.B. Du Bois's idea of a split psyche in black Americans, where there are competing impulses to identify with an African heritage or mainstream American society. He asks if this has ever been a problem for Young.

AY: Always. I'm just getting to the point where I'm beginning to resolve it a little. Now, my folks were the assimilationists. They didn't like spirituals. No blues (laughs). Anything Negroid, they shied away from. So it started in rebellion against this. In grammar school they sent me to all the New Orleans Symphony children's concerts on Saturday. I didn't enjoy it [but I] learned a lot from it. But when I also wanted to buy rock and roll blues records, they said this was cheap and I shouldn't bother with it. Well, we fought over that score and I won out.

Warren asks Young about the roles of black women and men in the civil rights movement.

AY: A man has to change the society. Women can maintain and strengthen, but the protest role, the role of shaping the world in a social and political sense, I think is the man's. And I think that the movement is giving men an opportunity to really exercise this and find themselves. But the women in the movement are not relegated to an inferior role. Relationships are developing between men and women. For instance, we had it when my wife decided that she wanted to go to jail. She wasn't arrested but she did decide that it wasn't enough for a man just to be taking part in the demonstrations, that she had some role to play also.

RPW: Let me read you a little passage: "The whole tendency of Negro history, not as history but as used as propaganda, is to encourage the average Negro to escape reality, the actual achievements, and the actual failures of the present. Although the movement consciously tends to build race pride, it may also cause unconsciously the recognition that group pride may be partly only delusion and therefore results in a devaluation of the Negroes by themselves for being forced to resort to a self-deception." This is from Arnold Rose, [Gunnar] Myrdal's collaborator.

AY: I think that there's something in Negro history. For instance, this was part of my self-discovery: nobody told me about Reconstruction. Nobody even introduced me to Du Bois until I was grown. There was a conscious effort in American history to devaluate whatever contribution the Negro has made, because we tend to have a kind of intellectual aristocracy among our historians. The contributions of masses of people, laboring people, of slave labor [are devalued]. I've tried to use Negro history but it hasn't been as propaganda. Nobody ever told me the influence that Frederick Douglass may have had on Lincoln, for instance, or on the whole abolitionist period. And I think that these are things we are using to let Negroes know that they are not completely without roots and heritage and connection.

Negroes, generally, have had no interest in their own history, except the few people that have really made a career of Negro history. The masses of Negroes were consciously trying to assimilate, and they wanted to get as far away from their past [as possible] because they wanted to become white. A friend of mine was saying that he sat down, very diligently, learning every movement of every symphony, that he felt he had to know Shakespeare thoroughly, and had to memorize quotations, under the notion that when he had done this, he would be completely accepted in a white world.

RPW: Let me ask you this question. Do you see any parallel between the situation of the Negro, a member of what they call a subculture—vis-à-vis the great American machine—and the situation of the white Southerner who is a member of a subculture, a defeated nationalism that has lived in a special box of prejudices—do you see any parallel there?

AY: It's probably very similar. You get Southerners that are new, very cosmopolitan, white Southerners that want to completely reject the Southern experience. And you get the Negro middle class that wants to completely reject his Negro experience from slavery.

Southerners—both white and Negro—probably have a lot more in common than they realize. It's the structures of our society, which segregated us on the basis of race, that really keep us from getting to know the fact that we probably are much closer to one another than anybody else in America.

RPW: A young lady with whom I was talking at Howard University some time back said she had more optimism for the Southern settlement than for the Northern settlement between the races on the account that there's a shared history, the same land the people have lived on. Beyond that, [there is a] possibility of a human recognition that she couldn't find in Harlem, or Detroit, or Chicago, she being raised on a Southern farm.

AY: This would be the general experience of most Negroes who move north, and certainly is mine. In the days when I was in the North, in school, most of my friends—since there were very few Negroes on the campus—turned out to be white Southerners. And I found that we had a great deal more in common than I did with many of the Northern students. I think this is true in the movement. We have watched Northern whites come down and try to work with us. But they almost never really get along as well as the Southern whites who are working with us.

For instance, just in the matter of the religious ethos that we share in the South, [there are] the old gospel hymns and spirituals, out of which many of the freedom songs come. White Southerners tend to sing these a little better. They feel them a little more. It's much easier for them, once they become liberated intellectually and socially, to become more deeply and personally involved in the movement.

Warren quotes an activist who says that the "grudging respect" with which some Southern segregationists view the courage of black protesters is a basis for potential racial reconciliation.

AY: It makes a great deal of sense. I hadn't thought of it that way. Even in the bitterest situations, we tend to put this trust in nonviolence to overcome this barrier. In Albany, Georgia, for instance, in spite of the fact that we are at war, in terms of politics and social structures, [Police] Chief [Laurie] Pritchard and I had a very close, personal friendship going through this time.

RPW: How did that work out, literally?

AY: Well, I almost became his counselor and his pastor over the tremendous guilt that he had over being involved in perpetuating a police state. And every time that I'd go into jail, he'd want to call me in and just talk some. For instance, when the seventy-five ministers went to jail, he talked a good deal about, "Oh, I don't want to put men of God in jail." He said, "You all don't know how it makes me feel to have to do this." He even asked if we could get Dr. King to intercede to get him a job as a federal marshal, so that he could get out of this system. At the same time, I had no illusions about his being very much a part of this system, and it represented a genuine schizophrenia on his part. I would think that even Adolf Eichmann would be probably a rather personable individual, if you'd sit down with him. I remember in Mississippi going to get some of our staff members out of jail, who had been beaten up. And I started a conversation with the sheriff and the chief of police. We were able to relate very warmly as persons. We talked about our families and we joked about the weather. Normal conversational banter. And I was convinced that these were real Christian gentlemen. And yet, here was a Negro girl on our staff who is one of the most sensitive and delicate creatures I know. They had beaten her for an hour and a half with blackjacks.

RPW: Same persons?

AY: The same persons. It shocked me when she came out of jail and her face was all bruised, her eyes swollen and blood still in her hair. I asked her who beat her and she said, "Those two that you were talking to right there." This is the problem we really are fighting: that the Southerner, who is a very warm and personable human being, when caught in this system, responds almost to a kind of mob psychosis. It's almost like a man disassociates himself from his conscience when he goes to war. In their dealings with Negroes, they are perpetuating a sacred way of life, so that anything they have to do to perpetuate this sacred way of life is okay. Now, if we can ever get the white Southerner and the Negro Southerner to be free of this system, which makes them respond this way, we will have much more rapport and a much better climate in the South than we have in the North.

RPW: [James] Baldwin has written that the Southern mob—the people actually on the street beating up Negroes, or perhaps the police in their jails cells—do not represent the will of the Southern white majority.

AY: The problem of the white majority in the South is it has no guts and no integrity left. Alabama responds to [Governor] George Wallace, and this means that Alabama, who elects George Wallace, has to bear the responsibility for his inflammatory speeches, which get children killed and which create a police state. Now, cornering these people individually, you get something completely different: the pleasant, personable, humorous Southerner who is also capable of great sadism. And I don't know what the source of that sickness is.

RPW: Let me ask this and see how you respond to it. I don't know how much money to put on this card, but I'll try: that the white Southerner is, in a way, like the Negro. He is a person who is outside of the dominant culture and is defending his identity. As the Negro has been trying to find his identity in his culture, he has felt none in the major American culture. But the white Southerner—who thought he had one once, you see, or looking toward his grandfather—now sees himself, his very identity, threatened. In a mistaken way he has elected to stake his identity on a pattern of life which involves segregation.

AY: The real political threat the white Southerner feels is in hardcore areas, in areas of Negro majority, such as the Mississippi Delta. And they couple with the myths, the sex myth, the communist myth, and all of these things tend to feed this neurosis a great deal. And so you get a kind of defensiveness that's very hard to cope with. I think both the church and the government make a mistake when they cope with it through judgment. Now, I certainly believe in federal enforcement of law and in the use of troops. But, for instance, the way in which [President] Eisenhower used troops in Little Rock was a defense of his ego and the fact that he was insulted. The issue of federal law enforcement was never really communicated to the South. I think almost the same thing happened to [John F.] Kennedy. He felt betrayed by [Mississippi governor] Ross Barnett. And he responded with a show of power. Now, at this time, neither Kennedy himself nor Eisenhower had ever made any attempt to communicate to the South the meaning of a republic. Nobody has ever attempted to do any education in the South, except the White Citizens Council and the [Ku Klux] Klan. And I think many of these people are—the little experience I've had in reading about these people—are genuinely sick. And they play on the social sickness for leadership. So that you find the South with nobody really trying to tell them what the moral and cultural issues are today.

Warren turns the conversation to the challenge of school desegregation in both the North and the South, and pitting the demand for rapid change against the argument, by some, for gradual integration.

AY: [The Negro] in Mississippi, he'd see the statistics that $206 a year was spent on white education—a white student in Leflore County—and $35 spent on a Negro kid. So he realizes that it's almost impossible to get this Negro's education up to $200, see? The rate of gradualism would just kill us. So he's got to integrate this $200 school system. Now, what the Northern Negro has done is taken the Southern analysis, integration being the answer to everything, and tried to slap it on a situation where the problem isn't so much segregation as it is urbanization. [In the North] you get education being de facto [segregated] because of housing. You get housing segregated, partially, because of jobs. You get jobs segregated

mainly because Negroes are not represented in the political structure. This is the reason we're centering more and more of our fight
on political representation. If Negroes represent 34 percent of the
population in Alabama, somehow they ought to have 34 percent of
the representation in the state legislature.

In New York, the same thing is true. It's white people who are
taking the blame for Negro education. When you get some Negroes to be representative and have the responsibility for actually
solving the problem, he will begin to see the problem in its depth.
But until you actually get representative government, or until Negroes are represented in the administration and in the government
bureaucracy, so that they take the responsibility for dealing with
some of these problems [with] racial overtones, you are going to get
segregation as the main focusing point. Now, I don't know whether
we have enough time to do this.

RPW: That's the problem right there. How do you contain the
problems to accomplish this?

AY: There is a trap that all leaders of mass movements fall into.
You've got to have slogans, you've go to have rallying points to keep
the little people informed, and yet, way down deep, you know that
the problems are not quite so simple. Two things can save you from
this. One is real creativity, and continually feeding your movement
new ideas. We, in the South, have been able to move from bus
boycotts to Freedom Riders to sit-ins to voter registration to massive, direct action. That has kept us from having any answers to
anything, and so the movement has continued to evolve and grow.
The other thing is [to have] enough humility to admit that you are
wrong. And Dr. King certainly exemplifies this.

RPW: In what specific way?

AY. Well, when you follow a slogan and it gets you into trouble.

RPW: Which slogan are you talking about now?

AY: Oh, let me see. I think of one case when Dr. King was really pulled into this with the Birmingham people demanding that twenty-five [Negro] policemen be hired by a certain date. This came out of a press conference, but it hadn't really been thoroughly discussed and analyzed. It was a slogan for public relations value. Something had to be done to give the people of Birmingham some hope that large-scale bombings and mass murders were not going to follow the [Sixteenth Street Baptist] Church bombing. The feeling in Birmingham is that policemen have been involved with the bombings. So that one of our answers, the slogan, was Negro policemen would guarantee us some law enforcement. So we asked for twenty-five Negro policemen. Now, Dr. King admitted that this was not possible, that we wouldn't stage demonstrations on the basis of this demand for twenty-five policemen.

Warren asks Young about psychologist Kenneth Clark's critique that nonviolent action sets up a kind of psychological vulnerability in people who try to make change peacefully in a violent society.

AY: Dr. Clark is reflecting a particularly behavioristic view of man, and a psychologist generally sees man more biologically than spiritually. Now this fellow from Vienna who developed the whole system of therapy out of his concentration camp experiences would say that his whole method is not the release and expression of hostility, but greater discipline ought to be required in a situation where sickness is imminent. He uses the illustration of an arc, when it's beginning to crumble. One of the things that you can do to keep it together is to put more weight in the center of it and this actually binds the pieces together. This would be our experience in nonviolence. While a certain amount of expression is necessary, I just don't believe in letting hostilities run rampant.

What we do is make it a virtue, in fact a superior virtue, to keep your hostilities in check.

Theologically, I would say that man is a creature of spirit. And we have so many day-to-day case studies of people who have become transformed because of their ability to love. In the act of attempting to do something that seems to be beyond their reach, we would say that, by the grace of God, they actually reach it. Now, it's not a permanent transformation. And this doesn't mean that those of us who are nonviolent don't get mad with our wives. But at least we have enough experience in coping with our emotions to know that it is to our advantage to control ourselves. We've actually made friends with the people that we are at war with. And we're saying that, for our movement, we are trying to create a community of love. A redeemed community, no less, where men can live together as brothers. And I've never known brothers to learn to live together by fighting things out. The path of amelioration, or forgiveness in religious language, is a much more realistic base for community.

RPW: What about this objection that one encounters, that such a philosophy may work in the South where you have [a Christian] ethos behind society? What about a disoriented noncommunity? Like big tracts of Detroit, Harlem, South Chicago, where this ethos has been lost? Where there's no ethos to appeal to?

AY: Fortunately, we've been able to take our ethos North with us. The Negroes in Detroit, see, came from the South. And when Martin Luther King came to New York and brought the tremendous mystique and charisma that has been entrusted in him, say in the Southern movement, these Negroes, a quarter of a million of them got out and marched behind him in Detroit. And they became a one-day community. All I'm saying is that leadership can make a community of the North.

RPW: You don't see that kind of leadership there though.

AY: It wasn't in Montgomery [Alabama] until it developed. Now, it develops, in part, through suffering. The big danger of Northern leadership is that it may not be tempered in time. Any delusions of grandeur that Martin Luther King may have had the first few months [of his time in the movement] were bombed out of him when they bombed his home. He had to face the fact that you can die doing this, so it's not something to play with. And it pushes him back to new depths. Then you begin to go along a little ways and you're slapped in jail. I trace some of his great new ideas to his jail periods. Certainly the finest articulation of our whole movement came out of his Birmingham jail experience, and I see that these periods of suffering are periods of great intellectual and spiritual deepening.

Septima P. Clark

March 18, 1964

Atlanta, Georgia

*Septima Clark had been a teacher for forty years when she was ap-
pointed the director of workshops at the Highlander Folk School, a
training ground for civil rights organizers located in the Tennessee
mountains. The year was 1956, and Clark had recently been fired from
a teaching job in South Carolina because of her membership in the
NAACP. Clark had been active in the NAACP since 1918, but after
the 1954* Brown v. Board of Education *ruling that struck down school
segregation, South Carolina lawmakers fought back by barring state
and city workers from the organization. Clark refused to give up her
membership and was soon out of a job.*

*Clark's move to Highlander was pivotal for her and, ultimately, the
civil rights movement. It was at Highlander that she developed the idea
of local "citizenship schools," where poorly educated African Americans
in the South could learn how to read, write, and pass the tests necessary to register to vote. The goal, though, was to create not just eligible
voters, but also informed, active citizens. During the civil rights movement, Clark helped launch hundreds of these schools and trained scores
of teachers to run them. Andrew Young, a leader of the Southern Christian Leadership Conference (SCLC), called the schools "the foundation"*

of the civil rights movement, "as much responsible for transforming the South as anything anybody did."

Highlander was a progressive, interracial school founded during the Great Depression to help poor Appalachians develop the skills and self-determination to improve their own communities. By the 1950s, it had become an important teaching and organizing hub for civil rights activists. The guiding philosophy of the school, as historian Charles Payne writes, was that "the oppressed themselves, collectively, already have much of the knowledge needed to produce change." It was a philosophy Clark embraced. "It is my belief," Clark said, "that creative leadership is present in any community and only awaits discovery and development." Historian Taylor Branch writes that Clark was known for her exceptional teaching skills, but also for "recognizing natural leaders among the poorly educated yeomanry . . . and imparting to them her unshakable confidence and respect." One of those people was Rosa Parks, who took one of Clark's leadership workshops. A few months later, in 1955, Parks helped spark the historic Montgomery bus boycott when she refused to give up her seat to a white man.

Highlander came under frequent attack from white segregationists. They accused the school of having communist ties. Clark herself was once arrested with other Highlander staff when they were falsely charged with possession of moonshine. In 1961, the state of Tennessee moved to shut down Highlander, and the SCLC—Martin Luther King Jr.'s organization—agreed to take over the school's citizenship program. Clark became the SCLC's director of education and Andrew Young became her new boss. She continued to travel across the South, establishing new schools, recruiting more teachers, and driving up black voter registration numbers in the process. When King won the Nobel Peace Prize in 1964, he insisted that Clark accompany him to Norway to accept the award. It was a testament to her impact on the movement.

Despite this recognition, Clark bristled under the sexism of her

SCLC colleagues; the daughter of a former slave, she balked at any whiff of arrogance from fellow organizers. Early in her relationship with Andrew Young, she criticized him for taking a private plane to the opening ceremonies of a citizenship school and preparing to eat on his own while none of the students had food. She would later say that, although she was a member of the executive staff, the men rarely listened to her. "Those men didn't have any faith in women, none whatsoever," she wrote. Clark saw sexism as a major weakness in the movement.

Septima Clark retired from the SCLC in 1970 but remained active. She was elected to the Charleston school board in 1975 and served two terms. In 1979, President Jimmy Carter honored Clark with a Living Legacy award. In 1982, she received South Carolina's Order of the Palmetto, the state's highest civilian award.

SEPTIMA CLARK: I was born in Charleston, South Carolina, on May 3, 1898. The thing that I remember most when I was a child was attending Sunday school in the city of Charleston. I remember that on Sunday afternoons, when I came from church and went to the corners where we separated from our friends, there was always a policeman there who very rudely told us to "get on, get on niggers." And all my life I've carried this thing in my mind, wondering what could I do to get better attitudes among policemen, or get them actually to protect us, as we walk through the streets.

Another thing that I can remember real well was that there was a part of our town called the Rotten Borough. In that part of town the people lived in these run-down shacks. The flies were prevalent because it was very near the river and the marshes. And in these shacks lived numbers of Negroes. They had to work hard during the day, in the heat of the day, and the flies were so great that they really covered the floor. As I walked through there sometimes, going down to the water's edge to catch shrimp, or to crab or to catch fish—as we did as children—I often wondered what could be done to get better housing for these people. And how could I work so that in time there would be something that we could say to the city fathers about this kind of thing?

I worked as chairman of the Committee on Administration in the YWCA, and I had a chance to work on some of these very things that I hated in my early life. I was made a representative of the whole YWCA program, and also of the community planning council. When the census was being taken—it was around '48 I guess, or it must have been '50—one of my co-workers talked about the terrible slums that she had to go into, and she was a white woman, wife of a Methodist minister. And she reported this thing to the mayor and to the alderman there. And now, a housing project has been built in that area and it is really good to know that this thing has come about, working through the years.

In Charleston today, I must say, we have a very good chief of police who will listen to you. I know because I've had a chance to meet with him and to talk to him about alcoholics, about men who were being unjustly treated on the streets, and about boys who dropped out of school. Today, while we still have a lot of problems, and we're still planning to have more meetings, I can say that we can talk with the policemen. And they have started a program of training with policemen in Charleston.

ROBERT PENN WARREN: How many Negro police in Charleston?

SC: We have quite a number of Negro policemen there now. And when the Negro policemen were first put on in Charleston, it's strange to say that one of our white club women made the search and found out how they could be used, and got the people to agree on this thing. They came in as policemen, not as a Negro policemen. They came in as policemen able to arrest anyone whose conduct needed just that. And two or three of them have been promoted to detectives, and they work throughout the state.

RPW: What people do you remember as having an influence on you, Mrs. Clark, through your childhood or youth?

SC: In my childhood, I can remember so well some of the teachers that taught me. And though my mother had very little money, she wanted to start her children at a private school. So I went to a private school. Later on I went to the public school. And all of our public schools during the time that I went to school, 1910 and even afterwards, all of the teachers were white. I can remember one teacher who taught music and who was exceptionally good. It was not until I was in junior high that we got our first Negro teacher and Negro principal. I wanted to be a teacher, and so I became a teacher after taking a teacher's examination at that time.

RPW: How long were you at the Highlander Folk School, Mrs. Clark?

SC: I stayed at the Highlander Folk School for seven years working with adults. It was there that I was able to develop the program that is now being taken over by the Southern Christian Leadership Conference called the Citizenship Education Program. And we have, at this moment, 595 teachers. We started with one teacher, fourteen students, and one hundred dollars. Today, we have a program that has 595 teachers. We've trained 1,078, but at the present time, 595 of the 1,078 are working. And they are in the eleven Southern states, with around 29,000-plus students from their classes and the communities they are in, registered to vote.

RPW: Let me switch to a question, Mrs. Clark, a historical question. In reading [Gunnar] Myrdal's big book on the Negro in America, I came across his [proposal] on what would have been compensation to the white slaveholders for the emancipated slaves. And expropriation of plantation land, with payment to the planters.

The resale of this land, not a gift, but sale to the landless, emancipated slaves, and the landless whites, on a very long-term, easy rate. One more thing, the movement of a large number of Negroes to free land in the West, and the setting up of communities outside of the South. Let me ask you, how would you feel about those items one-by-one? Let's start with compensation that would be offered for the emancipation of a slave. How do you feel about that?

SC: I do know that the slaves had nothing. They had no land and no money. But they did have something. They had a spirit, and they had the skill of working with the land. To mingle their blood and their sweat and their tears with. My father was a slave.

RPW: Your father was . . .

SC: My father was a slave on Joel Poinsett's farm. And he came out of that. And I really feel that not any of us would have liked a gift. We would rather work, and earn whatever we needed to get.

RPW: Now, what would you feel about a program which would have paid the slave owner for the emancipated slave, compensation for the emancipated slave?

SC: The slave owner, according to the stories that my father told me, had many things buried that they saved. And I don't see where they needed to be paid for an emancipated slave. Because they took away from the slaves all of the profit motive. They kept the land and every bit of the profit that came from the land. I wouldn't agree to pay them for the emancipated slave.

RPW: This on moral grounds or on practical grounds?

SC: I take my stand as a Christian principle. And that is on the real moral ground. I just don't see where I would want to, morally, pay any landowner for a human being. I just can't see it.

RPW: Suppose we can know that such a policy would have guaranteed peace in the South within a generation or so, and a reasonably humane society? And would we have avoided the problems of all the bitterness of Reconstruction, and the violence, and actually avoided segregation?

sc: It's very hard for me to believe that anything like this could have been avoided by payment to the landowners. I haven't seen money, as yet, actually bring about peace and harmony. But, when you put the *if* there—when you put the *if* in it—I would say, well, yes. *If*. Other than that, I would never agree to a landowner . . .

rpw: The only reason for doing it would be to establish a stable society.

sc: Yes.

rpw: You wouldn't feel offended then, if you knew you got a stable society as a result?

sc: If we can get a stable society, with Christian principles, I would not. And when I say Christian principles, I mean just that. I mean doing unto others as we would like to be done by. This is what I consider the Christian principles that I feel we have to take with us everywhere.

rpw: Let me quote or paraphrase a statement from James Baldwin: "The Southern mob does not represent the will of the Southern white majority." There's the crowd on the street breaking up demonstrations, or lynch mobs or police, in their illegal actions, they do not represent the will of the Southern white majority. Does that make sense to you?

sc: Yes, it does. In my mind—and I have felt this practically all through my years—there are many good white people throughout the South. Even in the state of Mississippi, where they aren't supposed to be, well, actually human. But I do think that there are some white people that the fear has kept them from speaking out or from acting. I think that the minority has the loud voice.

rpw: And the minority bullies the majority, is that it?

sc: It does, because of the great fear.

RPW: Of course, some Negroes say that keeping quiet from fear is a form of collusion, a way of joining the conspiracy.

SC: I guess that I say that, too. But I do know that there is a real fear. I had a very good friend who is the great-grandnephew of Harriet Beecher Stowe. He lived and worked in Birmingham, Alabama. And he wrote about the things that he actually saw. How people were burned at the stake. How they were castrated. It was hard for him to do anything else but run, and not to speak out any longer, but to leave. I guess we'll have to give the people a chance to grow where they don't fear death anymore. They may be joining the conspiracy. They join it because they fear death.

RPW: You had a very painful experience in Tennessee in the Highlander Folk School, didn't you?

SC: Yes I did.

RPW: Did you find any voice in Tennessee lifted in favor of the school?

SC: Yes, I'm very happy to say that the night that I was arrested, there were people who were concerned about my welfare. And at the trial, there were quite a number who came up and spoke for the school. I can remember riding with a taxi driver, and you know it's an all-white community. So I had to ride with the white taxi driver when I'd be coming in and going out. And he said that Miles Horton's wife—this is his first wife, Zilphia, who was a great singer—he said, "That was a good woman." He said: "When she first came here she came to our houses, and took our sick people out and carried them to the Folk School, and fed them. And then filled bags with food when she carried them back home. And Miles's mother taught us how to make quilts, and how to weave, until there were many who talked in favor of this school."

RPW: But they had no influence.

SC: But they had no influence. They were not able to speak loud enough to get above the talk of the rabble-rousers.

RPW: Where did the impulse to suppress the school come from, by your diagnosis?

SC: I felt that we had to fight three states. We had to fight not only Tennessee, but Arkansas, Alabama, and Georgia. Because while we were having a meeting in 1957, Governor [Marvin] Griffin of Georgia sent a man, Ed Friend, up there, who came in as what he called a water pollution expert to take pictures and spy on the group. We weren't doing anything we didn't want him to see. But he managed to have a fellow there that they considered a communist. And every time he would get near one of our speakers, he would snap a picture of them. So they made a slick paper of this thing and sent it all around. When Miles was investigated, too, at Nashville, there were men there from Georgia, Alabama, and Arkansas, who were trying to put pressure on the jury at that hearing.

RPW: Was the main question the biracial seminars then?

SC: When we were in the mountain courts, and the local courts with the magistrates and the justice of the peace, the issue was integration. And I think they did that to inflame the jury. But, when the case was then carried to the state Supreme Court, the integration angle was dropped and it became operation of the school for the personal benefit of Miles Horton, or the selling of beer without a license.

RPW: But those were subterfuges, weren't they?

SC: They were. And we know that those things were not true.

RPW: Do you feel, Mrs. Clark, that there's been a real change in the general climate of opinion in your times, about racial inferiority and superiority?

SC: I've lived quite a long life and I see a great difference in the climate. I've known the times when many Negroes felt very inferior.

In fact, I know of some today who still feel that way. I've had a chance recently to see some Negro women, when I go into towns, who won't even sit and eat with me. They still let the husbands eat with company while they go and eat in the kitchen. That's a carry-over, I think, from slavery. So this thing is still with us.

I started to say I've also seen a great difference with white people. My mother had many children and we lived in an integrated neighborhood. Charleston was not a zoned city; it is just becoming zoned. And so there was a man with his mother, who lived not too far away from us, and the mother was elderly and wanted some child to sleep with her every night. And there was always, to my mind, a kind of inferior thing. They would want to make you a pallet somewhere, but never want you to sleep in a bed with them, even though they wanted you for company. But today, many of those same people of that same family will offer you a bed in the room with them, or in a separate room in their house. The climate has changed all around. I think white people felt, at one time, that they had to have subordinates, but today it's not true all over.

RPW: What's caused this change, in your opinion?

SC: Two world wars and the introduction of federal programs. I can remember the first time when I was teaching, when the Agricultural Association came, and Negro farmers, dirt farmers, were going to get loans. Well, before that time, white farmers would go into a place and Negro farmers would stand outside. But after the Second World War, white farmers and Negro dirt farmers lined up in the same room, one behind the other, as they came—first come, first served. And that, I think, changed the people. Then there were new banking laws. Right after Mr. Roosevelt came in, banks were closed down. And when we went back into the banks, people were served on a first-come, first-served basis. And so that thing has spread.

From every rural section of the South and every dive in the

North, Negroes were taken to other countries and saw another kind of life. And they came back home to get some of this democracy that they were trying to save. There were more people coming from everywhere to demand the rights that were actually theirs. And as white people matured, they realized that these [Negro] people had saved their lives during the First and the Second World Wars.

Martin Luther King Jr.

March 18, 1964

Atlanta, Georgia

The Reverend Martin Luther King Jr. was already the leading voice for nonviolent social change in the civil rights movement when Robert Penn Warren interviewed him in Atlanta. Warren wrote extensively about the meeting in a chapter of Who Speaks? *that concentrated on eight major movement leaders Warren termed "the Big Brass." He was taken by King's personal magnetism, grace of movement, and the depth of thought he gave to the questions Warren asked. "The charisma is not the product of publicity," Warren wrote. "It is real."*

King was born in Atlanta in 1929. His father and grandfather were pastors at the city's prestigious Ebenezer Baptist Church, which King himself would come to lead. He earned degrees from Morehouse College, Crozer Theological Seminary, and Boston University. In 1953, King married Coretta Scott and a year later became pastor of Dexter Avenue Baptist Church in Montgomery, Alabama. It was there, during a bus boycott by the city's black residents, that King got deeply involved in the cause that would dominate his life.

By the time Warren met with King, in March of 1964, the minister had been repeatedly arrested in Southern towns and cities for his civil rights activities. He had written his famous "Letter from a Birmingham

Jail," delivered his "I Have a Dream" speech at the March on Washington, been named Time *magazine's Man of the Year*, and met with presidents Eisenhower, Kennedy, and Johnson. Later in 1964 King was awarded the Nobel Peace Prize.

The Southern demonstrations led by King and others—and the violent white backlash—helped spur Congress to pass the 1964 Civil Rights Act and the 1965 Voting Rights Act. With momentum from those victories, King pressed the civil rights movement to enlarge its vision. He rallied his forces to protest housing discrimination in Chicago in 1966, but the effort met with limited success. The centrality of King's leadership in the movement was also being increasingly challenged by other activists, especially younger and more militant organizers.

In 1967, King stepped up his opposition to the war in Vietnam. On April 4, he gave a speech at Riverside Church in Manhattan declaring that the nation's struggles with racism and poverty were inextricably linked with the war. Critics within the civil rights movement accused King of sacrificing their domestic aims by speaking out against the Vietnam War. King felt he could not do otherwise. Exactly one year to the day after the Riverside speech, King was assassinated in Memphis, Tennessee.

Robert Penn Warren met King at the headquarters of the Southern Christian Leadership Conference, the civil rights organization King founded in 1957. King seemed busy and Warren guessed that he was skipping lunch to make time for him. He opened the interview with a question about the Reverend Martin Luther King Sr., known to his family and followers as "Daddy King." The elder King had been pastor at Ebenezer for more than thirty years. His son became his co-pastor in 1960.

Daddy King was a gifted orator and had long been an active, implacable foe of segregation. In 1939, he led an ambitious voter registration drive in Atlanta over the opposition of more cautious leaders in the black community. He headed a successful effort to improve working conditions and pay for African American teachers. And he challenged

white authority figures to treat him with respect. Martin was with his
father when an Atlanta traffic cop called Daddy King "boy." Martin
said his father pointed at him and replied forcefully, "This is a boy. I'm
a man, and until you call me one, I will not listen to you." The aston-
ished officer hastily wrote out a ticket and left the scene.

ROBERT PENN WARREN: Do you see your father's role and your own
role as historical phases of the same process?

MARTIN LUTHER KING: Yes, I do. My father and I have worked
together a great deal in the last few years trying to grapple with the
same problem. He was working in the area of civil rights before I
was born. I grew up in the kind of atmosphere that had a real civil
rights concern.

RPW: There are vast differences, of course, in techniques and
opportunities and climate of opinion—all of those million things
that are different from one generation to the other. But you see a
continuity in the process, and not a sharp division between roles,
yours and his?

MLK: Yes, I see continuity. There are certainly minor differences,
but I don't think there is any sharp difference. I think basically
the roles are the same. Now, I grant you, my father did not come
up under the discipline of the nonviolent philosophy. He was not
really trained in the nonviolent discipline. But even without that,
the problem was about the same, and even though the methods
may not have been consciously nonviolent, they were certainly
nonviolent in the sense that he never advocated violence as a way
to solve the problems.

RPW: Yes, yes. Those are phases then, shall we say, in a process.
What is the next phase of the Negro movement?

MLK: My feeling is that we will really have to grapple with ways
and means to really bring about an integrated society. Nonviolent

direct action, working through the courts, and working through legislative processes may be extremely helpful in bringing about a desegregated society. But when we move into the realm of actual integration, which deals with mutual acceptance—genuine intergroup, interpersonal living—then it seems to me that other methods will have to be used.

RPW: In that phase, we can certainly see quite clearly responsibilities that belong to the white man, and obligations. Now, what problems, responsibilities, and obligations would you say the Negro would have in this phase?

MLK: Well, I would think the responsibilities of the Negro in this phase would be in the area of what Mahatma Gandhi used to refer to as "constructive work." Which is a program whereby individuals work desperately to improve their own conditions and their own standards. After the Negro emerges in and from the desegregated society, then a great deal of time must be spent in improving standards which lag behind, to a large extent, because of segregation, discrimination, and the legacy of slavery. The Negro will have to engage in a sort of "operation bootstraps" in order to lift these standards. By raising these lagging standards it will make it much less difficult for him to move on into the integrated society.

RPW: Two weeks ago a prominent newspaperman—a Southerner by birth—said to me: "Thank God for Dr. King. He's our only hope." He was worrying about violence. Now, this is very often said by white people. Dr. Kenneth Clark has remarked in print that your appeal to many white people is because you lull them into some sense of security. And I hear, too, that there is some resistance on the part of Negroes because they feel that your leadership has somehow given a sense of a soft line, a rapprochement, that flatters the white man's sense of security. Do you encounter this, and how do you think about this?

MLK: Well, I don't agree with it, (laughs) naturally. First, one must understand what I'm talking about and what I'm trying to do when I say "love," and that the love ethic must be at the center of this struggle. I'm certainly not talking about an affectionate emotion. I'm not talking about what the Greek language would refer to as *Eros*, or *famile*. I'm talking about something much deeper. I'm thinking of a very strong love. I'm thinking of love in action. Not something where you say, "Love your enemies," and just leave it at that. You love your enemies to the point that you're willing to sit-in at a lunch counter in order to help them find themselves. You're willing to go to jail. I don't think anybody could consider this cowardice or even a weak approach. So I think that many of these arguments come from those who have gotten so caught up in bitterness that they cannot see the deep moral issues involved.

RPW: Or the white man, caught up in complacency, refuses to understand it.

MLK: Yes, I think so. I think both.

RPW: There's a problem that many people now talk about, as more and more [civil rights] activity occurs in the big centers, like Harlem and Detroit and Chicago—desperate wondering as to whether any leadership now visible, or imaginable, can control the random explosion that might come at any time, that is stored up. Is that the big, central problem you all are facing now?

MLK: I think it's a real problem. And I think the only answer to this problem is the speed in which we move toward the solution of the problem. The more progress we can have in race relations and the more we move toward the goal of an integrated society, the more we lift the hope of the masses of people. This will lessen the possibility of sporadic violence. On the other hand, if we get setbacks, and if something happens where the Civil Rights Act is watered down, for instance, if the Negro feels that he can do nothing but move from one ghetto to another and one slum to another, the despair and the disappointment will be so great that it will be very difficult to keep the struggle disciplined and nonviolent. So it will depend on the rate and speed of progress, and recognition on the part of the white leadership of the need to go on and get this problem solved—and solved in a hurry—and the need for massive action programs to do it.

Warren asks King about public school segregation and the effects it has on white and black children.

MLK: When a white child goes to school only with white children, unconsciously that child grows up devoid of a world perspective. There is an unconscious provincialism, and it can develop into an unconscious superiority complex, just as a Negro develops an unconscious inferiority complex. Our society must come to see that this whole question of integration is not merely a matter of quantity—having the same this and that in terms of a building or a desk—but it's a matter of quality. If I can't communicate with a man, I'm not equal to him. It's not only a matter of mathematics; it's a matter of psychology and philosophy.

RPW: Let me ask a question that lies behind part of this, I think, at least for some people. [W.E.B.] Du Bois, many years ago, wrote about a possible split in the Negro psyche. The Negro is pulled, on one hand, toward almost a mystique of African heritage, or at least the special Negro cultural heritage here, to the mystique of blackness. On the other hand, the pull toward Western, European, Judeo-Christian-American cultural heritage, with the price of being absorbed away from the other cultural heritage, and even having the blood integrity lost entirely, possibly, in the end. Does this present itself to you as a real problem, as a real issue, or not?

MLK: It's a real issue and it has made for a good deal of frustration in the Negro community. People have tried to solve it through various methods. One has been to try to reject, psychologically, anything that reminds you of your heritage. This is particularly true of the Negro middle class, the desire to reject anything that reminds you of Africa, anything that reminds you of the masses of Negroes. And then trying to identify with the white majority, the white middle class. And so often what happens is this individual finds himself caught out in the middle, with no cultural roots, because he's rejected by so many of the white middle class, and he ends up, as E. Franklin Frazier says in a book, "unconsciously hating himself," when he tries to compensate for this through conspicuous consumption.

So there's no doubt about the fact that this has been a problem, but I don't think it has to be. I think one can live in American society with a certain cultural heritage, whether it's an African heritage or European, or what have you, and still absorb a great deal of this [American] culture. There is always cultural assimilation. This is not an unusual thing. It's a very natural thing. And I think that we've got to come to see this. The Negro is an American. We know nothing about Africa, although our roots are there in terms of our forebearers. But the average Negro today knows nothing about Africa. And I think he's got to face the fact that he is an American, his culture is basically American. One becomes adjusted to this when he realizes what he is. He's got to know what he is. Our destiny is tied up with the destiny of America.

Warren asks King about the meaning of the phrase "Freedom Now," in the context of historical change in society.

MLK: I think the slogan is a good one. It really means that the Negro has reached the point of feeling that he should have freedom

now. I don't think there's any illusion in the mind of anybody about the fact that you've got to observe the historical process, that this structural change cannot come overnight. But we must work at it and we must try to deal with it with such an urgency that we are challenged by the need for it—now. This [slogan] is more of a challenge to work, and [to] realize the urgency of the moment, than it is a belief that you can really get freedom within such a short period.

RPW: I sat with a group of students some months ago and asked if it's a question of social process. And a very bright boy, a senior in a good college, said, "I understand about social process, in time. But I can't bear to bring myself to say it."

MLK: Yeah, well, I find it is a problem. And we have lived so long with people saying, "It takes time," and "Wait on time," that I find it very difficult to adjust to this. I mean, I get annoyed almost when I hear it, although I know it takes time. But the people that use this argument have been people, so often, who really didn't want the change to come. Gradualism for them meant a do-nothing-ism, you know, and the stand-still-ism. So it has been a revolt, I think, against the feeling, on the part of some, that you can just sit around and wait on time when actually time is neutral. It can be used either constructively or destructively.

RPW: But some words have become symbolically charged with feelings where they can't even be used. Like the word "gradual" has become emotionally charged, symbolically charged.

MLK: That's right.

RPW: So the word can't be used.

MLK: That's right. Exactly. All of the emotions surrounding gradualism, and this whole thing of waiting on time, brings about resentment from the Negro and his allies in the white community.

RPW: Now, speaking of symbolisms: I was talking a few weeks ago with a very, very able Negro attorney. He's a very violent, bitter man.

And he suddenly said, "I live in a society where all the symbolism of the poetry I read, the Bible I read, is charged with the white man's values. God's white robes, you know. White light of hope. All of which are an affront to me." And he said, "I find myself schooling myself now to resist all the symbolism and invert it for myself."

MLK: Many Negroes go through this, now probably more than ever before. My only hope is that this kind of reaction will not take us right back into the same thing we're trying to get out [of]. There's always a danger that an oppressed group will seek to rise from the position of disadvantage to one of advantage, you see, thereby subverting justice. You end up substituting one tyranny for another. Our danger is that we can get so bitter that we revolt against everything white. This becomes a very dangerous thing, because it can lead to the kind of philosophy that you get in the black nationalist movements—the kind of philosophy that ends up preaching black supremacy as a way of counteracting white supremacy. I just think this would be bad for our total society. But I can well understand the kind of impatience, and the psychological conditions, that lead to this kind of reaction.

RPW: There's a special thing about this revolution that makes it unlike, as far as I can tell, any other. All previous revolutions have aimed at the liquidation of a class or a regime. This one does not aim at liquidation of a class or a regime. It's aimed at something else.

MLK: It's a revolution.

RPW: How would you define that aim then?

MLK: I would say this is a revolution to get *in*. It's very interesting. I think you're quite right that most revolutions, almost all revolutions, have been centered on destroying something. In this revolution, the whole quest is for the Negro to get into the mainstream of American life. It's a revolution calling upon the nation to live up to what is already there in an idealistic sense, in all of its creeds and all of its

basic affirmations. But it's never lived up to it. So this is the difference: it is a revolution of rising expectations, and it is a revolution not to liquidate the structure of America, but a revolution to get into the mainstream of American life.

RPW: A revolution to liquidate an idea, is that it?

MLK: That's right, to liquidate an idea which is out of harmony with the basic idea of the nation.

RPW: It's a new kind of revolution.

MLK: Yes, it's a new kind of revolution.

RPW: The problem may be to define this revolution in new terms, to contain the element of hate and liquidation, and exploit the element of hope. You want to drive one horse, not two, unless you want to kill one of the horses. Hate's a great dynamic in a revolution. That's human. The hate element is there. But it's a question of containing that. Or converting it to something else, because there's no legitimate object for it.

MLK: I think you're quite right. This is a part of the job of the leadership in this revolution: to keep that hope alive. To keep the kind of righteous indignation alive, or the kind of healthy discontent alive, that will keep the revolution moving on.

The conversation turns to incidents in which King was attacked by black people in Harlem. In 1958, a mentally disturbed woman stabbed King in the chest as he was signing books in a bookstore. In 1963, King's car was pelted with eggs when he was on a visit to the area.

MLK: The first one, I don't know if we'll ever know what the cause or basis was because [she] had a demented mind [and] really didn't know why she was doing it. It may be that she had been around some of the meetings of these groups in Harlem, black nationalist groups, that have me all the time as a favorite object of scorn, and hearing this over and over again, she may have responded to it when I came to Harlem. Or it may be that she was just so confused that she would've done this to anybody whose name was in the news. We'll never know.

But now, the other one where they threw eggs at my car, I think that was really a result of the black nationalist groups. They've heard all of these things about my being soft and my talking about love the white man all the time. [They think] that this is a cowardly approach. And they transfer bitterness toward the white man to me because they fear that I'm saying love this person that they have such a bitter attitude toward. It grows right out of that. In fact, Malcolm X had a meeting the day before and he had talked about me a great deal and told them that I would be there the next night. [He] said, "Now, you all are to go over there and let old King know what you think about him." And he had said a great deal about nonviolence, criticizing nonviolence, and saying that I approved of Negro men and women being bitten by dogs and [blasted by] fire hoses, and that I say, "[Do] not defend yourself."

So I think this response grew out of all of the talk about my being a sort of polished Uncle Tom. This is the kind of thing they say in those groups. Now, my feeling has always been that they never understood what I'm saying. Because they don't see that there's a great deal of a difference between nonresistance to evil and nonviolent resistance. I'm not saying that you sit down and patiently accept injustice. I'm talking about a very strong force, where you stand up with all your might against an evil system. You are not a coward. You are resisting. You've come to see that, tactically as well as morally, it is better to be nonviolent. Even if one didn't want to deal with the moral questions, it would just be impractical for the Negro to talk about making his struggle a violent one.

Warren mentions a public opinion survey conducted in Harlem in which a large percentage of African American respondents did not think of blacks as being a minority.

MLK: Is that so?

RPW: Because they see so few white people around.

MLK: That's right. They never go out of Harlem.

RPW: So the tactical appeal doesn't apply to them. They say, "We're the majority." That's a dangerous fact, isn't it?

MLK: That's a dangerous fact, yes. And you see, many people in Harlem never go out of Harlem. I mean, they'd never even been downtown. And you can see how this bitterness can accumulate. Here you see people crowded, and hovered up in ghettos and slums, with no hope. They see no way out. If they could look down a long corridor and see an exit sign, they would feel a little better. But they see no sense of hope. And it's very easy for one talking about violence and hatred for the white man to appeal to them. And I have never thought of this, but I think this is quite true: that if you talk to them about nonviolence from a tactical point of view, they can't quite see it because they don't even know they're outnumbered.

RPW: Let me ask one more question. When you were assaulted— and it's very hard, I know, to reconstruct one's own feelings—what did you feel? What were your first actual reactions at the moment they threw the eggs? Can you reconstruct that?

MLK: Yes, I remember my feelings very well. At first I had a very depressing response because I realized that these were my own people, these were Negroes throwing eggs at me. And I guess you do go through those moments when you begin to think about what you're going through, and the sacrifices and suffering that you face as a result of the movement, and yet your own people don't have an understanding, not even an appreciation, and [they are] seeking to destroy your image at every point.

But then it was very interesting. I went right into church and I spoke. And I started thinking not so much about myself but about the very people, the society that made people respond like this. I was able, very quickly, to get my mind off of myself and of feeling sorry for myself, and feeling rejected. I started including them into the orbit of my thinking—that it's not enough to condemn them for engaging in this act. But what about the society, and what about the conditions that are still alive which made people act like this? And I got up and said: "The thing that concerns me is not so much those young men. I feel sorry for them. I'm concerned about the fact that maybe all of us have contributed to [the problem] by not working harder to get rid of the conditions, the poverty, social isolation, that cause individuals to respond like this."

Wyatt Tee Walker

March 18, 1964

Atlanta, Georgia

Wyatt Tee Walker came early to civil rights activism and, according to Martin Luther King Jr., was "one of the keenest minds of the nonviolent revolution." Walker served as the executive director of the Southern Christian Leadership Conference (SCLC) from 1960 to 1964, greatly expanding the organization's size, capacity, and fund-raising efforts, and serving as a key direct action strategist. SCLC staffer C.T. Vivian said Walker "made everybody snap to attention. You were going to produce when Wyatt was around."

Wyatt Tee Walker was born on August 16, 1929, near Boston, Massachusetts. He was one of eleven children. Walker graduated from Virginia Union University with a BS in chemistry and physics, but he soon followed his father into the ministry. In 1953, he was called to minister at the historic Gillfield Baptist Church in Petersburg, Virginia, one of the oldest black churches in the nation.

Walker was a prodigious organizer all his life. When he was nine years old, he and his siblings, living in New Jersey, refused to be barred from a segregated movie theater. Over the course of his life, Walker was arrested seventeen times for civil disobedience. The first time was in 1958, when he entered a whites-only public library in Petersburg and tried to check out a book. Joining him were his wife, children, and a handful of other preachers and students. Historian Taylor Branch says the book Walker selected was a biography of Confederate commander Robert E. Lee because it amused him that "white southerners would arrest him for trying to read about their most cherished hero."

Historian Raymond Arsenault describes Walker as "one of the movement's most flamboyant characters." His courage and aplomb won the admiration of King early on. In the 1950s, Walker was president of the local chapter of the NAACP, the state director of the Congress of Racial Equality, and one of the founding directors of the SCLC. He also founded the Petersburg Improvement Association.

As a civil rights leader, Walker often found himself nose to nose with white supremacists. While supporting Freedom Riders jailed in Monroe, North Carolina, he encountered a beefy white man on the steps of the county courthouse. According to Arsenault, the man "picked the diminutive SCLC leader up and threw him down a flight of concrete steps into a bed of ivy surrounding a granite Civil War monument." Walker got up and climbed the stairs, only to be thrown down again. The third time, police arrested the man, and Walker entered the courthouse.

Walker was a skilled and meticulous tactician. He helped plan the SCLC's 1963 Birmingham campaign, which he dubbed "Project C" for "confrontation." Aimed at attacking segregation in the Alabama city, the campaign included mass demonstrations, sit-ins, and a boycott of white-owned businesses. Thousands of people were arrested, including King and hundreds of children.

Walker described the Birmingham campaign as "a tremendous organizational operation." One key goal was to provoke public safety commissioner Eugene "Bull" Connor, a vicious segregationist. Historian David Garrow says Walker tried to "precipitate . . . crucial crises in order to expose what the black community was up against." Walker said that he and fellow organizers had been counting on Connor's stupidity. "Bull Connor had something in his mind about not letting 'these niggers' get to City Hall," he said. "I prayed that he'd keep trying to stop us. . . . Birmingham would have been lost if Bull had let us go down to the City Hall and pray. . . . There would be no movement, no publicity."

Instead, the battle being fought in the streets of Birmingham became a national story and led to major concessions from city leaders, including desegregating lunch counters, removing "whites only" and "blacks only" signs from water fountains and restrooms, and releasing protesters from jail. White segregationists retaliated with a series of violent attacks, bombing King's temporary headquarters at the Gaston Motel and the home of his brother. Still, the campaign was considered a success. It inspired similar action across the South.

On a team of staff with outsized egos at the SCLC, Wyatt Tee Walker made no apology for his. "I didn't give a damn if people liked me," he once said in an interview, "but I knew I could do the job." He was devoted to King, whom he addressed, simply, as "Leader." He told Robert Penn Warren, "One big piece of evidence about the greatness of Martin Luther King is that a man as vain as I am is willing to play second fiddle to him. And I'm not ordinarily ready to play second fiddle to anybody."

By 1964, Walker's heavy-handed management style had become a problem for the independent-minded SCLC staff. He resigned from the organization not long after meeting with Warren. Walker soon took the helm of a new publishing company, the Negro Heritage Library, which sought to expand school curricula to include more African American history and culture.

At King's urging, Walker became senior pastor at Canaan Baptist Church in Harlem in 1968, where he served for thirty-seven years. King was the guest preacher at his installation on March 24, 1968, eleven days before his assassination. In 1975, Walker was awarded a doctorate in African American studies from Colgate Rochester Divinity School. An expert on gospel music, he published a number of books on music, social change, and religion. Walker remained a staunch activist throughout his life. He organized efforts to challenge apartheid in South Africa and led community development activities in Harlem.

Robert Penn Warren met the Reverend Walker at SCLC headquarters in Atlanta. He described Walker as a "voluble and eloquent" man who appeared to speak with candor and self-awareness.

ROBERT PENN WARREN: To many people it is astonishing that the leadership, by and large, of the Negro movement has come from people living in the South. How do you explain this?

WYATT TEE WALKER: There's a large degree of coincidence involved here. The nonviolent thrust of the Negro community in the South that we have seen in the last decade has been a part of the history of the world—the rise of the nations in Africa toward independence. I think there's something about this moment of history which has caught this present generation.

One of the biggest contributing factors to it is that we have come into a day of instantaneous communication. One of the things that kept the Negro community in the Deep South insulated against even knowing something better to want was the fact that he didn't have the information. There's an old expression, you can't miss what you never had. So this day of instantaneous reporting of events has given the Negro a chance to connect himself up with the whole stream of history.

Another contributing factor is that, in a very real way, the minds of Negroes have been unlocked. For instance, I think the white Southern race uses a lot of sophisticated arguments as to why the Negro is inferior, and why there ought to be separate education facilities, which are not at all the real reasons. I think the more insidious reason is that he has wanted to keep the Negro ignorant. You can't lay open a man's mind to the truth of the humanities, to the trend of civilization of the Western world in the last five hundred years, you can't bait his mind in thinking of Aristotle and Plato and Diogenes, without him wanting something better in life. To keep a man a slave you've got to keep him ignorant. Unslave his mind and you unslave, inevitably, his person.

RPW: As [Frederick] Douglass put it.

WTW: Yes. As you're making an analysis of Negro leadership, I think the people who hold the titular responsibilities, whether they have come by them out of design or by accidents in history, they are all people with finely tooled minds, who have a sharp sensitivity to the humanities. They are generally literate and well-read men who do their own thinking. I think if you could make just a spot survey or spot check of the people with whom you talk, that this is the general stripe of people you talk with.

RPW: That's true. This raises a question. In 1935, would such a leadership have been available among Negroes?

WTW: Well, I personally doubt it. It's difficult to second-guess history. I do not think it was possible in 1935 because a lot of what has been produced has come about out of the response to what World War II produced. You had a new temper developing in Negro boys during World War II. They got to see the world. And they had made an investment in making the world safe for democracy, et cetera, all of the slogans we had. And they came back with certain questions in their minds. They had been overseas and had freedoms that they never even conjectured in Mississippi and Alabama and Georgia and Louisiana. Then, in their own minds, they said: "If I fought and ran the risk of dying for all of America then I ought to have some share of it here." This shift in the South, from an agrarian economy to an urban industrial economy, has had a lot to do with the groundswell of discontent of the Negro community. The Negro was leaving the Deep South in droves, going to other large industrial cities in the North during the war.

RPW: What about the notion that we are encountering some-times, that the Negro is just discovering his identity, that this is part of this whole movement?

WTW: It's a very critical part, because I've seen, in my own lifetime—I'm not an old man, as you know—an internal color discrimination in the Negro community. And, being a mulatto, I guess I was sensitized to it because I had brothers and sisters who, I don't know why, gave being light-skinned some special value. Fortunately for me, I rebelled against this. I thought people were people on the basis of their intrinsic worth, the fact that they were humans. And I think this could have been one of the things that made me get the issue of humanity square in my own mind. I have seen that change sharply in the last fifteen or twenty years. I have known dark-skinned people in whose presence I would be afraid to say the word "black," seriously or humorously.

RPW: You mean now, or in the past?

WTW: In the past, fifteen years ago. Now I feel no reluctance whatsoever. In fact, it's part of the built-in humor of the movement that we kid each other about, calling each other half-white Negroes and black Negroes. In affectionate terms, you know.

RPW: Some weeks ago I was having an interview with a quite distinguished lawyer, who is a Negro, and he was saying to me that it's a real problem for him, living in a world of white symbolisms— the symbolism of white and black, dark and light, as symbols that convey value. He said, bitterly: "I find myself schooling myself to invert these symbolisms, which are hidden in all literature and in common speech."

wtw: I think this is symptomatic in the Muslim movement, you know.

rpw: This man is not a Muslim.

wtw: He may not be, but this is the other extreme, that within this movement they are exalting black, which is the reverse of exalting white. And I can certainly sympathize with this lawyer because I know, when I am watching television and reading stories, and in some of our expressions, my antenna is out to pick up these little value assignments on the basis of color. We talk about a little white lie, but a terrible lie is a black lie. I saw a television story about a good horse and a bad horse, and the good horse was white and the black horse was bad. And it's so skillfully woven into the whole fabric of our value judgments that I think sometimes it almost happens to us unconsciously.

rpw: These oppositions, light and dark, run through all sorts of things in our society, in our literature. It also is found in Africa. The symbolism, as some anthropologists say, antedates any contact with white European culture. In the Chinese theater, literally, a face is darkened to denote a villain and whitened for a hero.

wtw: You must understand that this is the normal emotional response for the American Negro because of the frame of reference in which he has been forced to move, because of the box in which the Negro has been moved, and this is his immediate interpretation of it. I think this goes back even to Platonic dualism. It's reflected in the New Testament writings of Paul; he talks about the children of light and the children of darkness. And we can even go back to the business of day and night, with the primitive mind not really quite grasping what makes night and what makes day.

rpw: Then we have a very strange situation, don't we, of a conditioned attitude toward natural symbols.

WTW: I think one has been superimposed on the other. We have taken the natural symbols and then, as the structure of race and color concepts developed, we superimposed them on nature symbols that were already available.

RPW: There we are. What reaction is appropriate, then, for a cultivated Negro or a not-cultivated Negro facing these symbolisms? What's reasonable and logical?

WTW: I would hope that I could be considered cultivated, but I don't think any Negro, no matter how much he's cultivated, ever really becomes emancipated. No matter how much my mind has been opened, no matter how much, academically, I recognize the fallacy of race, so much has been done to my emotional pattern by what we call the system—the segregation and discrimination—that I never really am free of it. And so you get, sometimes in fleeting moments, the reverse response, discrimination the other way. For instance, I think Negroes like myself have developed almost a mental catalog of the tone of voices of how a white face speaks to them, which in another circumstance, when a Negro speaks, would get no response whatsoever. But everything that a white person says is interpreted by the nuance of the tone of voice, or maybe the hang of the head, or the depth of tone, or the sharpness of the tongue. Things that in the ordinary, normal frame of reference would have no meaning take on tremendous and deep and sharp meaning.

RPW: You are documenting the remark made by more than one Negro, that to be a Negro is to have a touch of the paranoid.

WTW: Oh, yes. We have almost a total ambivalence. Even in this moment of history for the Negro, when he really accepts his identity more than he ever has before, there is still a retention of this ambivalence, which has many roads by which it has come. Some of it came out of survival, some of it came out of hatred for the white man, just the pure job of saying one thing that you knew he wanted to hear and really meaning something else.

RPW: Even the folklore, even Uncle Remus.

WTW: Yes, poking fun at the master without the master ever really understanding what he was saying. This runs through the idiomatic expression of the Negro, and the Negro spirituals, and the Negro religion.

RPW: What about this question, then, of the relation of white men to the Negro movement? We have very violent statements here and there. [James] Baldwin says the white liberal is an affliction. Others have said, "We will have no more connection with the white sympathizer, the white liberal. He has no place. He's a curse." This is a logical extension of that attitude, isn't it?

WTW: Yes it is. I do agree with Adam Clayton Powell Jr., one person whom I know has said this again and again, that the day has come when the white person has no role to play in the policy decisions of the Negro movement. But I do not go all the way with him to say that we do not need white allies. No, maybe I am middle-of-the-road on this point of view. I say that there are some decisions that the Negro will have to make tactically and strategy-wise, as far as the direction that his movement is going to take, and there are certain kinds of decisions in which I don't think a white man's attitude can have any impact whatsoever, and these decisions ought to be left alone to the Negro community. But if the white man wants to help with our revolution, he must come and join with us. I think we have passed through the stage of the Southern white liberal of fifteen years ago. I have an expression I use: we are afflicted with worn-out white liberals who, fifteen years ago, could have been killed for what they were saying [against segregation]. But they're saying the same things now that they were saying fifteen years ago, and as [American poet] James Russell Lowell has said, "Time makes ancient good uncouth." We are at a different moment in history.

RPW: Is it possible that the Negro movement could have success without a white consensus, though, in its favor?

WTW: Yes, I do think so.

RPW: How would you explain that?

WTW: Well, I know this is a minority opinion, but I sincerely believe it. The Negro has just enough pivotal position in the economy of our nation—the free enterprise system—and just enough visible identity, that in a united effort we could produce so creative a crisis that the consensus might be forced. Not a consensus of consent, but a consensus prodded by practicality. Coupled with the guilt burden that the white community must bear—that they do bear—particularly within white Christianity or white religious life.

RPW: But guilt is in the guts. If you have a feeling of guilt you already have an awareness of the moral issue and a desire for another attitude in yourself.

WTW: I had not defined it as closely as that. The feeling that I was trying to get at is when a white person says, "I know what the right thing is to do, but I just don't have the power to do it."

Walker turns the conversation back to the question of black acceptance of identity.

WTW: I wanted to say a few more words about that, because I think this is half of the battle, for the Negro to accept himself as he is. Now, maybe my philosophy or attitude about this is a little structured because I've talked about it a good bit on the public platform, but this business of this internal color discrimination was very sharp fifteen or twenty years ago, when I was a youngster. I was very aware of it. And I have seen a sharp disappearance. You do not find Negroes today who are light-skinned who assign to themselves any special value. And you do not find the counterpart, the sharp sensitivity of Negroes who are dark-skinned. In fact, it has gone a little bit the other way. There's a little more pride being taken now in a Negro being a visible Negro. If you're on the borderline, like some of us mulattoes are, you feel a little bit embarrassed, kind of like we've been cheated in this movement of the rise of the nations in Africa, and the respectability of being black and having kinky hair.

I think it's healthy, even though the pendulum has gone the other way, because I think it will even out. But, more than anything else, this is what the nonviolent movement has given the Negro: a basic belief in his own personal worth, no matter who he is. There is a means, now, by which he can make his witness for what he believes, without cursing and swearing and clubbing and shooting— using any of the traditional violent means when one wants to react against oppression. He has found identity not alone for himself but with the group. The Negro has a new solidarity. This is true not only of one Negro with a hundred other Negroes, but it's also true of Negroes South and North. I think Birmingham meant this more than anything else. There were many Negroes in the North who kind of felt sorry for those Negroes down South, but then didn't really feel a bond. But the bond has been forged now as never before.

RPW: In fact, there was, by all reports of sociologists and other observers, a great withdrawal on the part of Northern Negroes from Southern Negroes as they came north.

WTW: Yes, they wanted to be cut off not only from the stark circumstances that they had left, but also from their [history] of having been slaves. I think this is reflected, in another way, in the middle-class Negro, who begins to develop enough economic security that he wants to cut himself off from the Negro community. He finds himself unacceptable to the white community, and so his frustration is lost in—as I think Dr. King describes it—conspicuous consumption, completely devoid of any spiritual or moral values. And it has been a kind of entrapment that [the Negro] wandered into. I think it has been reflected in the early days, maybe even now in our present revolution, that a lot of the goals of the movement have been middle class, and not so much things that affect the simple and plain people of the land. But more and more the center of the movement, the focus of the movement, is shifting, particularly in economic terms, to matters of employment, those things which are going to be the day-by-day, flesh-and-blood considerations of the people of the land.

RPW: Moving away from civil rights, as such, toward the economic substructure, the psychological substructure. Is that it?

WTW: Yes. From civil rights to human rights. The right to be free from the fear of want and hunger, and free from the fear of not having shelter, free from the fear of ignorance.

Warren asks Walker to comment on W.E.B. Du Bois's concept of the split identity in the black psyche between identifying as an African and as an American.

WTW: In this present movement, what we have is going to lead toward a synthesis of the two. I do not think that Negroes, in the foreseeable future, are going to lose ethnic identity, if that's the proper way to describe it. I think for three to four to five and maybe six generations, there is going to be a visible Negro community. But I think the temper of history in the world, particularly with the rise of the African and Asian nations, is such that the color factor is going to recede in its importance. I don't think it's an undue optimism. Color will become an incidental means of identification, and the Negro will find his place in America as the Jew has, as the Irish, as the labor movement. The tide of history, of our times, is going to demand so much for human rights that the Negro will integrate himself into this new stream of history in such a way that he will not be lost visibly, but yet the stereotypes and the discrimination and the artificial obstacles that hampered him in his first hundred years of emancipation will recede almost into insignificance.

RPW: You envisage a pluralistic society in America, rather than a unified society in that sense?

WTW: I think what we're going to see in America is what the world is like in miniature, in one place. It's going to be a kind of United Nations because, even with the restrictions being imposed on new people coming from other countries, I think we're still going to have them come. Some way is going to be found. The technological advances of this nation, the agricultural skills, our reputation and our bent as builders—we get more out of the land, we have the largest leisure class, you know—it's going to be a mecca toward which people who have an opportunity are going to find their way. You're going to have more of a melting pot in America. I envision something like maybe a larger Hawaii, or a larger Jamaica, something like that. This is my hope for America, that it will become like Jamaica. I was in Jamaica last year, and you could clearly distinguish Orientals and people of English stock or European stock, I should say, some Americans, West Indians and Negroes—but everybody had the concept, not that they were Jewish or English or Chinese or Oriental or that they were Negro, but that they were Jamaicans.

RPW: Have you read [William] Faulkner's *Intruder in the Dust*?

WTW: Yes.

RPW: Do you remember that very ambiguous section about the Southern Negro and the Southern white and the theory of

homogeneity that they would represent somehow against an outside world? What sort of sense does that make to you, or how do
you interpret it?

wtw: Here you have a reflection of the geographical provincialism that still pervades, to this day, in the South. For instance,
the South feels it stands against the rest of the nation politically
and maybe economically. I think this is, to a large degree, the
same kind of thinking which causes us to have this Southern bloc
in Congress. I don't think in practical terms it really works out
like this. As I recall, vaguely, they were saying that the utopia of
the South would be that the Negroes would go along their slow
course to whatever their goals were, and the white people would
go along their course to whatever their goals were, and in one
Southern homogeneous setting the two would exist separately but
side by side.

rpw: That isn't apparently what Faulkner meant—a formal segregation. [He] meant some vision of reconciliation, some special
relationship based on a common history. How would you respond
to that notion?

wtw: I have said this at different times, and I think I have
heard others say this who have worked with us in the revolution:
that we believe the South is going to be a better place to live for
Negroes and whites than perhaps the North. Even though we are
passing through a period which is very tenuous and in a sense very
costly emotionally to both whites and Negroes, because of the sharp
social changes being demanded and forced, but after a period of
reconciliation—if I'm following your guess at what Faulkner meant,
if his projection was that Negroes and whites would live together in
a warmer relationship than they would elsewhere because of their
common bond—I think this is generally true. Because of a kind of
sentimentality of the South, and the ease with which relationships

have been built, the fact that white children were reared by Negro wet nurses, that perhaps both of us were refined in the cauldrons of the Civil War and Reconstruction, maybe because of that, out of our common geographical history, I could agree very strongly that I think there will be a unique relationship that Negroes and the whites in the South will enjoy, after the reconciliation of the revolution. More than is presently, or can be hoped for, by Negroes and whites in the North. I think the level of interpersonal relationships is closer than it could ever be in the North.

RPW: You referred to Reconstruction—do you remember [Gunnar] Myrdal's sketch of what would have been his recommendation for policy after the Civil War? He gave a five or six point policy that he thought would have saved us the last hundred years of race troubles. The policy runs like this: first, compensation to Southern slaveholders for emancipating slaves. Two, expropriation of plantations as needed, but payment for the land taken. Three, the sale of land to landless freedmen and landless whites—sell, not gift—over a long period of time. With education and some supervision during this transition, and other details too. Do you feel any emotional reaction to the fact that a payment was proposed to the slaveholders for the emancipated slaves?

WTW: No, I wouldn't have any at all because I guess I'm enough businessman, and practical-headed enough as a student of history, to know that the Negro slave represented dollars and cents to an economy which was being crippled by the dissolution of slavery. Now, I suppose it would be federally subsidized. But I would have no emotional response whatsoever, and I don't know just why other than what I said.

RPW: Now, many Negroes do have a violent response to that. Some people you know.

WTW: It wouldn't bother me at all.

RPW: They just say no, this is compounding a sin. By paying the man who . . .

WTW: As small as the investment might have been. Maybe he didn't pay anything for the slaves but at least he [provided] housing, as poor as it was, and fed them, and his whole economic venture depended upon the exploitation of free labor. I mean, there were some dollars and cents involved, whether it was right or wrong, and as I say, at this point, I'm a pragmatist. And further than that, if I may push the point: I don't know whether this would have been the panacea, but I think this would have been far better than what they did do.

RPW: Now, I'm getting something like this, which is a matter of speculation, and I want to see how you feel about it: the Southern white man is in a situation parallel to that of the American Negro. He's been having identity trouble. He is, on one hand, a Southerner with a special history, a nationalism, with a special body of beliefs and prejudices and sentiments. On the other hand, he is pulled into the American orbit in many strong ways. Now, to be himself, the naïve Southerner feels he must cling to a certain number of prejudices and attitudes which have symbolic value for him.

WTW: Yes, and to his history.

RPW: Segregation, for one. Segregation becomes the symbol of identity, to be Southern. Now, this I should say is a mistake, is [an] abandoning of history. Segregation is a very late idea, anyway. But the point I am getting at: do you see a parallel of the sort I have mentioned?

WTW: I think the difference is that the Negro has had no identity. It is not a matter of change for him as it is to crystallize an identity. And that is where I would see the significant differences, and where the Negro would have a lesser problem of adjustment, psychologically and emotionally, than the Southern white.

RPW: The Negro is moving successfully toward identity. The white man in the South is fighting a somewhat losing battle to maintain that identity. A falsely conceived identity.

WTW: And he's also being dragged forward by what I would call a new identity, with the concept of a total United States or total American, see? Which he's got to keep up with because of automation, industrial advances, the space age, and all this. If he's going to get in the mainstream, then he's got to give up some of this so-called Southern identity. And this is the thing that is giving him such a tremendous problem; you don't have a solid Southern posture anymore. You've got degrees of differences ranging from white all the way to black, with a thousand different grades in between. There are many, many Southerners who say, "Yes, I think the schools ought to be desegregated, but I don't think [Negroes] ought to come to our church." Or they say, "I think they ought to be able to sit anywhere they want on the bus, but I don't want them living in my block." Or, "I think they ought to have the right to have good schools, but I don't think they ought to participate in sports." There are so many contradictions at this point.

RPW: What happens if a Negro man, say, marries a white woman and she lives, societally, as a Negro?

WTW: She becomes accepted. A white person becomes assimilated into the Negro community in such a way that no white and no Negro could ever become assimilated into a white society. We haven't gone that far yet.

RPW: Aren't there some Negroes who have, by losing their identity?

WTW: Oh, yes. That's what we would call passing. Of course, that's not assimilation, that's disappearing.

RPW: Yes. What is your view of a person who passes—a Negro who—a so-called Negro, shall we say, who passes?

wtw: This may surprise you. If that's what he wants to do, more power to him. And I say, there's always the irrevocable question: if you could come back, would you come back as a white man or a Negro? I'd come back as a white man every time.

rpw: I heard the other day a professor of law, in a distinguished law school, saying, "It must be great to be a Negro now."

wtw: Well, this is a great hour for him.

rpw: This man is a white man, you see. He says, "It must be great to be a Negro now. You must have a sense of significant action that you couldn't have as a white man."

wtw: The white man may feel, I don't know—I never thought about it really—he may feel that he's at the mercy of history, whereas the Negro in a sense is guiding or directing . . .

rpw: Making history, is that it?

wtw: It's a theoretical question. I know people say to me, "You've done pretty well, why are you bothered? You've developed some of the culture of our nation, you're highly educated, you're not doing bad." My response is, suppose I had not had the obstacles to face that I've had as a Negro? There's no telling what I might have been. I might have been attorney general of the United States.

rpw: Let's reverse it. There are some Negroes who say that, in special cases, not as a general principle, segregation has meant a spur to achievement, to self-fulfillment.

wtw: I think that is true in special cases. But if the human spirit is what I think it is, I do not really believe that the coincidence, or the accident, of color really changes the nature of a man. I would have had the same kind of ambition and the same kind of drive and the same kind of incentive in striving for perfection that I do—and I happen to be a Negro. I don't think environment is as much a factor in the personality as many modern thinkers would suppose.

I'm about to take a leave of absence from my work with Dr. King. I am planning to go to work with a company that's putting out a sixteen-volume encyclopedia on Negro life and culture. This is the next frontier, to give to the Negro of this present generation, and the next, a sense of historical roots, which he has never had. It's going to solidify his new identity that he's building. I guess you know that I am a damned Yankee.

RPW: Yes, I know your origin.

WTW: I went to integrated schools all my life, and the only thing I can recall reading in history books about Negroes is that we were slaves, and that there were a few slave owners who didn't treat their slaves well, but for the most part a genuine warm relationship existed. That's all I can really recall. I've never had any [impulse to] deny the slave experience of the Negro. And this has grown out of my deep appreciation for what is, almost, the only thoroughly American music we have, the Negro spiritual and folk songs. Despite the terrible experience slavery was, it was an ennobling experience for the Negro, because he has proven that he could rise above it, that he took the rigors that it produced and somehow kept his spirit and soul together. So if we can get into, say, two-tenths of the Negro church community, we can get in a tenth of the public school system or get in half of the libraries, get in a tenth of the civic and human relations groups, with these volumes, which will talk about the Negro and his contributions to medicine, sports, religious life, Negro womanhood, literature—[people would learn about] the whole gamut of experiences that [the Negro] has been able to develop within his own culture.

Warren asks Walker to evaluate the role of the Nation of Islam in the civil rights struggle.

wtw: My feeling is that the Muslim movement and its so-called impact in race relations is almost nil. It's a specter, a paper tiger that the white press has created. For instance, I have a serious question as to how strong they are with all of the fear that they strike in some people's hearts. I know in Birmingham they say they've had a temple there for ten years, and they have to scrounge around to get fifty people. The only place where Malcolm X can get a crowd is Harlem. Maybe Newark, because it's in the shadow of New York, but you get him anywhere else, he's lost. Fifty percent of the Negroes don't even know what the Black Muslims are. They never heard of them. They don't know who Malcolm X is. But 90 percent of Negroes know who Martin Luther King Jr. is.

rpw: That's beyond dispute. It's a question of what impulses are implicit in these appetites and angers—an instinct for violence and revenge would be implicit.

wtw: This is where a great many people have misjudged the real temper of the Negro. Who can best say what the temper of the grassroots Negro is? Can Roy Wilkins say it? No. Jim Farmer? No. Whitney Young? Certainly not. Who is it that enjoys titular leadership of the Negro community, who really knows what the pulse of the central, plain people are? The one man who had a following and who has any kind of programmatic thrust that ever touches them, that's Martin Luther King Jr. Let me press it. There is not a single Negro leader, not a single white leader, who touches as many people individually as does Martin Luther King Jr. In Birmingham, in less than ten days' time, he personally saw hands and eyes and faces of better than a quarter of a million people. There isn't anybody who commands the kind of response, individual physical response, that he does. Now, I'm not even counting the compounded contacts that he makes when he's recorded his speeches and they play them over the radio, or if he's on television such as he was at the March on Washington. And I think this is unique in a man. It's so ordinary for us that we are slow to detect it.

Warren and Walker discuss the demonstrations and police violence in Birmingham.

WTW: What built the Birmingham movement was an accident that we parlayed into its most useful application. When we went to Birmingham—five months ahead I had started in at Dr. King's behest—preparing the community, organizing, mapping out the streets. We had four hundred people when we came to town April 2 [1963], who we knew were ready to go to jail for ten days apiece. We were going to stagger them through a period of time. On the first Sunday of the demonstration, which I believe was Palm Sunday, we had twenty-three people in the march. But you know how mass meetings are, they last a little while. We were about an hour behind schedule [when neighborhood people] began to stand around and wait to see what was going to happen. Well, it swelled to about fifteen hundred people. Only twenty-two people marched, see, but they followed these twenty-two down the street. And when United Press International took the pictures and reported it, they said [there were] fifteen hundred demonstrators, [with] twenty-two arrested.

Well, the twenty-two or twenty-eight was all we had. So then we devised the technique. We'll set the demonstration for [a certain time] and delay it by two hours and let the crowd collect. Now, this is a little Machiavellian, and I don't know whether I've ever discussed this with Dr. King, I doubt if I have. It was the spectators following [the march] upon whom the dogs were turned. It was only until three weeks later that the [fire] hoses were actually used on demonstrators. And that was only done one afternoon. But there were reports over and over again of . . .

RPW: The dogs, you mean, only one afternoon?

WTW: No, no. The hoses. One afternoon. After that, [the police] saw that didn't stop them and they just started to use rented buses and put [demonstrators] on buses. One afternoon, the Saturday before the truce, came some of the most graphic [news] pictures. On that Friday there had been some rock throwing by spectators, and we felt this did not grow out of the demonstration, per se, but at the policemen's insistence to make [the spectators] move back, get up on the curb, just rough treatment generally, and they resented it. And so out of a crowd of a thousand people some rocks and bricks came. So in response to this we felt that, in order not to have the nonviolent thrust scarred by rock throwing, we began to distribute our demonstrators to other points in the city, to other churches, and they left the church in twos and threes. And that day, even though there were some three or four hundred arrested, not a single demonstration originated at the Sixteenth Street [Baptist] Church. But the spectators waited from eleven that morning until about four that afternoon, waiting to see some action, waiting to see the demonstrators. And none ever appeared.

So they had gathered in [Kelly Ingram Park], which is a shaded area, and the firemen had set up their hoses at two corners of the park, one on Fifth Street and one on Sixth Street. And the mood was like a Roman holiday; it was festive. There wasn't anybody among the spectators who were angry. And they had waited so long it was beginning to get dark. So somebody heaved a brick. They had been saying, "Turn the water hose on, turn the water hose on." Somebody threw a brick and [the commissioner of public safety] Bull Connor started turning them on, see. So they just danced and played in the hose spray. This famous picture of them holding hands, it was just a frolic of them trying to stand, and some of them were getting knocked down by the hose. They'd get up and it would slide them along the pavement. Then they began bringing the hose up from the other corner, and Negroes ran to the hose. It was a holiday for them. And this went on for a couple of hours. It was a joke, really. All in good humor and good spirit. Not any vitriolic response on the part of the Negro spectators. Which, to me, was an example of the changing spirit. Where Negroes, once, had been cowed in the presence of policemen and maybe water hoses, here they had complete disdain. They made a joke out of it.

Roy Wilkins

April 7, 1964

New York, New York

Roy Wilkins was a prominent civil rights campaigner who was executive director of the NAACP in the 1950s and '60s, pivotal years in the movement. Wilkins helped oversee the NAACP's landmark legal campaign against segregated schools, and he worked closely with President Lyndon B. Johnson to help pass groundbreaking civil rights laws. Wilkins used his organizational and political skills to expand the NAACP from some 25,000 members to nearly half a million people.

A 1981 obituary in the New York Times *described Wilkins as a skilled politician and a statesman who avoided "both words and deeds that would seem to cast him in the role of a firebrand."*

Wilkins was born in 1901 in St. Louis, Missouri. He was the grandson of a Mississippi slave. His parents were both from the Deep South and were college graduates, which was unusual for African Americans from that region at the time. Wilkins's mother died of tuberculosis when he was four years old, and his father sent him and his two siblings to live with relatives in St. Paul, Minnesota. Wilkins grew up there and attended an integrated high school, where he edited the student newspaper. While black people were not treated as the social equals of whites, Wilkins experienced little in the way of formal segregation.

"I was sheltered," he said about the relatively benign racial climate in Minnesota. "A tremendous shock was waiting for me."

Wilkins studied sociology at the University of Minnesota and worked on his college newspaper as well as a St. Paul weekly for African Americans. After graduating in 1923, Wilkins moved to Kansas for a job on the Kansas City Call, *a black newspaper. He experienced Southern-style racism for the first time and became active in the local chapter of the NAACP, an organization his family in St. Paul had belonged to from its earliest days.*

Wilkins's activism in Kansas City got the attention of Walter White, the national head of the NAACP. In 1931, White hired Wilkins to work at the organization's headquarters in New York. He and NAACP lawyer Thurgood Marshall dressed as sharecroppers to study living conditions for black people on plantations in Mississippi. Their findings led to a federal investigation. In 1934, Wilkins took up the leadership of the NAACP's long-running crusade against lynching. The campaign was credited with raising national awareness about the atrocities and eventually curbing this form of racial terrorism.

Wilkins was also deeply involved in organizing and raising money for the NAACP's decades-long legal assault on segregation. Starting in the 1930s, teams of NAACP lawyers filed lawsuits in courts across the land—and especially in the South—to fight discrimination in the voting booth, in housing and education, and in law enforcement. Wilkins was not a lawyer; he was the man who paid the bills, organized the staff, and drummed up public support. Still, he said his "crowning glory" was the 1954 U.S. Supreme Court decision Brown v. Board of Education, *which banned public-school segregation.*

The NAACP elevated Wilkins to the top post of executive director when longtime leader Walter White retired in 1955. Wilkins's tenure marked the high point of NAACP influence in American politics. As the 1960s unfolded, the NAACP fought for the right of activists to engage in nonviolent protests. It frequently supplied bail money and legal help to people who were arrested in demonstrations. Wilkins took part in many of the historic civil rights protest marches, including those in the South headed by Martin Luther King Jr. Wilkins also helped organize the massive March on Washington for Jobs and Freedom in August 1963.

Wilkins developed a close working relationship with President Lyndon Johnson. He helped Johnson drive the historic 1964 Civil Rights Act and the 1965 Voting Rights Act through Congress.

Wilkins was well known and widely respected, but he did not possess the charisma of leaders like King or Stokely Carmichael. In the 1960s, many younger African Americans grew impatient with the seemingly slow pace of social change and disdained older moderates like Wilkins, who worked within the nation's power structures. In turn, Wilkins denounced the revolutionary rhetoric of the black power movement, calling it a new form of racism.

When he retired from the NAACP in 1977, Wilkins was seventy-six years old. The civil rights movement, and Wilkins's own organization, had been through a decade of decline. But he was widely praised for the half century of tireless and often thankless work he contributed as a civil rights executive—a man who kept the engine of the freedom movement running. In 1969, Johnson honored Wilkins with the Presidential Medal of Freedom. After his death, Congress awarded him the Congressional Gold Medal.

Historian James R. Ralph Jr. writes that Wilkins is often relegated to a supporting role in histories of the black freedom struggle. Although "Wilkins was less charismatic, more organizationally inclined, and certainly more cautious than other civil rights leaders," he writes, he was a "critical figure" in the movement.

In Who Speaks for the Negro? *Warren included Wilkins in a chapter on civil rights leaders entitled "The Big Brass." He described*

Wilkins as seeming unusually "unhurried" for such a busy man. "He is, clearly, a thoughtful man, with something detached and professorial in his tone," Warren writes. "You feel that he knows a good deal about human nature, including his own—and yours."

ROBERT PENN WARREN: What accounts for the timing of the so-called Negro revolution the last few years?

ROY WILKINS: This is the result of an accumulation of events, an accumulation of developments. First of all, we had the emotional stimulus of one hundred years since the Emancipation Proclamation in 1963. An emotional year, a centennial, an anniversary. [Negroes] looked around them and said, "It's been a hundred years and look where we are." Secondly, we have to reckon with the fact that it took a number of years to build up an educated cadre of youngsters, fathers, and grandfathers who cumulatively built resistance and resentment against things they suffered. This couldn't help but explode. You graduate a hundred high school graduates this year, you graduate a thousand five years from now, you graduate ten thousand, you graduate twenty-five thousand—you keep on graduating and finally you get to the place where that number of graduates will say, "This is untenable. I can't stand it. We must push." That was one factor.

You had a migration from the South to the North beginning with World War I. A large number of Negroes came up to Gary and Youngstown and Akron—industrial centers—and they settled down. They became voters and went to school and they sent their children to school. More importantly, in about 1930 they became political factors in the Republican machine in Cleveland, in the Big Bill Thompson Republican machine in Chicago, and in the Pendergast machine in Democratic Kansas City. All of this was a buildup to the 1960s.

You had two world wars, too. You had a war to save the world for democracy, in the words of Woodrow Wilson, and the Negroes came from the swamps and the plantations and the cotton fields and they went overseas and they saw Paris, and they saw Berlin, and they saw Europe, they saw London. And they came back and they knew there was a world outside of their particular county and there were a different kind of white people there. And in World War II, you had them fighting against the "master race" theory. And they could go back to Terrell County, Georgia, and find a master race theory, too. And this was not lost upon them.

And finally, in 1960, you had the pileup from the 1954 [*Brown v. Board of Education*] school decision, the defiance of it, the refusal to obey it, the attack upon the Supreme Court, the attempt to change the rules after the game had been won. The Negro thought he had won in 1954, his citizenship had been reaffirmed, that the constitutional basis of his life had been reaffirmed by the Supreme Court. [The ruling] said we can't discriminate on account of race. But discrimination went on. The Southern legislatures passed laws and they obstructed.

Finally, in the 1960s, the Negro broke loose and took direct action. He said, "We can't depend on legislatures. And we go to the courts and we take fifty years to go slowly through the courts and chip away at the separate but equal [doctrine]. And we win in 1954 but we don't win. So let's get out on the streets and take it directly to the seat of government." That's what happened. And I believe that's the reason you have the revolt in the 1960s and not in the 1950s.

RPW: I don't imagine it would be surprising to you if I should say that a good many Negroes flinch from your explanation. I know that the Negro shrinks from the use of this word gradualism, or even the concept of gradualism.

RW: Yes. He just doesn't like that at all. And yet, if he read the history of the labor movement, if he read just the history of the struggle for a child labor law, he would understand that while you never, never, never give up or compromise, things don't happen overnight.

RPW: This is a question, then, of what "Freedom Now" means.

RW: Yes, it does, and the answer is not very simple. "Freedom Now" means just that. It means away with the old concepts, it means a beginning of a real, solid, good faith beginning of new concepts. [Negro] students realize that you don't change overnight, but they want Mississippi or Alabama or South Carolina or Louisiana to set its face in the direction of change and to make meaningful steps toward change that, carried out successively, can lead to what they want. Now, all Negroes are very quick to detect those phony steps toward change, those pretensions, those delays, those take-it-or-leave-its, or those teaspoonfuls that they give you here and there, instead of giving you the whole pot of soup. Negroes have no truck with this sort of thing in this kind of revolution.

RPW: Let's take the word "revolution" for a moment. Behind the word, what is the reality? How does this correspond to the French Revolution or the American Revolution?

RW: I don't believe it corresponds to those because we are not here seeking to overthrow a government or to set up a new government. We are here trying to get the government, as expressed by a majority of the people, to put into practice its declared objectives. This is a slightly different kind of a revolution, it seems to me. We are also not in a revolution of despair—as has been said over and over again—but a revolution of rising expectations. In other words, the Negro wants in. He wants to share in American life. His outpouring in Washington on August 28, 1963, was an outpouring saying, "Let me into the good things of American life. Stop denying me." It was not a revolution.

RPW: There's another aspect that might mean the difference between other revolutions. Revolutions live on hope and they live on hate. The hope for change; otherwise it's a servile revolt or a desperate insurrection. It also lives on this mobilizing of force through hate. Now, if you look at Malcolm X, it's easy to take an extreme situation.

RW: I don't envisage the Negro employing hate as a tactic, as a recognized procedure to mobilize the support for his side or to win objectives for his side. I, of course, do not rule out the fact that, here and there, individually, there might be something akin to hate as a motivation for action. But I don't see the Negro in this country adopting hatred as a tactic. In the first place, if he had believed in hatred as a tool he would have done so long ago.

I once said about Malcolm X—he was talking about [Negro] rifle clubs in 1964, and violence and shedding blood—if the Negro had believed in that he would have used it a long time ago when he was much worse off than he is now. As a matter of fact, the Negro in this country is a very practical and pragmatic animal. He has never lost sight of the elementary facts of survival and he never has forgotten that he's a minority, numerically. So he does not have the power, except the moral power, to mobilize. To put it bluntly, how many guns can he get?

RPW: But, shall we say, that any movement is always a movement of power. It's a question of the nature of power, is that it then?

RW: Yes. And [the Negro] has on his side, and he has utilized magnificently, the moral power that he has. He has the power of moral righteousness on his side. And he has something else. The United States is vulnerable because of its declared purposes. Now, if it had an ambiguous Constitution, or if it had an ambiguous Declaration of Independence, this would be different. But the Declaration of Independence says "all men." America is on record as the haven of all the oppressed peoples of the world. This is the land where you can come and demonstrate your ability and achieve on the basis of your ability. If you're a Hungarian when you get here, you become an American. And if you're an Irishman when you get here, you become an American.

RPW: What do you think of the notion that some sociologists or historians have enunciated that the American Negro is more like the old Yankee or the old Southerner than any other element in our culture? He's an old American.

RW: Yes, he's a very old American and he's American in his concepts. He's liberal only on the race question. I mean, he's a conservative economically. He wants to hold on to gains in property and protection. I may be wrong, but I don't see him as a bold experimenter in political science or social reform. He may change once he gets in a period of equality. There are Negroes who are nonconformists, there are Negroes who are atheists, there are Negroes who are even Gaullists.

RPW: How much anti-Semitism do you think actually exists among Negroes?

RW: That's a hard question. Basically, the Negro is not anti-Semitic. Such anti-Semitism as he occasionally expresses stems from his own personal experience. Like a white man who tells you that Negroes are no good; I knew one once and he did so-and-so to me, or he wouldn't do so-and-so. And Negroes who make anti-Semitic remarks are those who may have run into, say, a Jewish storekeeper or a Jewish landlord or a Jewish woman who is the boss of domestic servants. These are the three areas in which they come into contact with Jewish families. If they have an unfortunate experience with a Jewish housewife, let's say, they are likely, as most weak people are, [to say], "This Jewish lady did so-and-so." Well, if they work for an Irish woman or a German woman or a Swedish woman and she did precisely the same thing the Jewish woman did, or had the same attitude, they would say, "Oh, that old white woman," you see.

I have traveled all over this country. I've met thousands upon thousands of Negroes, and have lived in their areas and I know them. They have never forgotten that, wherever they have been, whatever kind of trouble they've been in, the Jews have helped them, some Jews. Either Jewish individuals, or Jewish philanthropists, or Jewish rabbis. Invariably, when you go into a town and you ask the Negro community, who do you count among your friends in the white community? Among the first five people, always a Jewish rabbi. Always. He's the man who understands their problem and sympathizes with them, who speaks to their meetings. So anti-Semitism among [Negroes] is not virulent and not hateful, although, like any kind of racial feeling, it is detestable. But it's not the kind of hate-the-Jew attitude that you find in some people.

RPW: You don't think that they exploit it in the black nationalist movement?

RW: The Muslims have attempted it; they have used anti-Semitism. But I don't believe they have gotten far. They have mouthed a few catchwords, and those catchwords have been taken up by their followers. But I don't believe that it has become part and parcel of the Negro community. In fact, I am positive it has not. It just hasn't taken hold. Now, even in the Deep South you recognize that Jews have helped [Negroes]. Jews have extended a hand, Jews have made loans to them, Jews have granted them credit, Jews have fought the battle against discrimination where they could. Remember, Jews have been vulnerable in the South, too. They have not been able, at all times, to speak out. But in the present civil rights crisis that has developed since the Supreme Court decision in 1954, the Jewish community overwhelmingly has been on what we call "our side." Now, there are Jews who are not on our side, Jews who are opposed to us and who have nothing to do with the civil rights movement.

RPW: This raises a question about the role of the white man in relation to the Negro movement or Negro revolution. You will find such statements as, "The white liberal is an affliction." You will find [Negroes] saying, "Go away. Leave us alone and we'll run the show." On the other hand, in Mississippi, for instance, Robert Moses [described] the attitude of the Negroes there toward white helpers from the outside who want to overidentify [with Negroes]—this contempt of the white man's naïveté, his desire to buddy up, to be one. Do you see the problem?

RW: Yes, I see the problem. I'm familiar with it, and I disagree very greatly with it. Although I understand why it exists, in some cases. But I feel, first of all, that we ought to recognize that white people have been fighting for the liberty of the individual long before the Negro question of liberation ever came up. White people, long before the Magna Carta, were fighting against oppression and for the liberty of the individual. And they have fought, since we have had our country here, many battles not connected with race. They have fought for freedom of the press, and freedom of religion, and all the sorts of things. We ought to recognize that they have a heritage of protecting and enhancing the Constitution of the United States, irrespective of whether it applies to black people, white people, Northerners, or Southerners, and that there can be sincere white people who believe in these principles and want to fight for them. We ought not to shut them out of our movement because they don't fit into every niche and cranny of our thinking and our being, and they don't behave exactly as we feel they should behave as blood brothers. We're brothers, after all, in a cause: the cause of liberty.

We ought to recognize that in the present state of Negro-white relations, and the scramble that's going on, to get on record, and to be understood, and to be uncompromising, and to be militant, and to be demanding, and to be all the things that are now regarded as the things that you have to be, [Negroes] say a lot of things in public about white people have to conform to this, white people must give up, white people must recognize, white people must, must, must, must. This is a sure way to get on television and to get quoted and to cause tremors in some quarters. Or, if not tremors, head-scratching and soul-searching. But the Negro must recognize that there must be some sincere white people interested in the liberal cause and in the cause of freedom, irrespective of whether race is involved or not. They have given too much blood and made too many sacrifices for the right of freedom of religion, for the right of a trial by jury, for the right to vote and to have the kind of government that will represent their views, for freedom of the press and for all the things that they hold dear. They have fought for these things and bled for them and died for them. And if they now step forward and say, "We want to include in our beliefs also the belief in Negro equality, or equality of opportunity for the Negro, or placing the tent of the Constitution over our Negro citizens," if they now step forward and want to do this, I think we ought to examine, sincerely, whether they are opportunists, or phonies, or pretenders, or Trojan horses, or whether they are sincere. And I don't go with this idea of dismissing all white people as being insincere, or trying to climb on the bandwagon, or trying to make a profit, or trying to use you. Some of them are, freely admitted. But there are sincere ones and we can use them, just as all fighters for the extension of human liberty can use all hands.

Now, as to this thing about their apparent haste to ingratiate themselves in the new movement, here, again, I think we have to use caution. Because in one breath we are saying, "One of the great troubles in the race question is the lack of communication. They don't know about us," we say. "We know about them, we're so sure, but they don't know about us."

When they come over and try to find out about us, why don't we teach them, instead of saying to them, "We look on you with suspicion. You're just trying to ingratiate yourselves. You don't know how to get into the Negro world. You're awkward and we look down on you. We laugh at you." Is this the way, when we say the prime obstacle has been lack of communication, and people come who want to communicate?

RPW: Suppose, Mr. Wilkins, tomorrow morning we woke up and found that a good civil rights bill had been passed, and that there were fine enforcement agencies in operation and fair employment was enforced, and we had our schools all integrated. What remains?

RW: What remains for the Negro is to make himself with this opportunity, with these barriers down, with the help of new legislation. To speed on the process of self-development and self-discipline, so that he becomes a more contributing member of society than he is now, he assumes broader duties than merely within the Negro community. If he is a successful businessman, he becomes concerned with hospitals and health and traffic and profits and manufacturers and banks and all of the things that go to make for community and state and national development. This takes time, Mr. Warren, because when you come out of a ghetto—not only a physical ghetto but an intellectual and ideological ghetto—and you've been excluded from the mainstream of American life, it takes a while to find out how to function outside of the ghetto.

RPW: A sense of community identification in a full way.

RW: Yes. There are Negroes who now, already, have that identification in many communities. You find them assuming their roles and sometimes suffering derisive comments from their brothers on how they have removed themselves from racial life.

One of the things the South has neglected is to estimate what this Negro can contribute to the South. He's there; he has talent. Why should he have to migrate from the South to exercise this talent in Chicago or in Pittsburgh? Now, the South could save this talent and help to build the South. It needs the Negroes. It needs their man-power. It needs their life, their laughter, their warmth. It needs their indigenous identification with the South. They can be a tremendous asset to the South and they contribute, however, through a screen, through white people. But they could contribute for themselves.

RPW: Some weeks ago I was talking to Mr. Charles Evers. I asked him why he stayed in Mississippi. He said, "I think things are going to work out here fairly soon. We'll have a settlement here that's satisfactory, probably before you can get it in some other parts of the country."

RW: This is the echo of a hope that has existed in many areas in the South. Breakthroughs have been made in North Carolina. The University of North Carolina has quietly taken on a good many Negro students, without any fanfare. The University of Arkansas, interestingly enough, without any lawsuit, without any bitterness, without any tension, admitted Negro students to medicine and law and opened up the university to them. And you haven't heard a peep out of Fayetteville, Arkansas. Now, for Mr. Evers to say that he hopes that this will take place in Mississippi, it is the kind of thing that we all hope. I wonder how it can happen as I look at Mississippi's resources. I don't doubt that there are white people in Mississippi who would like to see some changes take place, but I see a massive political machine in Mississippi built strictly upon white supremacy and keeping the Negro down.

The biggest obstacle in the South is not the white, rank-and-file man who demonstrates occasionally against the Negro, it's the Southern political oligarchy. They're the ones that have the stake in this thing, and it's not only control over the Negro population. That's only incidental. I think if the white population ever woke up in the South to the fact that the political oligarchy has used the Negro scare in order to perpetuate control over the entire Southern hegemony, I think we'd see a real revolution there.

Warren turns the conversation to the role of the NAACP. He remarks on criticism by some younger civil rights activists—including members of the Student Nonviolent Coordinating Committee (SNCC) and the Congress of Racial Equality (CORE)—that the NAACP is too slow-moving and moderate.

RPW: You know the quotation attributed to you. "SNCC furnishes the noise. The NAACP pays the bills."

RW: Yes. We had just finished bailing out some of the SNCC kids in McComb, Mississippi, who went off on an independent tangent of their own, without consulting us, without plans. And then when they got the $6,000 bail bond trouble, why they screamed for the old NAACP to come down and help them out. And it applied, particularly, to our unfortunate experience with some members of CORE in Louisville, Kentucky. We were on a joint demonstration, which was billed, however, as a CORE demonstration. I wish I knew the secret of CORE's ability to get newspaper publicity. I'd like to hire whoever they have over there to come and work for us. We had a demonstration in Louisville in which 267 were arrested, and 255 of them were NAACP young people. That's another thing that sticks in our craw. Most of our young people have been involved in all these matters, but the credit has gone to other organizations. Anyway, only twelve people out of this so-called joint demonstration were identified with CORE. And yet, when all the shooting was over and all the hooting and hollering was done, we not only got none of the credit, but were left with the legal bill of some five or six thousand dollars. It's a little tough to find yourself vilified and sneered at as a kind of old lady, knitting over in a corner, while the revolution is being carried on by us strong men, and yet called upon to bear the financial burden.

RPW: How do you explain the white man who [knows] a Negro family where the boy or the girl has gone away to school and made a very good record, and the white man is as proud of that as he can be. Yet he will make sweeping generalizations about Negroes being no good, lazy, unable to learn. He applauds the fact that this girl or boy who went to the University of Chicago, or the University of Illinois, or Harvard or Yale, [but says], "I don't want Negroes to go to school with my children." A contradiction.

RW: Absolutely, a contradiction. What are you going to do with white people in Laurel, Mississippi, who cheer Leontyne Price at the Metropolitan Opera, and say she is a Laurel girl, she's a Mississippi girl, but who turn right around, in Laurel, and deny the opportunity to somebody who doesn't have a sponsor like Leontyne Price had? There is, I'm sorry to say, an increasing expression among some Negroes in this period of tension, general statements like, "White people are all alike," or, "You know, you can't trust white people." This skepticism is growing out of their continued frustration over the civil rights bill, the discrimination in employment.

What the Negro is saying is that he doesn't want to be discriminated against, beating his head against the business of automation, the reduction of opportunities for employment. He also knows that he isn't getting the training in new skills that he should get, and he isn't getting a crack at the new jobs. For example, in the South, where the Negro and the white have both been displaced from the land by industry and by diversified farming, and they have both gone to the cities, or gone to the towns where new industries have been established, the white men and women have been able to get jobs in the new industry without training, or they have got on-the-job training. But the Negro has had the door slammed in his face. He has had to go all the way up to Ohio and Pennsylvania and Illinois and Indiana and Michigan to try and hunt for a job, without any skills. He's right off the land. He lands there. He becomes a welfare case, or he's crowded into an already overcrowded apartment, or overcrowded house. He becomes a health menace. He becomes all of these things, and he causes frowns and apprehension in city councils of Northern cities, and among the mayors and the departments of welfare. And then the Southerners don't help the situation any by pointing a finger and saying, "See, we told you what he was. Now he's on your doorstep and you see." What they don't say to themselves is "I made him like that."

There are two things that are coming home to the Northern white people and that are working against the Southerners, although the results may not be seen tomorrow morning. One of them is that the Negroes coming North in their great unprepared, untrained, uneducated state, with their lack of a sense of participation in twentieth-century political, civic, and urban community life, because of deprivations—they have driven home to the Northerner what a terrible, terrible job the Southerner has done with the Negro for a hundred years, in not giving him access to the training—even rudimentary training—he should have had. What is happening is that the Northern white man is being converted to the Negroes' contention—hitherto made mostly by Negroes—that we've been mistreated in the South. The Northerners either looked the other way or listened to the rosy accounts of how well the Negroes were getting along and how well they were satisfied. [The Northerner] has always regarded the problem as being a thousand or more miles away. Now, it's on his doorstep.

[President Franklin] Roosevelt is supposed to have said to Winston Churchill—they were on a trip together in Africa and went through a British protectorate or a British colony—and FDR is supposed to have said, "Winston, when the hell are you going to give these people the chance to be themselves and stop treating them like colonies?"

And Winston is supposed to have replied, "FDR, when are you going to free the Mississippi Negroes?"

Well, the idea is that the Northern white politicians and industrialists and responsible people are going to pretty soon say to the Southerners over their gin and tonic, "You didn't do so well by the Negroes, because we've got a lot of them up here that came up from your state, and they this, that and the other." We contend that's all to our side. We contend, further, that there is going be a backlash from Northerners who are coming South, into the civil rights movement, and are being met with oppression and mistreatment—ministers, rabbis, students.

Two days ago, I spoke at a university in New Jersey and three students were introduced to me as alumni of the jails, one in Georgia and two from somewhere else. A year ago, I spoke at Coe College, deep in the heart of Iowa. And they had three alumni from jails in Mississippi. These kids come back, they spread the story to their families, their churches, their sororities, their campuses, and it's no longer Wilkins of the NAACP or Martin Luther King spinning a tale of horror and oppression. It's these kids coming back and saying, "This is what a policeman did to me. This is what the judge said. This is what my fine was. This is what my crime was supposed to be."

This is the kind of indictment that I don't believe the South ought to let stand. I believe that the cooler heads there, the ones who understand what it's all about, ought to take charge from the ones who are perpetuating these sorts of things.

RPW: There's been no leadership in the South in this whole matter, as far as I can make out. Except, well, the hard-core segregationists.

RW: Some has emerged, Mr. Warren. Some has emerged. We have noted that businessmen in a number of areas have said, "Now, this we don't want. We can't afford to have this upheaval. It's bad for business." The Tuscaloosa businessmen, for example, told Governor [George] Wallace, they pleaded with him. The Birmingham businessmen pleaded with Wallace: ease up on his University of Alabama stand. The Norfolk businessmen in Virginia, years ago, took charge of school desegregation in Norfolk. It illustrates that when business gets together, they can have an effect on the politicians, and the politicians, I maintain, are the big obstacles in the South.

Whitney M. Young Jr.

April 13 and 29, 1964

New York, New York

A social worker by training, Whitney Moore Young Jr. was an influential civil rights leader who worked within institutional systems such as corporations and government to seek equality for African Americans and raise money for the movement. Young served as the executive director of the Urban League from 1961 to 1971. The League was founded in 1910 to advocate for the rights and well-being of Northern blacks, many of whom had migrated from the South. Over the decade he led the organization, Young greatly expanded its size and influence.

As a close adviser to President Lyndon B. Johnson, Young promoted a "Domestic Marshall Plan," akin to the massive American-backed effort to rebuild the European economy after World War II. Young is credited as a major contributor to Johnson's "Great Society" domestic programs, which aimed to eliminate poverty and racial injustice.

Young was born in 1921 in Lincoln Ridge, Kentucky. His mother, Laura Rae, was a schoolteacher; his father, Whitney Moore Young Sr., was president of Lincoln Institute, a private black college. Young and his two sisters grew up on the Lincoln campus and went to segregated public elementary schools before completing high school at the Lincoln Institute. Young studied science at Kentucky State Industrial College *and engineering at the Massachusetts Institute of Technology. In World War II, Young rose to the rank of first sergeant in an all-black antiaircraft group, and mediated the sometimes tense interactions between white and African American troops. As Young told the* New York Times, *"That was the beginning of my work in that field, being an intermediary between whites and blacks."*

Young earned an MA in social work from the University of Minnesota, where he began working as director of industrial relations at the St. Paul Urban League. Young convinced white employers to hire African Americans for jobs that had been closed to them, including salesmen, telephone operators, and beauticians. He later ran the League's Omaha branch and served as dean of the School of Social Work at Atlanta University, where he was deeply active in the city's racial and political affairs.

When Young was appointed executive director of the National Urban League in 1961, the organization was in financial crisis. At business lunches, Young recruited support from prominent philanthropists, including banker David Rockefeller and Robert Sarnoff of RCA. In the ten years he ran the League, Young increased its budget tenfold and expanded the staff from three hundred to more than twelve hundred.

In 1962, Martin Luther King Jr. invited Young to address the annual convention of the Southern Christian Leadership Conference. While the Urban League was primarily concerned with social service, Young made the decision to co-sponsor the March on Washington for Jobs and Freedom in 1963. This was considered politically risky, as it was unclear to moderates how the massive demonstration would turn out.

In the crucial decade of the 1960s, Young worked to bridge the gap between the white establishment and black activists. He convinced major corporations and foundations to support the civil rights movement. He also shifted the League's focus from middle-class issues to problems of the poor.

Young initially disagreed with King's opposition to the war in Viet-nam, saying African Americans needed to concentrate on their own struggle for survival. But in 1969 he came out against the war, saying it diverted money that could be spent on domestic programs for the poor.

Young died unexpectedly while on a trip to Nigeria. President Richard M. Nixon ordered an air force jet to bring his body home. At Young's funeral, Nixon praised the civil rights leader as "a doer, not a talker."

Robert Penn Warren conducted two interviews with Young for Who Speaks for the Negro? *In the book, he described Young as a "persistent, heavy, aggressive force: impatient aggressiveness leashed and controlled by will."*

ROBERT PENN WARREN: Let me read you just a quote. It's a question with relation to the white man. This is a summary in a forthcoming book on race relations. I'll read the quote from it and we'll see whether it makes sense or not. "In James Baldwin's cosmology, there seems to be no decent white of any sort and no way a white man can prove his decency. If you are hostile, you're a racist. If you express friendship or sympathy, you're a liberal. If you commit yourself to action, this merely proves you're condescending towards the Negro [in order] to purge your own conscience."

WHITNEY YOUNG: My analysis would differ. First of all, I think that neither white people nor Negro people have any monopoly on virtue or on vices. My analogy of this situation is that the present plight of Negro citizens, and that plight is really a very serious one, results not so much from historic ill will or goodwill. Actually what we've had in our society is about 10 percent of white Americans who have been actively concerned, and who have been actively working toward integration; about 10 percent who have been actively resistant, who have worked to preserve the status quo, or to even send the Negro back to Africa; but about 80 percent of white Americans have been largely indifferent. This has been active apathy, active indifference, so it hasn't been ill will or goodwill; it's been *no* will that is largely responsible.

This is characteristic of Americans. We tend to focus on the pleasant and the beautiful and the gay, and to push into the subconscious that which is ugly and unpleasant, particularly if we feel some responsibility for it. So what's happened, largely, is that white Americans have ignored the Negro. They've not taken the Negro seriously. They've driven around the slums, and they keep their heads buried in the *Wall Street Journal* as a commuter train stops at 125th Street.

This is the significance, it seems to me, of the Negro revolution of 1963: all America was forced to look at the Negro. There was a confrontation, for the first time, in the lives of many people. And this is where 1964 becomes a year of decision making. We have assumed up until now that good racial relations meant the absence of tension and conflict, and not the presence of justice and equal opportunity. I don't think that anybody can generalize about all whites being this or all Negroes being this.

Obviously, many white people find themselves, out of fear and insecurity and ignorance, identifying more with the racists. They'll vote for [Alabama governor George] Wallace. But increasingly, white America, when it's confronted with the grim realities, with the tragic consequences of their indifference, with the threats to their way of life, with the inhumane kind of consequences that result from indifference in considering race relations as a spectator sport, will find themselves on the right side. I'm not distressed by the unrest, by the tension, by the conflict. In many ways this is healthy, because it's bringing the real attitudes and feelings to the surface where we can deal with them. Historically, Americans have only reacted to crisis. They've fixed a bridge when it fell in; there was an accident at the corner and they put up a stoplight.

RPW: There's one historical theory that says Negro gains have come as by-products of national crises of one kind or another. But in the last few years, there's been a great drive on the part of Negroes to separate the present revolution, or movement, or whatever we should call it, from this by-product status in history.

WY: I wouldn't say this entirely. I think we can attribute this heightened impatience, this accelerated kind of aspiration of the Negro, directly to a number of historical forces. I think we can attribute it directly, in part, to the mobility of Negroes made necessary by World War II, when Negroes were taken out of the South for the first time in their lives and traveled throughout the world. They got a taste of freedom, a taste of what it meant to be a man. They found out that their lives did not have to be lived in misery and abuse.

I think of the increased and perfected system of communications, which immediately threw on the screen what was happening throughout the world. I think the increased education of Negroes, I think the Cold War, the competition between America and Russia—America, attempting to prove more world leadership, was forced to commit itself publicly, over and over, to a certain concept of democracy and freedom. That did not go unheard by the masses of Negro people.

I think the emergence of African nations into independence and their subsequent reception in America by the highest government officials, their appearance on television frequently at the UN, gave to Negroes a new sense of destiny, a new sense of pride in race. It made them shake off their feelings of inferiority. This all led up to the incident in Montgomery with Mrs. Rosa Parks, where she sat on the bus for reasons even she cannot tell you now. Montgomery led up to Tuskegee, the sit-instructional—a direct result of the inability of the power structure to absorb the increasing number of intelligent Negroes. As long as it could absorb them into dependent positions, they could control them. But I don't think this can be separated from certain larger forces that were at work in society.

Warren remarks on the growing critique of white liberalism by black intellectuals. He asks Young if the Urban League, by design, is more inclined to work with whites who support the civil rights movement than are other organizations.

WY: Let me say first that it is quite true that the Negro today no longer conceives of his goal in life as simply a replication of white society. He is conceiving of integration more as a synthesis, rather than as a complete dropping of all that is Negro and the adoption of all that is white. What he's saying, in effect, is that all that is white is not good. It couldn't be good, or else we wouldn't have been kept in slavery and suppressed all these years—that there must be some moral bankruptcy here somewhere, there must be some value orientations that are not proper and good. He's saying, "I can bring something to a new society even though I cannot bring, certainly, superior technological know-how. Certainly I can't bring the money. I can't bring, in many cases, the same level of education." But out of suffering one develops something that goes beyond just jazz and music. One develops compassion, one develops a humaneness. Certainly the Negro has developed a tolerance, a patience that maybe the larger society can use. Maybe General Motors can use some of our compassion.

I have a theory, that with work and with thought, if we can't change status seeking and if we can't change conformity, at least we can change the norms to which people are conforming, and we can change the symbols that represent status. Instead of exclusiveness as it relates to a neighborhood or school or bus—exclusiveness being good—we can change that and make inclusiveness possible, we can somehow get people to see that only the hopelessly insecure and inadequate person needs to surround himself with sameness.

RPW: Let's take it then a little further. When Miss [Lorraine] Hansberry or when [James] Baldwin, or when others say: "White liberal, stay away. We are running this show." Or, "White man, we don't want to integrate," because he is for the Black Muslims.

WY: One of the tragedies in this whole civil rights struggle is the inability of the white person to distinguish leadership. For example, any Negro who achieves a certain amount of popularity or prominence, whether it's a Cassius Clay or a baseball player like Willie Mays, when he utters something about the race relations problem he is treated and thought of as an expert. While Lorraine Hansberry is a very gifted playwright, and while Baldwin is a very gifted writer, these are not people who either by their experiences or by their training or by their whole emotional orientation are by any means leaders of the Negro revolution. They are people who describe it, who react to it, who write about it, but who themselves are not equipped to suggest strategy, to interpret the social implications. Again, it reflects the lack of contact that the average white person has; the only Negroes that some white people know are the popular entertainers or writers or athletes, and so they're pretty much a victim, or beneficiary, as the case may be, of that person's interpretation.

It must be remembered that when the struggle was really hard and tough, Baldwin couldn't take it. He left the country. He wasn't even here. Many of these people who are now able to write about it, make a wonderful living on it. But let's not confuse this for leadership. You see *Time* magazine made that mistake. Baldwin should have been on the cover of *Time* magazine if *Time* magazine was going to do a story on contemporary American writers who are addressing themselves with some impact to the current American scene. But instead they had him on there talking about the Negro revolution. Well, then, you should have possibly had a Roy Wilkins or somebody. Again, this only reaches the intellectual kind of white person, who is moved by this, who has a great deal of guilt feeling and, who Baldwin knows well, are in a masochistic kind of mood where they don't feel like they're going to do anything, but at least they will permit themselves to be ridiculed and punished.

RPW: Now, by masochistic he means white people or Negroes now?

WY: White people. My point is that a great deal of the preoccupation of the white press, whether it's with Malcolm X or Baldwin or [U.S. Representative] Adam Powell, is a kind of guilt feeling. I'm willing to be punished. You take the Muslims, for example. There's many a white person who's irritated about the tension and the conflict, frightened by the threats of integration of their neighborhoods and all this. And along comes a man who says, "I don't want to integrate your schools. I don't want to integrate your neighborhoods. I don't want to integrate your daughters. I'm going to get rid of crime and welfare." There's many a white person who subconsciously says, "Look, this isn't too bad an idea." So instead of talking about Whitney Young and his efforts to integrate, let's play up the Muslims. But this is very stupid, because the truth of the thing is that there wouldn't be ten Negroes who would follow Malcolm X to a separate state, even if America was going to give him one. Africa doesn't want our welfare load any more than New York wants our welfare load. They aren't going to import them to Africa. The appeal that a Muslim has is the opportunity for a Negro who's been beaten down all day to get a vicarious pleasure out of hearing somebody cuss out white people. But this is not serious.

RPW: Back to Du Bois and his talk about the great split in the American Negro's psyche: the pull toward Africa, the pull toward the mystical black cultural heritage, as opposed to the pull in the other direction, to identify with the Western, European-American tradition, the Judeo-Christian tradition, even to be absorbed totally and lose his blood identity in that tradition. Now this great split, for some this is a real, live problem, right this minute. They tell me, at least.

WY: It's probably more a dilemma now than before. You see, in the past ten years, even fifteen years ago, Negroes made very little attempt to identify with Africa. There was no real effort. In fact they denied any real relationship. It's been only in more recent years, as Africa's come into independence, and all this. I think what's working here is not so much the conflict between retaining his black identity, as the feeling that this type of solidarity has been practiced by every other group in our society—-minority group—the Irish, the Italians, the Catholics, Jewish people did it. And so the pull is more toward this as a tactic, as a survival technique, than it is any basic conflict with, "Do I want to worship the idols in Tanganyika or do I want to worship Jesus Christ?" The Negro, basically, has not this kind of historical contact and relationship with Africa. He's never been really that close.

RPW: He's cut off.

WY: He's been cut off, yes.

RPW: This makes a difference. The question is what kind of difference and how much of a difference?

WY: The new pride in race is a very positive thing. Because as long as a person felt that his being a Negro made him inferior or made him an object to be despised, then being a Negro was something he couldn't help but subconsciously wish he wasn't. Now there is developing, as more Negroes attain their rights and are recognized, and as Africa has come up, there is this new pride in race. My concern is, can America move quickly enough to reward the Negro, give him his just rights, so that this pride will not degenerate into chauvinism, and into a kind of blind nationalism, which he feels is necessary for survival? I think part of the dilemma that the white liberal is facing is that what the Negro is saying today is that you've had all the institutions in our society, and had an opportunity to do something about our plight—the churches, the businesses, labor, every other group—but you haven't done it. So the Negro has assumed the initiative. If whites want to express their liberalism today, they must accept the fact that the Negro must lead, or that the Negro will accept him only as a peer. Now what worries me is that most white people spend their time today bemoaning the methods and the tactics that Negroes are using instead of saying, "I don't like the sit-ins," or "I don't like the blocking of traffic, so I'm going to [support] the Urban League's massive Marshall Plan to get better housing and better education and better jobs."

RPW: You mean that the white man is saying this.

WY: The white man is spending more time concentrating on the inconveniences and the disturbances than he is on the basic causes of the problem. To begin with, the poverty, the one out of four who are out of work, the one out of six who are in poor housing, the 500,000 Negro kids between the ages of sixteen and twenty-one who are out of work and out of school.

If 1963 did nothing else for us, it said this: that no longer can we generalize about our friends and our enemies in this whole struggle. In the past, we've said Northerners are liberal and Southerners are bigoted, and management is bigoted and labor is liberal. We found, in the 1960s, some of the most sophisticated and brutal bigots in the North and in labor than we ever found in the South. And we found the reverse was also true. As long as they could express their liberalism in terms of indignation about a lynching in Mississippi, this is one thing. When it came to moving next door to them, this was something entirely different.

RPW: Let me take a phrase or two out of some of your writings that I have been reading. In the speech "The Social Revolution, Challenge to the Nation" you have a phrase that you will be able to put into its proper context: "responsibilities of the victims of injustice." What are such responsibilities of the American Negro?

WY: I have been concerned, as the Urban League has been for years, with the fact that with rewards, with rights, go responsibilities. I've been inhibited in elaborating on this, especially before all-white audiences, by two facts. One, the fact that I'm not sure that the average white American is aware of the great sense of responsibility that Negro citizens have already shown throughout history in providing for their own, long before many of the welfare programs and social security benefits were open to them. Negro citizens, through their churches and their organizations, were forced to provide for themselves, and there has been a history of self-help within the Negro community that I think is largely missed in history, and is largely unknown to the white American. To concentrate too much on this would make it appear that this is a new experience for him. So when I talk about Negro responsibility, it's reminding them of their continued and increased responsibilities as they get new resources, as they move into middle-class status, as they develop a stable family life in order to help out, as other immigrant groups have helped their own who are less fortunate.

The other reason that inhibits me somewhat in talking about the responsibility of Negro citizens, as much as I should like to, is

that the—so many of the columnists and so many of our newly appointed advisers in the press and . . .

RPW: You mean self-appointed.

WY: Self-appointed advisers have taken this line almost solely.
And these are people who have, in the past, been largely indifferent
to the plight of Negro citizens and to discrimination against them.
They've been people who fought against civil rights laws (I'm thinking of columnists like David Lawrence and Fulton Lewis) and who
have done little to see that the Negro acquires his civil rights. These
are people who now speak of Negroes assuming certain responsibilities before these rights are to be given. And also there is a tendency on the part of so many of these people to make it appear that
before the Negro citizen as a group can get—even deserves—his
civil rights, each and every Negro must measure up to some kind of
standard of morality and decency and responsibility.

I know that in my speeches, and in many of the speeches of
Negro leaders to an all-Negro audience, the speech is an entirely
different speech. Seventy-five percent of it is a reminder to the
Negro citizens that the removal of barriers alone will not ensure
first-class citizenship. If the white community wants to hear responsible Negro leaders speak more to their people about their
own responsibilities, then let them speak to the white community
about their responsibilities. And I never want people to forget the
amazing sense of responsibility that Negroes have shown throughout history—probably more than any other ethnic group, given the
provocations and the conditions—of the responsibility of remaining loyal to the country, not being taken in by the communists,
responsibility for not getting violent and for being restrained in the
face of all kinds of provocations, the responsibility of taking care of
their unwanted children when white parents could either arrange
for abortions or could get their kids sent off into institutions that

were closed to Negroes. And we have historically taken care of our aged, who didn't have the benefits of social security, because domestic workers couldn't get social security. We've had to do this.

RPW: There are complaints, now and then, by responsible Negroes that the actual cash outlay, in terms of philanthropy, in terms of support for organizations, is less than might be expected from Negroes. This complaint occurs pretty often from responsible sources. There's another kind of responsibility to one's own that's different from the kind you've enumerated.

WY: There are two factors here. No race throughout history that, within its generation, knew poverty has ever distinguished itself by its generosity or its humanity. There's an old saying that once you've been hungry, you're never full. And there's the constant haunting fear of a return to poverty, of your children suffering the same fate. Remember, this is the first generation of Negroes who have had anything approaching reasonable security. It was only after World War I, and Negroes began to get some jobs in war plants, and even so it's just a handful. But I still think that, given the Negro income and given the fact that Negroes have to spend so much time and so much money fighting for elementary rights, we have to give to the NAACP—which we can never list on our income tax returns, and you can't even list the Urban League if you live in the South without being called in and questioned about a lot of other irrelevant things, even though it's a tax-exempt organization.

You have to really measure the Negro's giving in terms of the number of Negro doctors who serve, clients who never pay them, the numbers of lawyers who serve who never get paid, and the fact that we haven't really developed any substantial wealth. We have a few businesses and the demands on them are terrific. The average Negro who is a school principal or who is the administrator of a social agency occupies a status in the Negro community that's

completely unrealistic, but it makes him an attraction for everybody. Every church in that community wants a donation.

RPW: There's another quotation from the same speech I'd like
to refer to: "As we win the battle for civil rights, we can and might
well lose the war for human rights." You know the context of that?

WY: Here, again, is a real fear that I have that so many Negro
citizens may have been led to believe that the solution to the problems of poverty which they face will be reached when the civil rights
bill is passed or when the ["whites only"] signs are taken down. This
is dangerous because a type of disillusionment may set in. I am fear-
ful that Negro citizens will not understand the need for a diversified
approach in this whole attack. There are many forces at work today
that, on the surface, are really indifferent to race: the forces of [in-
dustrial] automation, what's going to happen as a defense budget is
cut down and defense industries are closed. I doubt seriously if the
American public will immediately convert that same money into
the social sphere. All this will pose some real problems.

*Warren turns the conversation to the question of whether black
people want true integration, or rather equal treatment and equal
opportunities.*

WY: I don't think the masses of Negroes are anxious for integration, per se. What they're anxious for is first-class accommodations,
housing, education, health facilities. But they are deeply convinced
that segregation automatically makes it possible for a group to receive inferior services. Never throughout history has a suppressed
group ever been given superior services. But the thrust for integration isn't so much a thrust for association as it is a disbelief in quality services in a segregated city.

It may be sort of a strategy that some of our sincere liberal friends might have adopted, in order to assuage the fears of white people, [to say] that the Negro really doesn't want to integrate; what he wants is equal facilities, and if we give him that then he will not try to move into our neighborhoods and into our societies. We ought to press for the reverse. That is, what a terrible thing it would be for white people if Negroes do not attempt to move into their neighborhoods. Because it means they, too, will be left with a culture of sameness, and that is so uncreative. White people will soon see the value of diversity, as against the perpetuation of sameness, and will be encouraging this.

My concept of integration doesn't mean that any group gives up all that it has and adopts all that another group has. My concept of integration is that we explore and identify, within each group, the positives that have been developed out of that group's culture. The Negro, out of suppression, has developed a kind of compassion and humanness, certainly a kind of patience and tolerance that General Motors could use. I'm not just talking about his music and his rhythm. I'm talking about some other qualities that the larger society can use. So my concept of integration is that we reject the negatives: the poverty of the Negro, his lack of education, the lack of culture that he's developed. That we reject in whites the meanness, the selfishness, the inability to give up privilege and advantage. And we move toward another society, you see, that's much better, that reflects a synthesis of these.

RPW: We can't legislate the future.

WY: No, but I think we can plan this. My theory here is that the kind of separate societies that have been developed in our communities have not happened through chance. This has been consciously, deliberately planned. What they did was play upon the status needs of people, and they set a norm of exclusiveness as a criterion of success. This was done deliberately, through very clever advertisement of certain subdivisions, and a conscious effort to keep out Negroes. And this way, we can change the norm that's been true of all human history, in terms of classes as well as races, and sometimes all a matter of class and very little a matter of race, in some societies. I'm talking about the kind of situation where [Nobel Peace Prize laureate] Ralphe Bunche is told he can't get a hotel reservation in Atlanta, Georgia, while a drunken white man in overalls walks in and registers. Now that's about race, not class.

RPW: That's race. That's race.

WY: I'm saying that a community can set any standard it wants to, a schoolkid, a neighborhood, as long as it doesn't set a standard of race, and the Negro then should be asked to measure up, and can measure up and get in it.

RPW: We have no argument. But the question is how far the race question intersects and fuses with the other considerations? That you cannot have a solution merely in terms of race, is the question I'm raising.

WY: I've discussed this in the centennial edition of *Ebony* magazine in an article, my concern about the class situation within the Negro community. My concern was that we were developing a gap here, and that the choice that the Negro faced, all too often, was a choice either between bread and water or champagne and caviar, either sending his kids to slum, ghetto, inferior schools or to plush prep schools, either living in a hovel or living in a suburb. My concern is that this is creating a vacuum here, and it is denying the lower-class Negro of leadership potential. It is a situation, not so much of an attempt to escape the Negro, on the part of the middle class, but an attempt to escape the ghetto, which is symbolic of a lot of other things in his society that he wants to escape.

The class problem is basically an economic problem. America is not yet so cultural, so sophisticated, so aesthetic. When you really think of the suburbs, in cities like Chicago and other places, they are inhabited by the gangsters—all white. There are some twelve suburbs in Chicago. The most fabulous suburb in Chicago, that's all white. It has nothing to do with any kind of class, moral, or cultural value at all—it's money.

RPW: Oh yes. How much of that split between the Negro mass and the Negro upper-middle, upper class—is that split wider or not than it was ten years ago?

WY: Oh, it's much wider. And the reason it's wider is that the jobs are disappearing, jobs that would normally be [for the] lower middle class, and lower class, are disappearing.

RPW: This is not what is said by many Negroes, of course. They will deny that a split is widening. They say it's narrowing.

WY: I'm talking about a purely economic fact of life, now. We have more middle-class Negroes than ever before, but we have more poor people than ever before. And the figures will show that we have more unemployment and more impoverished Negroes today than we had ten years ago. But we also have more in the middle class. So, just from the economic standpoint, the gap is there.

RPW: The question is, what is the spiritual gap? Is it widening or narrowing?

WY: Two things are happening. On the one hand, there is a greater sense of pride in race and there is a solidarity, as far as goals are concerned. But there is also developing this gap on an economic basis that sets up social and geographic distances. In the North it poses another problem, in that the ability to communicate and to understand common goals and make common cause was much greater in the South, where regardless of the affluence of an individual Negro, or his education, he was still denied the same things as a poor Negro. So the poor Negro and the middle-class, educated Negro could make common cause easily. This brought a sense of restraint and balance and everything else to the group seeking its rights.

Now when you get to the North, the Negro of affluence can, increasingly, escape. He can move away from the ghetto. He can go to the theaters, he can go to the restaurants, and the better schools. It makes the identification of the common cause between the lower-class Negro and the middle-class Negro much more difficult to identify. What this means is the lower-class Negro in the North can be suspicious of the intervention of the middle-class Negro. He makes him prove why he is involved in civil rights, why he is concerned about it. This means that many Negroes who aspire to get involved become discouraged because they aren't warmly and immediately accepted by the masses. It also means that the ambitious demagogue or rabble-rouser in the lower class is able to influence the masses more easily and to discredit responsible leadership.

RPW: [There is a] great problem of leadership that is caused by this fact—that's the real danger, isn't it?

WY: This is the real danger, especially as long as the climate is so fraught with poverty and with the type of conditions that would make demagoguery easy, as long as there's mass unemployment, as long as there's poor housing, and all of this makes a natural breeding ground. The arguments are so plentiful. Also, the Negroes have learned through observation of the Southern demagogue, how he has exploited the fears and the ignorance of poor white people, using race as a factor. He watched [Mississippi politician and segregationist Theodore] Bilbo. He saw [Georgia governor] Gene Talmadge, with his red suspenders, do the same. And now that Negro, who's opportunistic, uses what he has learned so well in the South to exploit and to capitalize on the impoverished, illiterate, unemployed Negro.

RPW: Has this led to serious cracks in leadership in terms of bids for power, do you think?

WY: It's made it much more difficult for responsible leadership to intervene and to get the emotional response out of the masses of Negroes. But another thing in that picture is the mass media have helped in the buildup of the demagogue. The only person that the masses see on television, on the front pages of the newspaper, speaking for their hopes and their dreams and their aspirations, is a demagogue. And this contributes to the difficulty of the responsible leader getting the confidence, and even getting the awareness, of the masses that he is working on behalf of.

RPW: What do you think of the remark that one encounters now and then that the people who should be most alarmed about Malcolm X are the Negro leaders, responsible Negro leaders, and not whites.

WY: No, I disagree with this. I think the people who should be most alarmed are white people, because Malcolm X is but a symptom. There are many Malcolm X's around. There are people who have a genius for cussing out white people, and we will have many more [of them] developing. This is a symptom of an evil and a frustration and a feeling of despair and hopelessness in a society. The other thing is that white people will find Malcolm X interesting and amusing and certainly newsworthy, not because they really feel that he can mount a massive military activity against them, but because he is preaching a kind of separatism, and a kind of Negro self-help and isolation, which many white people find very appealing. There is a lot of wishful thinking. What they forget is that Hitler and Mussolini were able to develop great efficiency, and build roads and hospitals, by preaching hate. And that, eventually, this hate will turn against people. But Negroes, per se, find Malcolm X entertaining. They get a vicarious pleasure out of hearing him curse out white people. They've been kicked around all day, and they are quite amused by the way the white press, and the white community, seem to get aroused. This tickles them, how he can get front-page coverage and he can scare people. But in the Negro community, wouldn't ten people follow Malcolm X to a separate state.

RPW: Not to a separate state.

WY: No, even if America gave him one. And Africa doesn't want our caseload, welfare load, any more than New York wants it. They want chemists and physicists and engineers, so they're not fixing to open up their doors to impoverished Negroes in New York.

RPW: What would you say to this remark by Adam Clayton Powell, that the leadership of all the old-line organizations is finished? They have no political significance anymore.

WY: Mr. Powell is reflecting, in his attack on national Negro leadership, his frustration and his own inability to reach this kind of national status. He would like a great deal to be seen not as just a leader of a district here in New York City, or Harlem; he would like to be seen as a national leader. And he has been constantly rejected in this role. I guess what really set this thing off was the March on Washington, when Adam Powell was not called up in any major role. Adam Powell has a choice. He has to decide whether he's going to do like the Southerner, whether he's going to keep his position in Washington by doing daily, dedicated, visible work for Negroes, and make a real contribution, or whether he's going to use the technique of the demagogue, and stay in office simply by building up a straw man called the white man, who's out to get him.

RPW: It's very funny how discussions of him provoke, in some quite responsible Negroes, great evasions, unlike your reply.

WY: I understand the reason. In a war, and many Negroes conceive of this as a war, you should not criticize anybody who's cussing out white people for whatever reason. And there are a lot of

Negroes who find Adam Powell entertaining because they think he is upsetting white people. If white people didn't attack Adam Powell so much, Negroes would not rally to his defense so much.

The established Negro leadership has the support, when the issues really get serious and crucial, not facetious. The March on Washington, for example, [was a] success which was spearheaded by the established organizations through their machinery. You see, these are the only organizations, particularly the Urban League and the NAACP, that actually have the machinery in terms of local affiliates, and established know-how in community organization, and the basic confidence of the Negro community. So there is an emotional reaction, which many reporters pick up and identify [as proof that] these are the people Negroes are following. But when it gets down to meat, bread, and potatoes, they show up at the Urban League office. When they really get in trouble, need a lawyer or something, they go to NAACP. But as long as it's an entertaining evening, then they'll listen to some of this other stuff.

RPW: Tell me this: how much of a liability has the white affiliation of the Urban League and NAACP been, do you think?

WY: I think it's made us vulnerable to certain attacks. But deep down inside, Negroes know that they cannot go it alone. They cannot establish their own General Motors, their own A&P chain of stores, their own chain of banks. That we are dependent, that certainly the two societies are interdependent. And the reason that I know Negroes are never taking this type of philosophy seriously is that none of the people who espouse it ever suggest that they, themselves, will withdraw from an association and all dependency on white people. Mr. Powell, for example, doesn't withdraw from the Democratic Party, and Negroes certainly don't dominate it. He doesn't withdraw from Congress, and Negroes certainly don't dominate it. He doesn't turn down the salary that he receives from

Congress, and I'm sure Negroes pay a very small percent of it. Malcolm X and the Muslims don't tell their Negro followers, who pay them big dues, that they should quit their jobs if white people are in charge. Nobody says Negroes ought to move out of their houses unless they're owned by Negroes. So it falls down at the level of serious consideration.

RPW: What about the role of this poor fellow, the white liberal, who's been so beaten around the ears lately by Jimmy Baldwin and some others, who's called a plague and a nuisance? What is the role of a white man in such a thing as the Negro revolution, movement, or whatever you choose to call it? What is his reasonable role?

WY: Well, I think the role of the white liberal now is to mass a real assault to get the Negro included in basic social reform movements of this country. You see, the liberal's role earlier was to help bring about some of the social welfare measures and labor legislation, some of the things that went on during the New Deal period of Franklin Roosevelt. But when these things got established, then the labor, you see, became conservative and liberals really had nothing to hold on to, because they had not extended the social revolution to the Negro in the sense that the Negro was any more than a partial beneficiary. He was not in the strategy of policy making; he had not been included as a participant in the social reform. Liberals missed a real bet, I think, when they did not immediately jump on the Urban League's proposal for a massive Marshall Plan. This is a point at which the liberal could have intervened and been very meaningful. Instead, he let the other people call this preferential treatment, and so the Negro situation moved on into some more extreme demands where the liberal found he could not identify.

Now we're at a point where the Negro ought to be able to say to the liberal: "Look, I'm upset about the discrimination in the labor movement, but I know that I must not be *against* the labor movement. I'm upset about some other things, but I know that we have to work together on the common goals of better housing and better education and better social legislation."

In turn, the liberal ought to be able to say to the Negro, "I am opposed to the activities of the Triborough Bridge stall-in, but I am all for these other things, and on this we must keep together."

I think the Negro is like a person just learning to walk. He's trying out his legs and doesn't want anybody to help him. The liberal will have to be not just tolerant and patient, but he will have to be mobilizing now to provide this other help that the Negro's going to need. And then when we get back [together], he will have to insist on working with the Negro, and in some cases letting the Negro provide the leadership.

RPW: The Negro must provide, clearly, fundamental leadership. It's his show.

WY: That's as far as the basic civil rights are concerned. But when it comes to the social reforms that are needed in this country, for all people, this isn't a question of the Negro providing leadership; it's a question of sharing in cooperative leadership of these people. What's happened is, even very liberal papers like the *New York Times* came out and, instead of grabbing hold of the Marshall Plan, they again called it preferential treatment. A few days later they applaud the Appalachian [plan], a special effort for these people, they urge massive help be given to Alaskans after the earthquake, they applaud special help to the Hungarian refugees and the Cubans. But with the Negro, they come back and say, no, he must be treated as an individual, not as a community.

As the revolution has moved to the North, the liberal in the North is now being called upon to express his real feelings—not just in terms of indignation about lynching in Mississippi, but about people living next door to him and about people going to his schools. Are we just beginning to get what the real feelings of people happen to be and they're coming to the surface? The Triborough Bridge incident, for example. These [white] commuters who were being delayed twenty minutes to get to their martinis out in Westchester, their reactions were as vile, their language was as vicious and as vulgar and as hate-filled as any language that I have ever heard in Mississippi. And the hatred on their faces and the way they threw the things out of the car at the people would have done justice to any Klan meeting. Now on the surface we say, "Gee, this is terrible." But I think, ultimately, that if you're going to get at the roots of a problem and correct it, you have to get at the real feelings of people, and for a while it may look ugly. What's happening here, now, is that all Americans are on trial to reveal either their great decency or their great evilness.

RPW: Do you find any truth in the speculation made by a good many Negroes in the South that the crisis will have passed there long before it's passed here, that there's more basis for a rapprochement, for a working-together there than there is in, say, the great metropolitan northern centers?

WY: Yes, I'm one of these people who believes that when the South really gets over this hump of having to have segregation as a crutch to compensate for their other feelings of inferiority about the economy of their system, and their lack of a lot of other things, once they get over this hump and they see that they can't keep the Negro down without keeping themselves down, there's enough basic feeling, tone, and experience between white and Negro citizens that they will move off on a level unlike anything in the North, and there will be a much sounder relationship. I think this is based on a theory that the most vicious expression of hatred toward a person is to ignore him. Not to hate him. It takes feeling to hate. The thing that destroys people is not to hate them or to love them, but to ignore them and make their lives meaningless. I think the average Northerner, because of the separateness—and you know there's more segregation in housing in the North than in the South—because of the separateness, because so few whites have had contact with Negroes, their feelings [are] largely intellectual feelings. It's related to some abstract concepts of justice and equality, but they are still handicapped by [not having] a real experience with a Negro who's a peer, who's educated. Where the average Southerner has had to deal with him.

The conversation turns to the idea of minimum quotas for black people in access to employment and housing.

WY: No Negro has said to me that he wants to see a white person replaced. We think there ought to be equal opportunity in *un*employment as well as in employment. We're twenty-five percent or fifteen percent of the unemployed, and whites are five or six. And we think that this situation ought to be changed. I'm not buying the saying that the problem of unemployed Negroes will be solved only when there's full employment for all Americans. I know there won't be full employment for all Americans in the foreseeable future. In the meanwhile, I don't think that we can continue to have this large number of Negroes unemployed.

Integration is seen by too many white people either as something to be abhorred and fought, resisted completely, because it will bring in its wake all kinds of problems, or it's seen as something that's to be delayed until, say, the day after I die. Or else it's something to be grudgingly tolerated, as one takes castor oil. It's inevitable, I know I've got to take it, and it's probably good for me, but I don't want it. This is consistent with the American inability to think deeply. We look for easy solutions. We react to crisis; we don't benefit from past experiences. We wait for accidents to happen on a corner before we put up a green light, or for the bridge to fall down before we repair it. [The American] sees everything as a problem—not as an idea to be explored but as a problem to be dealt with, and grudgingly to be met, at a real personal sacrifice. That's why we've got to begin to think of integration not as a problem, but as an opportunity for a country to prove the validity of its system, of its economic system, of its Judeo-Christian convictions, of its democratic way of life. The Negro is a barometer of the validity of all of these, and this is the first real test that this country has had. Because in the final analysis, as Franklin Roosevelt said, the test of a country is not to what extent it can give more to those who have, but to what extent it can give to those who have not. Unless this country is able to meet this challenge, then a serious question can be raised about all these institutions. Because too many Americans, when asked what does being an American mean, will talk about refrigerators and cars, and will not talk about basic freedoms and opportunities. This is a real test of all that we hold very dear. If it doesn't work for the Negro in this country, then it's not likely to be the most appealing and attractive article for 75 percent of the world's population, that's nonwhite, that's shopping around for some way of life to adopt.

James Baldwin

April 27, 1964

New York, New York

James Baldwin was a literary prodigy. Born in Harlem in 1924, Baldwin was the eldest in a family of nine children. He wrote that as his mother gave birth to each child, "I took them over with one hand and held a book with the other." Baldwin says he was "plotting novels" almost as soon as he could read. By the time Baldwin sat down for a conversation with Robert Penn Warren, he had become, as critic Hilton Als put it, "America's leading black literary star." Baldwin was a bestselling novelist and a bracing social critic. By 1964, he had published three novels, Go Tell it on the Mountain *(1953),* Giovanni's Room *(1956), and* Another Country *(1962), and three deeply influential essay collections:* Notes of a Native Son *(1955),* Nobody Knows My Name: More Notes of a Native Son *(1961), and* The Fire Next Time *(1963).*

    Baldwin was a preacher in his teen years, following in his stepfather's footsteps, but he left the pulpit when he was seventeen. He gave up on Christianity, writing in 1963 that "whoever wishes to become a truly moral human being . . . must first divorce himself from all the prohibitions, crimes, and hypocrisies of the Christian church. If the concept of God has any validity or any use, it can only be to make us larger, freer, and more loving. If God cannot do this, then it is time we got rid of him."

Baldwin moved to Paris in 1948, at the age of twenty-four, seeking freedom from the tyranny of chronic racism in America. His physical response to that racism "was like some dread, chronic disease," he wrote, "the unfailing symptom of which is a kind of blind fever, a pounding in the skull and fire in the bowels." Nine years later, Baldwin returned to the United States to confront that tyranny through the burgeoning civil rights movement. Baldwin wrote, "I could simply no longer sit around Paris discussing the Algerian and black American problem. Everybody else was paying their dues, and it was time I went home and paid mine."

From the late 1950s through the late 1960s Baldwin traveled widely across the South, reporting on the movement for magazines like Esquire, Mademoiselle, *and* Harper's. *He also took part in direct action and befriended many civil rights leaders, including Medgar Evers in Mississippi, Martin Luther King Jr. in Atlanta, and Malcolm X in Harlem. Baldwin worked on voting rights campaigns, marched in demonstrations, and toured the country giving lectures and interviews. He sat with Hollywood glitterati and giants of the civil rights movement during the 1963 March on Washington for Jobs and Freedom. That same year, he appeared on the cover of* Time *magazine, which declared that no other writer "expresses with such poignancy and abrasiveness the dark realities of the racial ferment in North and South."*

Despite his deep connection to the black freedom struggle, Baldwin was sometimes kept at arm's length by its leaders. According to his biographer David Leeming, Baldwin was not invited to speak at the March on Washington because he was openly gay. Baldwin also drew heavy fire from leaders of the Black Power movement, who criticized him as an integrationist. In Soul on Ice, *Eldridge Cleaver wrote that Baldwin had a "grueling, agonizing, total hatred of the blacks, particularly of himself, and the most shameful, fanatical, fawning, sycophantic love of the whites." Cleaver said Baldwin was "the white man's most valuable tool in oppressing other blacks."*

Though his influence waned toward the end of the civil rights movement, Baldwin remained a prolific writer and his legacy remains deep. Along with novels and essays, Baldwin published plays, poetry, and countless reviews. He spent much of his life living abroad, mainly in France, though he continued reporting and teaching in the United States and traveling widely. In 1970, he bought a villa in St. Paul-de-Vence on the French Riviera, his main residence for the last seventeen years of his life. Baldwin died of cancer there, on December 1, 1987.

In her eulogy for James Baldwin, Toni Morrison noted that his life "refuses summation—it always did—and invites contemplation instead." As if speaking to him, she continued, "No one possessed or inhabited language for me the way you did. You made American English honest—genuinely international. You exposed its secrets and reshaped it until it was truly modern, dialogic, representative, humane. You stripped it of ease and false comfort and fake innocence and evasion and hypocrisy. And in place of deviousness was clarity. In place of soft plump lies was a lean, targeted power."

Robert Penn Warren was familiar with that power when he set out to record interviews for Who Speaks? *He often used quotes from Baldwin to probe the mind-set of his interview subjects. Historian David W. Blight observes that in reading the book, "it may seem as though Warren is carrying Baldwin's essays around in his pocket, as a kind of perverse as well as respectful ammunition."*

Speaking with Baldwin at a restaurant in New York City, Warren was struck by how Baldwin looked as he gathered an idea. "His eyes widen slightly," Warren writes, "a glint comes in them, he sits up in his chair, and the nerves, you are sure, tighten, and there is the acceleration of pulse beat and respiration. He is not looking at you now, or talking at you, at all: his eyes are fixed on something over yonder." Warren notes that while Baldwin had left the church years earlier, he "smuggled out the Gift of Tongues." With Baldwin, he writes, "we are to think of the blaze of light that rends the roof and knocks us all—all America and all American institutions—flat on the floor."

ROBERT PENN WARREN: In what sense, Mr. James Baldwin, do you think the [Negro] revolution is a revolution?

JAMES BALDWIN: Well that's a tough one to answer 'cause I'm not always sure that the word "revolution" is the right word. I myself use it because I don't know of any other. It's not as simple as a revolution of one class against another, for example. It is not as clear-cut as the Algerian revolution against the French. It is a very peculiar revolution because, in order to succeed at all, it has to have as its aim the reestablishment of the Union. And a great, radical shift in American mores, in the American way of life. Not only does it apply to the Negro, obviously, but it applies to every citizen in the country. This is a very tall order and desperately dangerous, but inevitable in my view because of the nature of the American Negro's relationship to the rest of the country, of all these generations, and the attitudes the country's had toward him, which always was, but now has become overtly and concretely, intolerable.

RPW: You say different from a revolution like the Algerian, which means a liquidation of a regime.

JB: That's right. But it doesn't apply here at all. Because this is [for Negroes] to liberate themselves and their children from the economic and social sanctions imposed on them because they were slaves here. Now if Washington, DC, had the energy to break the power of people like Senator [James] Eastland and Senator Richard Russell, so the Negroes began to vote in the South, we would make a large step forward. It seems to me that the South is ruled still by an oligarchy, which rules for its own benefit, and not only oppresses Negroes and murders them but imprisons and victimizes the bulk of the white population.

RPW: You said once in print that the Southern mob does not represent the will of the Southern majority.

JB: I still feel that. It's mobs that fill the street. Unless one's prepared to say that the South is populated entirely by monsters, which I'm not. Those mobs that fill the street are a reflection of the terror that everybody feels, at least on the lowest level. And those mobs that fill the street have been used by the American economy for generations to keep the Negro in its place. In fact, they have done the Americans'—North and South, by the way—dirty work for him. And they've always been encouraged to do it. No one has ever even given him any hint that it was wrong. And of course they are now completely bewildered. And can only react in one way, which is through violence. The same way that an Alabama sheriff, facing a Negro student, knows he's in danger. Doesn't know *what* the danger is and all he can do is beat him over the head or cattle-prod him. He doesn't know what else to do.

RPW: All revolutions of the ordinary, historical type have depended on the driving force of hope and the driving force of hate. Now, when this is directed against a regime to be liquidated, it's one thing; when it's inside of a system, which must be reordered but not destroyed, then the hope/hate ratio might change. I think how the hate is accommodated in this [Negro] revolution.

JB: The American Negro has had to accommodate a vast amount of hatred since he's been here. And that was a terrible school to go through. I myself am accused of hating all white people and saying that all Negroes do. I, myself, don't feel that so much as I feel a bitterness.

You can despise [white people]. You may even have given moments when you want to kill them. But here it's your brothers and your sisters, whether or not they know that they are your brothers and your sisters. And that complicates it. It complicates it so much that I can't quite see my way through this.

As for the hope, that is fuzzy too. Hope for what? You know, the best people involved in this revolution certainly don't hope to become what the bulk of Americans have become. So the hope, then, has to be to create a new nation under intolerable circumstances and in very little time and against the resistance of most of the country.

RPW: You mean the hope is not to simply move into white middle-class values? Is that it?

JB: Well even if that were the hope—it isn't as a matter of fact—it would not be possible. In order to accommodate me, in order to overcome so many centuries of cruelty and bad faith and genocide and fear, all the American institutions and all the American values, public and private, will have to change. The Democratic Party will have to become a different party, for example.

RPW: How do you envisage the result of this movement, if successful? What kind of a world do you envisage?

JB: I envisage a world which is almost impossible to imagine in this country. A world in which race would count for nothing. In which Americans grow up enough to recognize that I don't threaten them. Part of the problem here has nothing to do with race at all. It has to do with ignorance and it has to do with the culture of youth.

Warren asks Baldwin about the origins of growing racial pride among some African Americans.

JB: For the first time in American history, the American black man has not been at the mercy of the American white man's image of him. This is because of Africa. For the first time, the West was forced to deal with Africans on a level of power. And that image of the shiftless darky was shattered. Kids, people had another image to turn to, which released them. It's very romantic for an American Negro to think of himself as an African. But it's necessary in the re-creation of his morale.

RPW: In the matter discussed a while ago by [W.E.B.] Du Bois, and many other people since, of the split in the psyche of the American Negro—you have written something about it along this line—the tendency to identify with the African culture or African mystique, or the *mystique noir,* or even the American Negro culture as opposed to American white culture. The tendency to pull in that direction as opposed to the tendency to accept the Western, European-American white tradition, as another pull. Do you feel this is real for yourself?

JB: How do I answer that? It was very hard for me to accept Western European values because they didn't accept me. Any Negro born in this country spends a great deal of time trying to be accepted, trying to find a way to operate within the culture and not to be made to suffer so much by it, but nothing you do works. No matter how many showers you take, no matter what you do. These Western values absolutely resist and reject you. So that, inevitably, you turn away from them or you reexamine them. Because it is something that slaves knew and the masters haven't found it out yet; the slaves who adopted that bloody cross knew the masters could not be Christians because Christians couldn't have treated them that way. This rejection has been at the very heart of the American Negro psyche from the beginning.

Warren asks Baldwin about the attraction to Africa that an increasing number of black people had expressed, and whether he shared in that feeling.

JB: Which Africa would you be thinking of? Are you thinking of Senegal or are you thinking of Freetown? And if you are thinking of any of these places, what do you know about them? What is there that you can use? What is there that you can contribute to? These are very grave questions. I don't think that the void is absolute or that no bridge can be made. But we've been away from Africa for four hundred years and no power in heaven will allow me to find my way back.

Warren observes that some young, black voter registration activists from the North admired the purity of expression of semi-literate, Southern black farm workers.

JB: I would really agree with that. I've seen some extraordinary people just coming out of some enormous darkness. And there is something indescribably moving and direct and heroic about those people. And that's where the hope, in my mind, lies. Much more than in someone like me who was much more corrupted by the psychotic society in which we live.

RPW: This impulse is a very common one in many different circumstances though. You will find many white people romanticize some simpler form of life—the white hunter in the far west, or the American Indian or even the Negro.

JB: Or the worker.

RPW: Or the worker. This is an impulse of many people who feel we live in a complicated world, which they don't quite accept, don't want to accept, and turn to some simpler form of reality.

JB: I'm not so sure it's simpler, though. I'm not convinced that some of those old ladies and old men I talk to down South—I know they aren't simple. They are far from simple. And the emotional and psychological makeup which has allowed them to endure so long is something of a mystery to me. They are no more simple, for example, than Medgar Evers was simple. There was something very rustic about him, and direct, but obviously he was far from a simple man. My own father, who was certainly something like those people, was very far from being a simple man.

Warren asks about the possibility of political solidarity between black and white sharecroppers in the South.

JB: I have the feeling that the difference between the Southern white sharecropper and a black one is in the nature of their relationship to their own pain. And I think that the white Southern sharecropper, in a general way in any case, would have a much harder time using his pain, using his sorrow, putting himself in touch with it and using it to survive, than a black one. And there's a level of melancholy, and even tragedy in Negro experience, which is simply denied in white experience. I think this makes a very great difference in authority, a difference in growth, a difference in possibility. The Negro is not forbidden, as all white Southerners are, to assess his own beginnings. He may find it impossible or dangerous or fatal to do so. But a white Southerner suffers from the fact that his childhood, his early youth, when his relationship to black people is very different than it becomes later, is sealed off from him and he can never go back, he can never dig it up, on pain of destruction, nearly. This creates his torment and his paralysis.

RPW: Some Negroes in Mississippi and Alabama hold out hope for this understanding, for the rapprochement between the Southern poor whites, the sharecropper type, the laborer, and the poor Negro.

JB: Well I don't see much hope for it because, in the first place, the labor situation is too complex and too shaky. All workers in this country are in terrible trouble. Not enough jobs. And the jobs that exist are all vanishing. And this does not make for good relations between workers, as we all know.

Warren asks if the leadership of the civil rights movement has become more centralized or less effective.

JB: For the first time in the history of this struggle, the poor Negro has hit the streets, really. And it has changed the nature of the struggle completely. Pressure is being brought to bear by the people in the streets, especially by the poor and by the young, so that [movement leaders] are always in a position of having to assess, very carefully, their tactics. If the people feel betrayed, you've lowered their morale and then opened the door on a holocaust. I think that the Negro in America has reached a point of despair and disaffection. People talk about certain techniques being used that are destroying the goodwill of white people. But nobody gives a damn any longer about the goodwill of people who have never done anything to help you or to save you. Their ill will can hardly do more harm than their goodwill. And this is a very significant despair.

RPW: Yet you want to avoid a holocaust?

JB: Oh, indeed. We want to avoid a holocaust. But, you see, that's not simply in the hands of Negro leaders. That's in the hands of the entire country. If you have people up [in the United States Senate] filibustering about whether or not you are human, then obviously you are going to have a reaction in the streets.

RPW: Do you follow the line of thought that Dr. Kenneth Clark takes that Dr. King's [nonviolent] method in the South has some merit but is inapplicable in the North?

JB: Yes. I'm afraid I'm forced to agree with that. Negroes in the

South still go to church, some of them. And Negroes in the South, which is much more important, still have something resembling a family around which you can build a great deal. But the Northern Negro family has been fragmented for the last thirty years, if not longer. And once you haven't got a family, then you have another kind of despair, another kind of demoralization, and Martin King can't reach those people.

RPW: But he doesn't know he can't reach them?

JB: Martin does know it. He can't abandon them, either. And it's not that his influence is absolutely negligible. No, he is still a national leader and an international figure.

RPW: He can pack a hall in Bridgeport.

JB: Well, he can pack a hall in Bridgeport but it depends on what you are packing the hall with. The boys in the poolroom stay in the poolroom. And it's more important to reach them and do something about their morale. I'm not blaming Martin for this; it's not his fault at all. But to reach them is really very difficult. Malcolm X can reach them. Those kids are not Christians, and it's very hard to blame them for not being Christians, since there are so few in this Christian country.

The differences between the North and the South were really evident when the chips were down. They had different techniques of castrating you [in the South] than they had in the North, but the fact of the castration remained exactly the same, and that was the intention in both places. And, furthermore, it is impossible to be separate but equal. Because if you are equal then why must you be separate? It's that doctrine which has created almost all of the Negro's despair and also the country's despair. So I think that the instinct to destroy that doctrine is quite sound.

RPW: Separate but equal?

JB: Yes, that's right. It's really an attack on the white man's assumption that he knows more about you than you do, that he knows what's best for you, and that he can keep you in your place for your own good and also for his own profit.

RPW: What is the responsibility of a Negro, as you read it, to establish equality or justice? As you see, some of the white man's responsibilities are glaringly apparent. What responsibilities does a Negro have?

JB: One has to take upon oneself a very hard responsibility, [and it] is something you do with the young [people]. It has to do with a sense of their identity, a sense of their possible achievements, a sense of themselves. For this, one has to take upon oneself the necessity of trying to be an example to them, to prove something by your existence. Part of the problem of being a Negro in this country is that one has been beaten so long, and been helpless so long, one tends to think of oneself as being helpless. So the primary responsibility would be to convey to the people, whom one sort of helplessly represents, that they are not helpless. And that if they are not helpless, then they must try to be responsible, and to create a leadership out of these boys and girls in the streets, which indeed is happening. I think it's our responsibility, as their elders, to bear witness to them and to take risks with them. Because if they don't trust their elders then we're in trouble.

RPW: Well, I'm going to ask a question now that probably has no answer. How many Negroes read your books?

JB: (laughs) Well it's an impossible question to answer. But I do know this, that my brother, who lives in Harlem, says that whores and junkies and people like that steal the books and sell them in bars. There have been a lot of hot things sold in Harlem bars but I've never heard of hot books being sold in Harlem bars before. So I gather that means something.

Ruth Turner Perot

May 7, 1964

Cleveland, Ohio

Ruth Turner (now Ruth Turner Perot) taught German in the Cleveland, Ohio, public schools before heading up the local chapter of the Congress of Racial Equality (CORE) from 1963 to 1966. A native of Chicago, Perot earned degrees from Oberlin College and Harvard University's Graduate School of Education. She helped CORE's national office develop its black power philosophy, which she once described in a speech as "an audacious, prideful affirmation of self without which Negroes cannot assume a respected position in an integrated American society." Perot was eventually appointed assistant to CORE's national chair, Floyd McKissick.

In her interview with Warren, Perot described a 1964 demonstration against the building of a segregated school in Mentor, Ohio. One of the Cleveland chapter's founders, the Reverend Bruce Klunder, was crushed by a bulldozer when he tried to block its movement. She and Warren also discussed rioting in two Cleveland neighborhoods as tensions rose over desegregation. Perot later moved to Washington, DC, and founded or led organizations dedicated to improving health care for communities of color.

In a 2016 conference co-sponsored by the Robert Penn Warren

*Center for the Humanities at Vanderbilt University, Perot recalled
being interviewed by "an elderly white gentleman" who could be "as-
sertive" about his ideas, but she appreciated the opportunity to think
deeply about issues "I didn't have time to think about."*

*In retrospect, Perot says she wishes she had challenged Warren's as-
sertion that some in the African American community were apathetic.
"You can't even use that word to describe people who are oppressed,"
she said, "because as soon as we got the chance we blew up." Perot also
wished she could amend her youthful impatience with Martin Luther
King Jr.'s understanding of race issues in the North. "I would have
taken every word of that back," Perot said. "I know now that I was as
wrong as two left shoes."*

ROBERT PENN WARREN: Tell me about how you came to leave teaching and devote yourself fully to the work of CORE. Was this a long
process or a sudden decision? How did it come about?

RUTH TURNER: Well, I was the chairman of the chapter here
in Cleveland from November 1962 to June 1963. The events in
Birmingham brought about the rather sudden decision. I felt that,
after what occurred there, I could no longer continue teaching German at a time like this. I began looking for ways in which to work
in the civil rights movement on a full-time basis.

RPW: People I've talked to about the Cleveland situation, and
some in Cleveland, are very pessimistic about the immediate future
here. Do you want to talk about the local situation a bit? It seems
highly polarized now.

RT: I think it is very unfortunate. We have a polarized community here by virtue of the fact that a vacuum has been created in
the white community, through apathy. That vacuum has been filled
by people who would rather prevent the civil rights movement
from achieving its goals. The people in leadership positions such as

the president of the board of education, our mayor, would rather scream communism than address themselves to the real grievances that lie behind the protests. They are the ones who have organized around the principle of keeping down the movement and totally misunderstanding the movement. The outlook, then, for the immediate future looks a little bleak. However, the long-range future may be a different story.

RPW: There is considerable white support within a certain segment. Isn't the clergy here [involved]?

RT: Yes, there is considerable white support. The clergy has come out very strongly in favor of the goals of the freedom movement. There is also considerable support in suburban communities. But our major problem is that the white community in Cleveland has seen only one way to express itself, and that is through a misunderstanding of the goals of the movement.

RPW: What is the role of the white liberal in the freedom movement?

RT: Of course, we have quite a bit of discussion about whether the people who are really involved in our movement are liberals. We would call them the "white committed." And we feel that their role, as it has been exhibited in Cleveland, is a very strong, supportive role. There is a definite role for the white committed person—the person who is willing, as the Reverend Bruce Klunder was, to lay down his life for the cause in which he believed. There certainly is a role for that person.

RPW: You were present at that event, weren't you?

RT: Yes, I was. I didn't see it but I was at the scene at the time.

RPW: I understand that you did a great deal to try to quiet the mob after the event—the attack on the driver of the bulldozer?

RT: Yes. That occurred when the construction had stopped and the policemen were attempting to send the mob home. We knew

they were angry. They were justifiably angry. They had been pro-
voked considerably by the actions of the police that day. Yet we felt
there was no cause to be served by exploding there in the community. We attempted to quiet them and to send them home.

RPW: Could you see a situation where this explosive violence,
which you helped to stem, could serve a useful purpose?

RT: The whole purpose of nonviolent demonstration and protest action is to channel the justifiably intense feelings of people
who have gone through, and who lived under, the system. We try
to channel them in ways which will be creative and will bring about
constructive changes.

RPW: I noticed from *Time* magazine that Mr. Lolis Elie in New
Orleans, with whom I had conversations like this, now says if vio-
lence comes this summer, he would take no step to curb it in New
Orleans.

RT: Well, I think there's a point at which the curbing can no longer be done. It is primarily the duty of the law enforcement agencies
to curb violence. This is a heavy responsibility for citizens. I feel
that we should take those steps that we can, but I'm also realistic
enough to know that if wide-scale mob violence breaks out, I would
no longer be in a position to curb it. And I think this violence has
to be seen as an expression of such tremendous discontent, and of
tremendous frustrations that have built up over a long period of
time. And no one person can stop them.

RPW: The other day I was talking with Mr. William Stringfellow.
He's a white man, very much interested in and committed to the
freedom movement. He says, in predicting violence in Harlem this
summer, that the white man's role is to accept it. To put his hands
down and take the brickbat, or the knife, or whatever it is. I asked,
"What about the cops then? What should the cops do in that case?"

RT: Well, unfortunately, the policemen, if they behave in other places like they do here, are also unfortunate tools of a power structure which has failed to understand the dynamics of the protests, and consequently are not understanding anything about the people with whom they deal. That's why police brutality takes place. And, of course, police brutality breeds more violence. Clearly, at some point, the policemen ought to step in to prevent loss of life and limb. But they should not be there to [protect just] one side. An example here is that on Murray Hill, where a mob rioted out of control, a white mob, the police made no attempt whatsoever to curb them. Permitted them to riot. Refused to take horses there because they said it would incite the mob to more violence. And yet, in Lakeview, with a smaller number of people, they did use their horses, they charged the crowd, and did what they said they couldn't do elsewhere.

RPW: How much trouble do you have with Negro apathy?

RT: The apathy toward civil rights is being broken down. The very fact that we had a 92 percent effective school boycott here in Cleveland points up that the Negro community can be brought out of apathy, and is, in fact, less apathetic than the white community.

It's quite understandable to me that, as most of the people here have to worry about where the next meal and where the next rent payment is coming from, they have little time left over to concern themselves with the rights of other men. I think this is a matter of economic deprivation. Some of that we'll not be able to overcome. But at the same time, I'm encouraged by the fact that we can communicate with 92 percent of Negro parents to get them to keep their children out of school. This shows to me that apathy can be broken down. And we're going to do it.

RPW: Is it strange to you, as it is to me, that Memphis, Tennessee, the capital of the Mississippi Delta cotton country, has a very highly organized Negro vote that's very effective as a bargaining tool, and Cleveland does not have it?

RT: I would account for that in the following way: the entire Negro community in Memphis was forced to learn the brutal facts of segregation through civil rights demonstrations long before the entire community of Cleveland was. Cleveland has always been known as a citadel of tokenism. It has always been the place where people thought they were doing all right, and unless you have concrete evidence to the contrary, you'd like to believe that. We have given them concrete evidence to the contrary in the last few months. In the last few months there's been a lot more awareness in the Negro community that police brutality does, in fact, exist. They see it on television. The fact that we now have a movement here in Cleveland—at least the beginnings of it—is going to make a difference in terms of our political organization.

RPW: Was there ever a kind of Negro vote here, which could be delivered to one political party?

RT: Surely, surely. And that's been the pattern in most Northern cities. The Negro was organized politically, all right, but it was organized by the machine, and the machine delivered the votes, and no one ever challenged that. Now we're challenging that. We're asking the community to act as an independent body and to use their vote.

There's another problem here that we have to consider. Even though the machine here is white-dominated, the Negro community was easily fooled by the fact that the Negro still seemed to be in prominence. We had Negro councilmen. We had Negro judges. And, consequently, it looked as though the Negro vote was being delivered for Negro purposes, when in fact it's the same kind of maneuvering that went on in the South, one step removed. I think it's going to require a good deal more organization in the North to break down the pattern than it did in the South, where the racial lines were so much more obvious.

Warren asks Turner to imagine what American society would look like if economic and racial segregation could be eradicated overnight.

RT: If that's possible (laughs), it seems like we could settle back and live happily and normally again. Except we have a problem of attitudes to overcome. Unfortunately, the minds of too many Americans are so narrow that they wouldn't be able to gain that much from living next door to a Negro, or working next to one. And we'd also have to turn our attention to the problem of overcoming the backlog, overcoming the tremendous gap that has existed over these four hundred years. That will have to be done by giving priority, giving special preferential treatment to Negroes, by equipping them to overcome the gap that has existed between the white and Negro community.

RPW: What kind of backlog are we talking about? What kind of difference between the communities are we talking about? Let's push that a little bit.

RT: You still have a problem of people not being prepared to take the jobs that are now open to them because of the fact that they haven't had the proper education or background. So special training programs, crash programs, would have to be initiated.

RPW: You can't separate the race question from the economic context?

RT: The two are very much intertwined. You're saying that you're erasing the conditions, and yet you've still got the problems which come from all these centuries of Negroes not being treated as equals, and consequently considering themselves not equals. You've got all the business of brainwashing, of lack of respect of oneself, to overcome. You've got the problem of a white society, and white standards, and white textbooks, and the fact that the Negro's not been able to see himself as participating in the society.

Warren brings up the argument that the only way to end racism and discrimination is for whites and blacks to become assimilated into one racially mixed group.

RT: I won't buy that. I refuse to accept it. Because it seems to me, then, that we are accepting the American standard of the melting pot. In other words, in order for me to accept you, you've got to be like me. As a country, we have got to reach the point where we can accept individuals as they are and not force them to our own standards. I would reject that theory, totally.

RPW: What do you feel, as a Negro, about the problem of symbolisms in a white culture? White as symbol, and darkness carrying symbolisms of less value, or of evil?

RT: I feel it very strongly. And this is one of those psychological things that has to be overcome after the conditions are erased. White lies are not nearly as bad as black ones. Black sheep and white sheep. It was probably done purposely at some point.

RPW: Purposely? What about those African tribes where you have a dance of good and evil, and the dancer representing good wears white headdress and white robe and the dancer representing evil wears black?

RT: Yeah, but there are also some Asian cultures where white is a sign of mourning, and we don't read about those in our history books, and we don't hear about them and talk about them, as in our society.

RPW: Well, night is the time of terror and day is the time when the terrors of the jungle or the cave disappear. That is not a put-up job by the nasty white man, this symbolism.

RT: That may be but it's been very useful for his purposes, in view of the fact that the white/black symbolism was made so important in slave times. It was made so important that Negroes tried to bleach their skin to get away from it and straighten their hair. And some still do. Clearly it has had an effect. It's no accident, it seems to me, that Christ is always portrayed as a blond, blue-eyed person in white robes. Baptism is always taking place with white [robes]. This is cultural and can't be overcome. But in terms of the effect that it has had on the Negro psychology, it has to be overcome. We have not appreciated the beauty of blackness. A panther is appreciated for his blackness but a Negro woman is not, at least not in white culture.

RPW: It was in the Southern white culture.

RT: Yes, but sub rosa and in a very degrading kind of way. Never openly, and never portrayed in newspapers, and never on television, and never talked about, never advertised in magazines, no. It was never praised in any of the media. Beauty contests never considered blackness as a criterion for beauty. Negro girls were not encouraged to participate, and are still not encouraged to participate in beauty contests because, somehow, being black does not mean that you're a candidate for beauty.

RPW: Let me change the topic a little bit to the question of leadership. In all mass movements or revolutions there is a kind of tendency toward overreaching. Do you see this process, now, going on in the Negro leadership, an overreaching for power or for policy?

RT: In a sense, yes. Someone like Malcolm X, who actually is not really saying anything so very basically different from what we are. I mean, he's adding the dimension of the use of violence if all else fails. The solutions he spells out are attractive solutions. They are solutions to which I respond in moments of real depression.

RPW: This includes the racial separation as part of his policy— you approve?

RT: No, I'm talking about the solution that he spelled out in Cleveland not too long ago, which was the ballot or the bullet, making the point that if the ballot didn't work pretty soon, then the bullet would follow.

RPW: Would the bullet work?

RT: I feel a heavy responsibility to the community. If I organize around the bullet, I'm asking for something that can approach mass extermination. I think that it is courting disaster.

RPW: Most revolutions—all revolutions, I guess—in the past have been directed toward the liquidation of a class or a regime, haven't they?

RT: Yeah, I think that's right.

RPW: If the Negro revolution is a revolution, what's it liquidating?

RT: I think it's liquidating something quite different, and that's why I think this is a quite different kind of revolution. It's liquidating injustices. I don't think those injustices are carried, necessarily, by a particular class of people in this country. Although it is quite true that the wealthy are in control, I don't think the problem is to be solved by liquidating the wealthy, the class of people who are now in the position of power. We're talking here about basic and fundamental changes that have to take place throughout the fabric of our society. That goes beyond class.

RPW: It's sometimes said that hate and hope are the great motivating powers of social change. What about that in relation to the present situation?

RT: Hate and hope? In the particular movement in which I am involved, hate doesn't have much of a function. Hope does, despair

does. You're acting on despair with hope. You're acting on frustration with hope. None of us really have time to hate. It's too all-
consuming. Similarly, we don't have time to love.

RPW: How far do you follow Dr. Martin Luther King's view of
the philosophy of nonviolence?

RT: I'm not a committed pacifist, nor do I adopt nonviolence
as a philosophy of life. I adopt nonviolence presently as a tactical,
necessary philosophy. But I will not take it as an ultimate and an
absolute.

RPW: Do you think Dr. King's influence in the North is now
waning?

RT: I do, because I do not feel he addresses himself to the basic
problems that Northerners, in a sense, are in a better position to
grapple with than Southerners. I don't think he's a politician, nor
does he think like one. You have to, because we're playing in a game
of power, and we have to understand the dimensions and the implications of it.

RPW: What kind of power does a Negro have to negotiate from?
Will you explain that to me, please?

RT: He has a certain amount of political power. I think he
has a great amount of economic power. Power of withdrawal, for
example—withdrawing trade from those [businesses] that don't co-
operate. He has a great moral power because the Negro is the only
group which is raising the real moral questions of our time.

RPW: Then we are back to the element of the struggle in which
Dr. King places emphasis. The moral power is the same as his theory, isn't it?

RT: Yes, except that I'm talking about it in a different kind of
way. I'm not saying that the Negro should be a suffering servant for
the American conscience.

RPW: Does King say that?

RT: I feel that he does. We have to also be aware that the American conscience has become quite deadened by insensitivity and by luxury, in many instances. And we have to be prepared to use other methods to reach the American.

RPW: One more question. The tendency of any mass movement or revolutionary movement is to concentrate leadership finally in one man, one leader. Do you see that going on now? The movement toward a concentration of leadership, a concentration of power?

RT: No, on the contrary, I see a proliferation of power and leadership. I think that is one of the healthiest signs of this movement, that there are people all over the place who're emerging as leaders. And I think as long as that's the case, then we have something very creative and positive here. I would dread to see the day when that power and that leadership are located in one person.

Malcolm X

June 2, 1964

New York, New York

Robert Penn Warren interviewed Malcolm X at a time when the Harlem-based leader had just broken away from the Nation of Islam and started his own black nationalist organization, the Muslim Mosque Incorporated. Malcolm X was more controversial than many civil rights leaders because of his militant opposition to white supremacy. He pledged to use "any means necessary" to achieve freedom, justice, and equal opportunity for African Americans. Malcolm X inspired many people who were tired of the slow pace of social change, or skeptical that nonviolent protest could triumph over entrenched racism.

Malcolm Little was born in 1925 in Omaha, Nebraska. His father was a Baptist preacher and an outspoken follower of the black nationalist leader Marcus Garvey. When the family moved to Michigan, white terrorists burned down the Littles' home. Three years later, Malcolm's father was found dead on a street in Lansing; the family suspected he'd been murdered by white vigilantes. Malcolm's mother, Louise, was committed to a state mental institution when her son was twelve. He and his siblings were scattered among foster families.

Malcolm Little dropped out of school and made his way to New York, where he became a pimp and a petty criminal. He was sent to prison in 1946 for burglary. He read voraciously while behind bars and converted to the Black Muslim faith. He joined the Nation of Islam (NOI) and took on the name Malcolm X, eliminating that part of his identity he called a white-imposed slave name.

In 1952, Malcolm X was released from prison. He rose rapidly in the Nation of Islam, becoming the sect's main spokesman and field recruiter. The NOI's leader, Elijah Muhammad, preached an unorthodox interpretation of Islam mixed with a creed of antiwhite mythology, total racial separation, black economic self-sufficiency, and personal responsibility.

Alex Haley, a writer who collaborated on The Autobiography of Malcolm X, *said the minister's powerful personality was key to his success. "He was just simply electrical," Haley said in a 1988 interview. "Everything he did, almost, was dramatic, and it wasn't that he was trying to be, it was just the nature of him."*

As Malcolm X's national prominence grew, a rift developed between the charismatic young leader and the sixty-six-year-old Elijah Muhammad. The conflict deepened when Muhammad suspended Malcolm X for remarking that President John F. Kennedy's recent assassination represented "the chickens coming home to roost" because whites had created a climate of violence in America. Malcolm X left the Nation of Islam in March 1964.

Malcolm X soon embarked on a life-changing pilgrimage to the Muslim holy city of Mecca, in Saudi Arabia. He was astounded by the racial diversity he saw among Muslims. The trip led him to modify his views on black separatism, and he started calling for a wider, more inclusive movement against white supremacy.

Warren met Malcolm X at the Hotel Theresa in Harlem, the minister's headquarters. According to Malcolm's biographer Manning Marable, it was during a time when Malcolm X was "besieged—by writers, by other activists seeking favors and alliances, and by people who just wanted to have a piece of history." Warren had been warned that the interview would not exceed fifteen minutes, but Malcolm X became so engaged in his conversation with the Southern writer that they talked for more than an hour. Literary scholar Michael Kreyling describes the conversation as a "wrestling match," while Marable describes it as a "mutually revealing conversation." In Marable's view, Malcolm X was "clearly toying" with Warren, "a guilty white liberal" who paid too much attention to Malcolm's "incendiary rhetoric" and not enough to the "social program he was advancing." Indeed, Warren was both fascinated and somewhat unnerved by Malcolm X. He was skeptical of the minister's actual significance to the larger movement and startled by his "sudden, wolfish grin."

According to Warren's daughter, Rosanna, Malcolm X invited her father back to walk the streets of Harlem with him and see how the Muslim Mosque's organization worked. The return visit never happened. Malcolm X was assassinated on February 21, 1965, by members of the Nation of Islam.

Since his death, Malcolm X has become an icon of the black freedom struggle. President Barack Obama had a bust of Martin Luther King Jr. in the Oval Office, but he credits Malcolm X for asserting in a profound way the fundamental worth of black lives. The writer Ta-Nehisi Coates says Malcolm X's moral leadership continues to assert "the right of a people to protect and improve themselves by their own hand."

ROBERT PENN WARREN: From what I have read, which includes books I could find and a good many articles on the Black Muslim position and on yourself, it seems that the identity of the Negro is the key fact that you deal with. Is that true? Is that impression correct?

MALCOLM X: Yes. Not so much in the sense of the Black Muslim religion. Both of them have to be separated. The best religion is the religion of Islam. When one accepts the religion of Islam, he's known as a Muslim. He becomes a Muslim. That means he believes that there's no God but Allah and that Muhammad is the apostle of Allah. Now, the main problem that [the] Afro-American [has] is a lack of cultural identity. It is necessary to teach him that he had some type of identity, culture, civilization before he was brought here. Well, now, teaching him about his historic or cultural past is not his religion. This is not religious. The two have to be separated.

RPW: Yes. Or what about the matter of personal identity, as related to cultural and blood identity?

MX: I don't quite understand what you mean.

RPW: I'm trying to get at this: that a man may know that he belongs to, say, a group—this group or that group—but he feels himself lost within that group, trapped within his own deficiencies and without personal purpose. Lacking personal identity, you see.

MX: Yes. Well, the religion of Islam actually restores one's human feelings, human rights, human incentives, human talent. The religion of Islam brings out of the individual all of his dormant potential. It gives him the incentive to develop his dormant potential so that when he becomes a part of the brotherhood of Islam, and is identified collectively in the brotherhood of Islam, with the brothers in Islam, this also has the psychological effect of giving him the incentive as an individual to develop all of his dormant potential to its fullest extent.

RPW: A personal regeneration then . . .

MX: Yes.

RPW: Is associated automatically with this?

MX: Oh, yes. Yes.

RPW: Sometimes, in talking with Negroes in other organizations and other persuasions, I've found out that there's a deep suspicion of any approach which involves the old phrase "self-improvement."

[They prefer] to state the matter on objective, impersonal matters such as civil rights, integration, or job programs, and not on the question of self-improvement, or you might say individual responsibility. But you take a different line.

MX: Definitely. Most of the—or I should say many—of the Negro leaders actually suffer themselves from an inferiority complex, even though they say they don't. And because of this they have subconscious, defensive mechanisms which they've erected without even realizing it. So when you mention something about self-improvement, the implication is that the Negro is something distinct or different and, therefore, needs to learn how to improve himself. Negro leaders resent this being said, not because they don't know that it's true, but they're looking at it personally. They think that the implication is directed at them. And they duck this responsibility. Whereas, the only real solution to the race problem in this country is a solution that involves individual self-improvement and collective self-improvement wherein our own people are concerned.

RPW: Could you tell me, or would you be willing to, or do you think it's relevant, some detail of your own conversion to Islam?

MX: Well, I was in prison.

RPW: I know that fact, yes. I'm asking about the interior feeling of the process.

MX: I was in prison and I was an atheist. I didn't believe in anything. And I had begun to read books and things. In fact, one of the persons who started me thinking seriously was an atheist, another Negro inmate whom I'd heard in a discussion with white inmates, and who was able to hold his own at all levels. And he impressed me with his knowledge. I began to listen very carefully to some of the things he said. He switched my reading habits away from fiction to nonfiction, so that by the time one of my brothers told me about Islam, although I was an atheist, I was open-minded. And I began to read in that direction, in the direction of Islam. Everything that I read about it appealed to me. One of the main things that I read about it that appealed to me was, in Islam, a man is regarded as a human being. He's not measured by the color of his skin. At this point, I hadn't yet gotten deep into the historic condition that Negroes in this country are confronted with. But, at that point in my prison studies, I studied Islam as a religion, more so than as I later came to know it in its connection with the plight or problem of Negroes in this country.

RPW: This is getting ahead a little bit but it seems to apply here. If Islam teaches the human worth of all men without reference to color, how does that fact relate to the message of black superiority and the doom of the white race?

MX: The white race is doomed not because it's white but because of its deeds. The people listening very closely to what the Muslims have always declared, they'll find that, in every declaration, there's the fact that, the same as Moses told Pharaoh: "You're doomed if you don't do so-and-so." Or as Daniel told, I think it was Balthasar or Nebuchadnezzar: "You are doomed if you don't do so-and-so." Now, always that "if" was there. Which meant that the one who was doomed could avoid the doom if he would change his way of behaving. Well, it's the same here in America. When the Muslims deliver the indictment of the American system, it is not the white man per se that is being doomed.

RPW: It's not blood itself that's being—there's no blood damnation then?

MX: No. But, see, it's almost impossible to separate the actions, or to separate the oppression and exploitation—criminal oppression and criminal exploitation of the American Negro—from the color of the skin of the person who is the oppressor or the exploiter. So he thinks he's being condemned because of his color, but actually he's being condemned because of his deeds, his conscious behavior.

RPW: Let's take the question like this: Can a person, an American of white blood, be guiltless?

MX: Guiltless?

RPW: Yes.

MX: You can only answer it by turning it around. Can the Negro, who is the victim of the system, escape the collective stigma that is placed upon all Negroes in this country? And the answer is no. Because Ralph Bunche, who is an internationally recognized and respected diplomat, can't stay in a hotel in Georgia. Which means that, no matter what the accomplishment, the intellectual, the academic, or professional level of a Negro is, collectively he stands condemned. Well, the white race in America is the same way. As individuals, it is impossible for them to escape the collective crime committed against the Negroes in this country, collectively.

RPW: Let's take an extreme case like this, just the most extreme example I can think of. Let us say a white child of three or four, who is outside of conscious decisions or valuations, is facing accidental death. Is the reaction to that child the same as the reaction to a Negro child facing the same situation?

MX: The white child, although as a person has not committed any of the deeds that have produced the plight that the Negro finds himself in—is he guiltless? The only way you can determine that is, take the Negro child who's only four years old. Can he escape—though he's only four years old—can he escape the stigma of discrimination and segregation? He's only four years old.

RPW: Let's put him in front of the oncoming truck and put a white man on the pavement who must risk his life to leap for the child. Let's reverse it.

MX: I don't see where that . . .

RPW: Some white men would leap; some wouldn't leap.

MX: It still wouldn't alter the fact that, after that white man saved that little black child, he couldn't take that little black child in many restaurants, hotels, right along with him. Even after the life of the black child was saved, that same white man will have to toss him right back into discrimination [and] segregation.

RPW: Suppose that white man is prepared to go to jail to break segregation? Just keep it on the individual, this one white man.

MX: You can't solve it individually.

RPW: But what you're having toward the one white man who goes to jail, say, not once but over and over again, say, in . . .

MX: This has been going on for the past ten years. White individuals have been going to jail. Segregation still exists. Discrimination still exists.

RPW: Yes, that's true. But what is the attitude toward the white man who does this, who goes to jail?

MX: My personal attitude is that he has done nothing to solve the problem.

RPW: What's your attitude toward his moral nature?

MX: Not even interested in his moral nature. Until the problem is solved, we're not interested in anybody's moral nature. But what I'm boiling down to say is that a few isolated white people, whose individual acts are designed to eliminate this, that, or the next thing—but, yet, it is never eliminated—is in no way impressive to me.

RPW: That is, you couldn't call that man a friend?

MX: If his own rights were being trampled upon as the rights of Negroes are being trampled upon, he would use a different course of action to protect his rights.

RPW: What course of action?

MX: (Laughs) I have never seen white people who would sit, who would approach a solution to their own problems, nonviolently or passively. It's only when they are so-called "fighting for the rights of Negroes" that they nonviolently, passively, and lovingly approach the situation. But when the whites themselves are attacked, they believe in defending themselves. Those types of whites who are always going to jail with Negroes are the ones who tell Negroes to be loving, and be kind, and be patient, and be nonviolent, and turn the other cheek. So if I did see a white man who was willing to go to jail, or throw himself in front of a car on behalf of the so-called Negro cause, the test that I'd put to him, I'd ask him: "Do you think when Negroes are being attacked they should defend themselves, even at the risk of having to kill the one who's attacking them?" If that white man told me, "Yes," I'd shake his hand. I'd trust in him. But I don't trust any white man who teaches Negroes to turn the other cheek, or to be nonviolent, which means to be defenseless, in the face of a very brutal, criminal enemy. No. That's my yardstick for measuring whites.

RPW: What is defenseless at this point?

MX: Any time you tell a man to turn the other cheek or to be nonviolent in the face of a violent enemy, you're making that man defenseless. You're robbing him of his God-given right to defend himself.

RPW: Let's take a concrete case on the question of defenselessness, just to be sure I understand you. In the case of Dr. Aaron Henry of Clarksdale, Mississippi, his house has been bombed and has been shot through and that sort of thing. Well, he is armed.

I've been in his house. I know he's armed. His guards are sitting there with [guns] in their hands at night. And everybody knows this. Now, I can't see how anyone would ask him not to defend himself. If defense is literally defense, as it's taken in ordinary legal times. A mounted aggression for purposes of defense is another thing in society, you see what I'm getting at? A man sitting in his own house . . .

MX: I think that the Negro should reserve the right to execute (knocks on table) any measure necessary to defend himself. He should reserve the right to do that, just the same as others have the right to do it.

RPW: Political assassination, for instance?

MX: I don't know anything about that. I wouldn't even answer a question like that. But I say that the Negro, when they cease to look at him as a Negro and realize that he's a human being, then they will realize that he is just as capable, and he has the right to do anything that any other human being on this earth has a right to do to defend himself.

RPW: There are millions of white people who would say, right away, that any Negro should have the same legal rights to defense that a white man has.

MX: And I think you'll find, also, that if the Negro ever realizes that he should begin to fight—for real—for his freedom, there are many whites who will fight on his side with him. It's not a case where people think he'll be the underdog or be outnumbered. But there are many white people in this country who realize that the system itself, as it is constructed, [cannot] produce freedom and equality for the Negro. The system has to be changed. It is the system, itself, that is incapable of producing freedom for the twenty-two million Afro-Americans. Just like a chicken can't lay a duck egg. A chicken can't lay a duck egg because the system of the chicken isn't constructed to produce a duck egg. And just as that chicken system is not capable of producing a duck egg, the political and economic system of this country is absolutely incapable of producing freedom, and justice, and equality, and human dignity for the 22 million Afro-Americans.

RPW: You don't see in the American system the possibility of self-regeneration, then? You don't see any possibility of gains or better solutions through Negro political action, or economic action?

MX: Well, any time the Negro becomes involved in mature political action, then the resistance of the politicians who benefit from the exploitative political system as it now stands will come—will be forced—to exercise more violent action to deprive the Negro of his mature political action.

In my opinion, mature political action involves a program of reeducation and information that will enable black people, in the black community, to see the fruits that they should be receiving from the politicians who are over them and, thereby, they are able to determine whether or not the politician is really fulfilling his function. And if he is not fulfilling his function, they then can set up the machinery to remove him from that position by whatever means necessary. To me, political action involves making the politician who represents us know that he either produces or he is out, and he's out one way or another.

RPW: There's only one way to put a politician out ordinarily, it's to vote him out.

MX: I think that the black people in this country have reached the point where they should reserve the right to do whatever is necessary to see that they exercise complete control over the politicians [and] the politics of their own community, by whatever means necessary.

RPW: Let's go back to the matter of your conversion, or some of the details of that. Was it fast or slow?

MX: It was fast. Strange as it may seem, I took an about-turn overnight.

RPW: Really? Overnight, just like that?

MX: Yes. And while I was in prison and wasn't a Muslim, I was indulging in all types of vice, right within the prison. And I never was ostracized as much by the penal authorities while I was participating in all of the evils of the prison, as they tried to ostracize me after I became a Muslim.

RPW: Why was that?

MX: The prison systems in this country actually are exploitive and they are not in any way rehabilitative. They're not designed to rehabilitate the inmate, though the public propaganda is that this is their function. But most people who work in prison earn money through contraband. They earn extra money by selling contraband, dope, and things of that sort to the inmates, and so that really it's an exploiter.

RPW: This was a matter of defending their commercial interests, their economic interests, and not a matter of fear of the Muslim movement, is that it?

MX: It's both. They have a fear of the Muslim movement and the Muslim religion because it has a tendency to make the people who accept it stick together. And I had one warden tell me, since I've been out, and I visited an inmate in prison right here in New York, Warden Fay up at Green Haven told me that he didn't want anybody in there trying to spread this religion. And I asked him if it didn't make a better inmate out of the Negroes who accepted it. He said, "Yes." So I asked him what was it about it that he considered to be so dangerous. And he pointed out that it was the cohesiveness that it produced among the inmates. They stuck together. What you did to one, you did to all. So they couldn't have that type of religion being taught in the prison.

RPW: Just a matter of maintaining their own control then?

MX: Yes.

RPW: Has there been any change in your religious beliefs since your break last fall with [Nation of Islam leader Elijah Muhammad]?

MX: I have gone through the process of reevaluating, giving a personal reevaluation to everything that I ever believed and that I did believe while I was a member and a minister in what we call the Black Muslim movement.

RPW: May I ask how you've come out of that evaluation?

MX: First, I might say that when a man separates from his wife, at the out-start it's a physical separation but it's not a psychological separation. He still thinks of her, probably, in warm terms. But after the physical separation has existed for a period of time, it becomes a psychological separation, as well as physical. And he can then look at her more objectively. My split, or separation, from the Black Muslim movement at first was only a physical separation; my heart was still there and it was impossible for me to look at it objectively. After I made my tour in the Middle East and Africa, and visited Mecca and other places, I think that the separation became psychological as well as physical. I could look at it more objectively, and separate that which was good from that which was bad.

RPW: What did you find, if I may ask, good and what's bad in this reevaluation?

MX: Now it's possible for me to approach the whole problem with a broader scope, a much broader scope. When you look at something through an organizational eye, whether it's a religious organization, political organization, or a civic organization, you see what the organization wants you to see. But you lose your ability to be objective. But when you aren't affiliated with anything, and then you look at something, you look at it with the best of your ability and see it as it is.

RPW: For example, what specific thing do you now see as is and not through organizational eyes?

MX: I can look at the problem of the 22 million Afro-Americans as being a problem that's so broad in scope that it's almost impossible for any organization to see it in its entirety. And because the average Negro organization, especially, can't see the problem in its entirety. They can't even see that the problem is so big that their own organization, by itself, can never come up with a solution. The problem is so broad that it's going to take the inner working of all organizations. It's going to take a united front of all organizations, looking at it with more objectivity, to come up with a solution that will stand against the whites.

RPW: Would you work, then, with the Southern Christian Leadership Conference, Dr. King's organization?

MX: Even as a Muslim minister, in the Muslim movement, I have always said that I would work with any organization. But I can say it with more honesty now. Then, when I said it, I would make the reservation that I would work with any organization as long as it didn't make us compromise our religious principles. Now, I think that the problem of the American Negro goes beyond the principle of any organization, whether it's religious, political, or otherwise. The problem of the Negro is so criminal that many individuals and organizations are going to have to sacrifice what they call their organizational principles if someone comes up with a solution that will really solve the problem. If it's a solution they want, they should accept the solution. But if it's a solution they want—as long as it doesn't interfere with their organization—then it means they're more concerned with their organization than they are with getting a solution to the problem.

RPW: I'm trying to see how it would be possible to work with Dr. King's philosophy of nonviolence, you see.

MX: See, now, nonviolence with Dr. King is only a method. That's not his objective. His objective, I think, is to gain respect for Negroes as human beings. And nonviolence is his method. Well, my objective is the same as King's. Now, we may disagree on methods, but we don't have to argue all day on methods. Forget the methods or the differences in methods, as long as we agree that the thing that the Afro-American wants and needs is recognition and respect as a human being.

RPW: Have you changed your view about separatism, political separatism, the actual formation of an independent state of some kind?

MX: The solution for the Afro-American is twofold, long-range and short-range. I believe that a psychological, cultural, and philosophical migration back to Africa will solve our problem. Not a physical migration, but a cultural, psychological, philosophical migration back to Africa. Restoring our common bond will give us the spiritual strength and the incentive to strengthen our political and social and economic position right here in America, and to fight for the things that are ours by right, here on this continent. And at the same time, this will also tend to give incentive to many of our people then to want to also visit, and even migrate, physically, back to Africa. Those who stay here can help those who go back, and those who go back can help those who stay here, in the same way that when Jews go to Israel, the Jews in America help those in Israel and the Jews in Israel help those in America.

RPW: Is that the long-range, the second thing is your long-range solution, is that it?

MX: The short-range involves the long-range. Immediate steps have to be taken to reeducate our people into a more real view of political, economic, and social conditions in this country. And in our ability, in a self-improvement program, to gain control politically over every community in which we predominate. And also over the economy of that same community, as here in Harlem. Instead of all the stores in Harlem being owned by white people, they should be owned and operated by black people. The same as in a German neighborhood, the stores are run by Germans; in a Chinese neighborhood, they're run by Chinese. In the Negro neighborhood, the businesses should be owned and operated by Negroes and, thereby, they would be creating employment for Negroes.

RPW: You are thinking then of these localities as being operated by Negroes, not in terms of a political state, a separate nation?

MX: No. The separating of a section of America for Afro-Americans is similar to expecting a heaven in the sky somewhere after you die.

RPW: It's not practical then?

MX: To say it is not practical, one has to also admit that integration is not practical.

RPW: I don't quite follow that.

MX: The idea of a separate state is not practical. I'm also stating that the idea of integration, forced integration, as they've been making an effort to do in this country for the past ten years, is also just as impractical.

RPW: You can envisage Negro sections or Negro communities, which are self-determining, as a better solution?

MX: Until a reeducation program is devised to bring our people to the intellectual, economic, political, and social level wherein we can control, own, and operate our own communities economically, politically, socially, and otherwise—why, any solution that doesn't involve that is not even a solution. Because if I can't run my neighborhood, you won't want me in your neighborhood.

RPW: You are saying, in other words, you see neighborhoods and communities that are all Afro-American, and self-determining, but these are parts of a larger political unity, like the United States?

MX: Because once the black man becomes the political master of his own community, it means that the politicians of that community will also be black. Which also means that he then will be sending black representatives, not only to represent him at the local level and at the state level, but even at the federal level. See, all throughout the South in areas where the black man predominates, he would have black representatives in Washington, DC. Well, my contention is that the political system of this country is so designed, criminally, to prevent this, that if the black man even started in that direction—which is a mature step, and is the only way to really solve this problem and to prove that he is the intellectual equal of others—why, the racists and the segregationists would fight that harder than they're fighting the present efforts to integrate.

RPW: They'll fight it, yes. Let me ask you two questions around this. One, there are Negroes now holding a prominent place at the federal level.

MX: They've been put there . . .

RPW: Like Dr. [Robert Clifton] Weaver and . . .

MX: I don't mean . . .

RPW: Mr. [Carl] Rowan, and people like that.

MX: I don't mean those kinds of Negroes, who are placed in big jobs as window dressing. I refer to a Negro politician as a Negro who is selected by Negroes, who is backed by Negroes. Most of those Negroes have been given those jobs by the white political machine, and they serve no other function other than as window dressing.

RPW: Ralph Bunche, too?

MX: Any Negro who occupies a position that was given to him by the white man. If you analyze his function, it never enables him to really take a firm, uncompromising, militant stand on problems that confront our people. He opens up his mouth only to the degree that the political atmosphere at the time will allow him to do so without rocking the boat too much.

RPW: Is your organization supporting the voter registration drive in Mississippi this summer?

MX: Yes, we're going to give active support to voter registration drives, not only in Mississippi, but in New York City. I just can't see where Mississippi is that much different from New York City. Maybe in method or . . .

RPW: I don't either.

MX: No, I don't see, I never will let anyone maneuver me into making a distinction between the Mississippi form of discrimination and the New York City form of discrimination. It's all discrimination.

RPW: Are you actually putting workers in Mississippi this summer?

MX: We will. They won't be nonviolent workers.

RPW: Nonviolent in which sense? Upon attack or . . .

MX: We will never send a Negro anywhere and tell him to be nonviolent.

RPW: If he is shot at, shoot back?

MX: If he's shot at, shoot back.

RPW: What about the matter of nonselective reprisals? Say, if a

Negro is shot in Mississippi, like Medgar Evers, for instance, then [what about] shooting a white man, or trying to shoot a responsible white man?

MX: I'll tell you. If I go home and my child has blood running down her leg and someone tells me that a snake bit her, I'm going out and kill the snake. And when I find the snake, I'm not going to look and see if he has blood on his jaws.

RPW: You mean you'll kill any snake you find?

MX: I grew up in the country, on a farm.

RPW: So did I.

MX: And whenever someone said that a snake was eating the chickens, or bothering the chickens, we'd kill snakes. We never knew whether that was the snake that did it.

RPW: To read your parallel then, you would advocate nonselective reprisal; kill any white person around.

MX: I'm not saying that. I'm just telling you about snakes.

RPW: Yeah, okay (laughs). All right. We'll settle for that.

MX: Well, I mean what I say.

RPW: Mm-hmm. I know what you say. I know how the parables work. Let us suppose that we had—just suppose . . .

MX: Then, perhaps, you know the other: when the snakes out in that field begin to realize that if one of their members gets out of line, it's going to be detrimental to all of them, they'll take the necessary steps to keep their fellow snakes away from my chickens, or away from my children, if the responsibility is placed upon them.

RPW: Suppose we had—maybe it's a big supposition— but suppose we had adequate civil rights legislation and fair employment . . .

MX: I might even answer that, if I may. I believe when a Negro church is bombed, that a white church should be bombed.

RPW: Reprisal.

MX: I believe it, yes. I can give you the best example. When the Japanese bombed Pearl Harbor, the United States struck back. She dropped the bomb on Hiroshima. Those people in Hiroshima probably hadn't even—some of them, most of them—hadn't even killed anybody. But still she dropped that bomb. I think it killed eighty-some-thousand people. Well, this is internationally recognized as justifiable during war. Any time a Negro community (knocks on table) lives under fear that its churches are going to be bombed, then they have to realize they're living in a war zone. And once they recognize it as such, they can adopt the same measures against the community that harbors the criminals who are responsible for this activity.

RPW: It's a question of a Negro, say in Birmingham, being outside of the community, being no part of the community, so he takes the same kind of reprisal he would take in wartime?

MX: He should realize that he is living in a war zone and he is at war with an enemy that is as vicious, and criminal, and inhuman as any war-making country has ever been. And once he realizes that, then he can defend himself.

RPW: Suppose you had an adequate civil rights legislation enforced, suppose you had a fair employment practice code enforced. Suppose we had the objectives demanded by most civil rights organizations now actually existing, then what?

MX: (Laughs) Suppose.

RPW: Just suppose.

MX: (Laughs) You'd have civil war. You'd have a race war in this country. See, you can't force people to act right toward each other. You cannot legislate attitudes. And when you have to pass a law to make a man let me have a house, or you have to pass a law to make a man let me go to school, or you have to pass a law to make a man let me walk down the street, you have to enforce that law, and you'd have to be living, actually, in a police state. It would take a police state in this country, I mean a real police state, right now, just to get a token recognition of a law. It took, I think, fifteen thousand troops and six million dollars to put one Negro in the University of Mississippi. That's a police-state action. All of the civil rights problems during the past ten years have created a situation where America, right now, is moving toward a police state. You can't have anything otherwise. So that's your supposition.

RPW: All right. Then you see no possibility of a self-regeneration for our society then?

MX: When I was in Mecca, I noticed they had no color problem. They had people there whose eyes were blue and people there whose eyes were black, people whose skin was white, people whose skin was black, people whose hair was blond, people whose hair was black, from the whitest white person to the blackest black person. There was no racism; there was no problem. But the religious philosophy that they had adopted, in my opinion, was the only thing, and is the only thing, that can remove the white from the mind of the white man and the Negro from the mind of the Negro. I have seen what Islam has done with our people. Our people who had this feeling of [being a] Negro, and it had a psychological effect of putting them in a mental prison. When they accepted Islam, it removed that. Well, white people whom I have met, who have accepted Islam, they don't regard themselves as white, but as human beings. And by looking upon themselves as human beings, their whiteness to them isn't the yardstick of perfection or honor or anything else. And, therefore, this creates within them an attitude that is different from the attitude of the white that you meet here in America. It was in Mecca that I realized that white is actually an attitude more so than it's a color. And I can prove it because, among Negroes, we have Negroes who are as white as some white people. Still there's a difference.

RPW: I was about to ask you about, what is a Negro?

MX: Yeah, it's an attitude. I'll tell you what it is. And white is an attitude. And it is the attitude of the American white man that is making him stand condemned today before the eyes of the entire dark world, and even before the eyes of the Europeans. It is his attitude, his haughty, holier-than-thou attitude. He has the audacity to call himself even the "leader of the free world," while he has a country that can't even give the basic human rights to over 22 million of its citizens. This takes audacity. This takes nerve. So it is this attitude, today, that's causing the Americans to be condemned.

RPW: You know the book by [Professor E.U.] Essien-Udom called *Black Nationalism*? I know you must.

MX: I was with Essien-Udom in Nigeria last month.

RPW: I wish you'd tell me about him. Who is he?

MX: Well, he's a Nigerian. At present he's a professor at Ibadan University.

RPW: Ah! I didn't know where he was. I knew he was a scholar.

MX: Yes.

RPW: Do you agree with his analysis that the Black Muslim religion, Islam in America, has served as a concealed device to gratify the American Negro's aspirations to white, middle-class values?

MX: I don't think that the objective of the American Negro is white middle-class values because what are white middle-class values? And what makes the whites who have these middle-class values have those values? Where did they get it? They didn't have these same values four hundred or five hundred years ago. Where did they get their value system that they now have attained? My contention is that if you trace it back, it was the people of the East who brought them out of the Dark Ages, who brought about the period, or ushered in, or initiated the atmosphere that brought into Europe the period known as the Renaissance or the reawakening of Europe. And this reawakening, actually, involved an era during which the people of Europe, who were coming out of the Dark Ages, were then adopting the value system of the people in the East. Many of which they were exposed to for the first time during the Crusades.

Well, these were African-Arab-Asian values. The only people of Europe that had a high value system during the Dark Ages were those on the Iberian Peninsula, in the Spanish-Portuguese area, southern France. And that high state of a culture existed there because Africans, known as Moors, had come there and brought it there. So that value system has been handed right down in European society. And today, when you find Negroes, if they even look like they're adopting these so-called middle-class values, standards, it's not that they are taking something from the white man, but they are probably identifying again with the level or standard that these same whites have gotten from them back during that period.

RPW: You know, there's a theory that's sometimes enunciated by people like Reverend Wyatt Walker, or Whitney Young, that the Black Muslim is primarily created by the white press. He exists, but his importance was created by the white press.

MX: Wyatt doesn't say that as much as Whitney Young does.

RPW: Both of them say it; both of them said it to me, anyway.

MX: Well.

RPW: "A paper tiger" is what Wyatt Walker calls it.

MX: Yeah. Well, I can answer them like this. Wyatt Walker can walk through Harlem, no one would know him. Whitney Young

could walk through Harlem, no one would know him. Any of the
Black Muslims can walk through Harlem, and there's people who
know them. I don't think that anyone has been created more by
the white press than the civil rights leaders. The white press itself
created them. And they, themselves, in their pronouncements will
tell you they need white allies, they need white help. They are more
dependent on the white community than any other group in the
community.

RPW: Almost word for word, what you have said, I could turn
around as Wyatt Walker said to me about, not you personally, but
about the whole Black Muslim movement. That if you go outside
of New York City, Dr. King is known to 90 percent of the Negroes
in the United States and is respected as a hero of one kind or another. That the Black Muslims, outside of one or two communities
like New York, are unknown.

MX: If that's their opinion, that's their opinion. I myself have
never been concerned with whether we are considered known or
unknown. It's no problem of mine. I will say this: that anytime
there's a fire in a Negro community and it's burning out of control,
you send any one of them, send Whitney Young in to put it out
(laughs).

RPW: What do you think of Abraham Lincoln?

MX: I think that he probably did more to trick Negroes than any
other man in history.

RPW: Can you explain that?

MX: I have read where he said he wasn't interested in freeing the
slaves. He was interested in saving the Union. Well, most Negroes
have been tricked into thinking that Lincoln was a Negro-lover
whose primary aim was to free them, and he died because he freed
them. I think Lincoln did more to deceive Negroes and to make the
race problem in this country worse than any man in history.

RPW: How does [John F.] Kennedy relate to . . .

MX: Kennedy, I relate right along with Lincoln. Kennedy was a deceitful man. He was a cold-blooded politician whose purpose was to get elected. And the only time Kennedy took any action to even look like he identified with Negroes was when he was forced to. Kennedy didn't even make his speech based on this problem being a moral issue until Negroes exploded in Birmingham. During the whole month that Negroes were being beaten by police and washed down the sewer with water hoses, and King was in jail begging for the federal government to intervene, Kennedy's reply was, "No federal statutes have been violated." And it was only when the Negroes erupted that Kennedy came on the television with all his old pretty words. No, the man was a deceiver. He was deceitful and I will never bite my tongue in saying that. I don't think he was anything but a politician, and he used Negroes to get elected and to get votes.

RPW: What about [Franklin D.] Roosevelt?

MX: Same thing. No president ever had more power than Roosevelt. Roosevelt could have solved many problems, and all he did was put [Negroes] onto welfare, WPA, and other projects that he had. If it hadn't been for Hitler going on the rampage, Negroes would still be on the welfare.

RPW: What about Eleanor Roosevelt?

MX: Same thing. Eleanor Roosevelt was the chairman of the United Nations Human Rights Commission, I think it was, at a time when the Covenant on Human Rights was formed. This country didn't even sign it. They signed the Declaration of Human Rights. But if they had signed the covenant, they would have to get it ratified by the Congress and the Senate, and they could never get the Congress and the Senate to agree to an international law on human rights when they couldn't even get Congress or the Senate to agree on a civil rights law. So Eleanor Roosevelt could easily have told Negroes the deceitful maneuvering of the United States government that was going on behind the scenes. She never did it. In my opinion she was just another white woman whose profession was to make it appear that she was on the Negro's side. You have a lot of whites who are in this category. Therefore, they have made Negro-loving a profession. They are what I call professional liberals, who take advantage of the confidence that Negroes place in them and, therefore, this enhances their own prestige, and it gives them key roles to play in the politics of this country.

RPW: What about James Baldwin?

MX: Jimmy Baldwin. He's a Negro writer who has gained fame because of his indictment, and his very acid description of what's going on in this country. I don't agree with his nonviolent, peaceful, loving approach. I just saw his play, *Blues for Mister Charlie*, which I thought was an excellent play until it ended. The ending of it has the Negro, again, forgetting that a lynching has just taken place.

RPW: You know Ralph Ellison's work?

MX: Not too well. All I know is that he wrote *The Invisible Man*.

RPW: Yes, have you read that?

MX: No, but I got the point. Usually when a man is invisible he knows more about those who are visible than those who are visible know about him. And my contention is that the Negro knows more about the white man and white society than the white man knows about the Negro and Negro society.

RPW: I think that's true.

MX: The servant always knows his master better than the master knows his servant. The servant watches the master sleep, but the master never sees the servant sleep. The servant sees the master angry. The master never sees the servant angry. So the servant always knows the master better than the master knows the servant. In fact, the servant knows the house better than the master does. And my contention is that the Negro knows this country better than the white man does, every facet of it, and when he wakes up he'll prove it.

Bayard Rustin

Summer or fall, 1964

New York, New York

Bayard Rustin has been described as the "invisible man" of the civil rights movement. He was an influential adviser to a number of leading African American activists. He was a master strategist and tactician. He was the key organizer of the historic 1963 March on Washington. And it was Rustin, as much as anyone, who introduced Gandhi's principles of nonviolent political action to the movement. But this colorful and controversial man is often lost in the shadows of civil rights memory.

Some writers and historians say Rustin was content with his behind-the-scenes status as an organizer and movement intellectual. Others contend he stayed true to a broad social agenda that benefited all marginalized people at a time when the black civil rights establishment was growing more politically narrow and parochial. Many note that Rustin's open homosexuality made him an object of suspicion to some leaders of the movement, especially socially conservative black ministers in the South.

Bayard Rustin was born in 1912 in a suburb of Philadelphia. He was raised by his grandparents, both Quakers who helped found a local chapter of the NAACP. He attended Wilberforce University in Ohio and Cheney State Teachers College in Pennsylvania, historically black colleges. Rustin moved to New York City in 1937 to attend City

University. He immersed himself in Harlem's rich African American culture and in the city's gay community. Tall, handsome, and athletic, Rustin was an accomplished singer who performed with notable musicians such as Josh White and Paul Robeson.

As a pacifist, Rustin refused to serve in World War II and spent more than two years in federal prison. After his release, Rustin got a job on the field staff of the Fellowship of Reconciliation (FOR), a Christian pacifist group. Rustin studied Gandhi and visited India. Upon his return he roamed the United States, lending his formidable strategic and organizational skills to civil rights groups. Along the way, Rustin's refusal to back down in the face of Jim Crow discrimination landed him in jail time after time.

In the 1950s, Rustin began a long period working for a small pacifist group called the War Resisters League. In 1956, he became a mentor to a young activist preacher in Montgomery, Alabama, named Martin Luther King Jr. Rustin was principally responsible for helping King create the Southern Christian Leadership Conference. He played a key role in shaping the nonviolent civil rights philosophy that King would make famous.

In 1963, the legendary civil rights leader A. Philip Randolph—long Rustin's mentor and supporter—tapped him to organize a massive protest in the nation's capital. The March on Washington in August of that year drew some 250,000 people and was capped by King's "I Have a Dream" speech. Rustin's event became a landmark in American history.

Robert Penn Warren interviewed Rustin in the New York City offices of the War Resisters League. Warren opens the conversation by noting that Rustin was dedicated to overall social reform, not just racial equality.

ROBERT PENN WARREN: I'm just going to plunge in. It's very commonly said that you are almost rare in that your involvement in the civil rights movement has been primarily in terms of [class and economics], rather than in terms of race. You have that special kind of intersection of these two concerns.

BAYARD RUSTIN: Well, I think that's true. As you probably know, I was at one time a member of the Young Communist League. I became a member, fundamentally, because at that time it was my feeling, even if mistaken later, that it was only the Communists who were sincerely concerned—this was at the time of the Scottsboro case and this kind of thing—and I felt that others were not militant enough. This also came from the fact that I had, for some time, felt that certain problems which the American Negro faced could not be solved as race problems, but that many aspects of our society would need to change prior to the Negro's gain of certain status. Therefore, when I left the Communist Party, I went to work for the Fellowship of Reconciliation, which had with it the Reverend A.J. Muste, who for many years had been a social reformer. After that I then went into the socialist movement.

RPW: What date was it, the year of your going into the Fellowship of Reconciliation?

BR: 1941. The Communist Party violated what were, to me, two sacred trusts. One was peace—I'm a Quaker—and that an imperialist war became, overnight, a people's war [to the Communists]. Plus, the fact that they then called me in and told me not to work against discrimination in the armed forces any longer. This brought me to my senses. I saw that these people were not truly interested in justice wherever it existed, but in justice if it was in keeping with the foreign policy of the Soviet Union.

The emergence of intense industrialization—bringing more and more Negroes into our large cities, the movement of the white middle classes out of our cities, the emergence of automation, and other aspects of the technological revolution—has all the more

convinced me that when Negroes are ill-prepared to do many types
of work it is essential to have certain basic forms of social change
in our economic and social institutions—if it is possible to accommodate not only the Negro, with whom I am concerned, but the
poor white. [Otherwise] Negroes and whites will be fighting each
other in the streets for a few jobs, which do not, in fact, exist for
the underprivileged. Therefore, it is imperative that we, Negroes
and whites, build in this country a new political movement. I do
not mean a political party, but the kind of political movement
which got the civil rights legislation through Congress. This was a
movement made up of civil rights groups, other minority peoples,
and the best elements in the trade union movement. The churches
played a magnificent role—Catholic, Protestant, and Jewish—as
did the intellectual students. There was a great consensus of all the
best elements in our society, which broke the back of the filibus-
ter and got legislation through Congress, the first important social
legislation since 1938. Now, I would like to see that same kind of
coalition of forces backing a number of things, which mean quite
fundamental change.

RPW: You would see it in terms of existing political parties, is
that right?

BR: I would see it in two terms. That existing elements in both
political parties would come together, but in a sense that is realign-
ing the political parties and making, over and above the general
political party structure, a force which, as it moves, then moves the
parties. For an example, I think that, negatively, [Barry] Goldwater
is having some of that effect. And, positively, I think the civil rights
movement is forcing things a little more open. Mr. [Strom] Thur-
mond leaving the Democratic Party and going into the Republican Party is another illustration of this kind of thing. It's not only

important that there should be such a political force. The important thing is, what is it dedicated to? And I think it has to be dedicated to full employment. It has to be dedicated to public works. Not public works as in the '30s, where you just give men jobs until the economic situation opens up, because many of these men will never again be employed. It has to be in terms of training. I think, also, we have to redefine what work is now.

An illustration of what I mean is this: I believe that now we must recognize that the work of the young people is to develop their minds and skills for the benefit of society. There is no more sacred work. Therefore, I think that high school and college students who cannot afford it should have not only their books paid for and their tuition paid but, if necessary, get a salary in order to make it possible for them to consider school their work. I think in these ways we're going to have to redefine work. In addition, it means that we are going to have to have some democratic planning in the society, in order to know what to prepare people for as machines take over in various [occupations], and that means some basic reassumptions. One is the assumption that if the private sector of the economy is not capable of keeping people at work with dignity, then the public sector must come in and play a larger role. I think this also means that we must evolve a society of Negroes, and other poor people, to be healthy people. Where the society says to these people, we know you do not have education, we know you cannot get certain types of work, but nevertheless you must be healthy. Therefore, the state sees to it that anyone who cannot afford it has medical care. And here's the strange thing in this whole struggle that the Negroes are now making for justice: I reject the idea of working for justice for Negroes as being impractical, as well as immoral, if one does that alone. One now has to see it as a problem of attempting to deal with the inconsistencies and the wrong assumptions in the entire society.

Warren asks Rustin about efforts to guarantee a higher proportion of jobs to black people: not necessarily quotas, but target figures.

BR: Well, I am in favor of attempting to do everything at this moment for upgrading and finding work for Negroes. But, in the long run, I do not believe that the quota is an answer. Given the attitudes of many people toward Negroes, I think you will get resistance to this. Because a man, regardless of what color he is, if he doesn't have a job he tends to fight to get it before the other fellow. So the answer lies in Negroes and whites, North and South, pulling together around the slogan of full employment, now, for all. Otherwise, I think that we're going to have the kind of thing we have in Newark, New Jersey, where Negroes and whites are fighting over the few jobs that are available. You have 52 percent of the city Negro, and almost three times as many Negroes unemployed, as whites. But the white man who is employed is extremely nervous about any philosophy that tends to suggest that maybe he's dispensable, and he's got enough sense to know that something basic must be done.

RPW: Let me turn to the riots this summer [in Northern cities], which you know a great deal about and I know were deeply involved in, emotionally. Let's take one question: we know these things are socially conditioned; the participants are conditioned by society in a certain way. Where do other responsibilities come in, on the part of police, on the part of the city fathers, on the part of the Negroes of influence?

BR: It's most important to understand the three stages of a riot first. Number one, the rioting was the result of pent-up frustration that grew from the economic conditions, the absence of hope, and the confusion that one finds in ghettoes, the inability to sleep at night in the summer because you sleep in shifts, and the inability to sleep because the trash is not collected at proper hours. Garbage collectors come in the middle of the night. Now there was a second stage, and that is the stage that all criminal elements use. When they see something going on, regardless of what caused it, they move in because they're criminals—black criminals or white criminals—whatever it happens to be. The third stage is the stage where certain political groups, for their own objectives, try to keep the situation stirred up.

Now if one goes back to stage number one, the responsibility on the part of black and white people of goodwill is, as rapidly as possible, to relieve these frustrations by working for jobs, for decent housing, and for quality schools. If one comes to point number two, one is then in a very difficult position in regard to police. They have to maintain some degree of law and order. The problem that I think made a number of people in Harlem angry was the police used force far beyond that which was necessary. Now, I don't think the police did this because they got into a back room and said, "Let's be nasty." I think it is because they are afraid of the ghetto. They are frightened men and they do what all men do when frightened, behave as if the truth were not true. This is the ticklish part. I think what we were trying to get the police to do in New York was to recognize that, until we can deal with these fundamental questions, no matter how well they behave, it is never good enough. If they had set up a board, it could review cases of so-called brutality, and if we had a responsible Negro on that board, that people knew, this would make [police brutality] less possible.

So far as the third stage is concerned, where the political folks come in to make hay—as when the progressive labor people, for their own means, attempted to keep a parade going on Lenox Avenue when they knew there would be problems—that has to be dealt with by the Negro community's intelligent leadership. It was not for the police to put an end to this. It was those of us who went and got people off the streets, who organized the youth to keep them off the streets to make that parade absolutely impossible. They had, finally, thirty people.

RPW: Now, what about the relation between say the—we'll say white riots, like they had in New Hampshire, like the English riots of unoppressed young people—what kind of psychological ground do they have in common, if any, between that and the Harlem, Rochester, Philadelphia riots?

BR: We're talking about two different things that have a common root. I would call the poverty in Harlem physical poverty, which comes from the absence of plenty. There is another form of violence, which comes from the poverty of plenty. At the root of both of these is the same thing: the feeling on the part of young people that they don't belong, they don't know what their place in society is, that somehow they are a subclass which has nowhere to go. And there is a great deal of frustration among white youngsters, even rich ones, children who tear up a house in Long Island and who take dope in Westchester, and it springs from the basic fact that we don't have hope, we don't have a future, we don't know who we are. And I think there is less excuse for their doing that, because in addition to everything that they've got, the Negro also has physical discomfort. But I think it springs mainly from the same thing.

RPW: Let me cut back to the question about the word "responsibility," in quotes, as it has been used in various ways in relation to leadership of the movement.

BR: Well, I feel that the word "responsible" is a bad word because it has moral overtones, and I think we have to make it clear that we disagree with people, tactically and otherwise, but not morally, necessarily, that we are not impugning their morals. So I'd like to use the word "relevant." Is it really workable, is it getting us somewhere? Because a great number of people have quite as much moral commitment and dedication as I have, but I just don't think what they're doing is relevant and meaningful in the situation.

RPW: Birmingham was a violent situation. If it hadn't been violent, no civil rights bill. What do you say about the use of violence?

BR: Who used the violence? That is the question. By and large, Negroes did not resort to violence in Birmingham. Violence was directed toward them. Dr. Martin Luther King insisted [on nonviolence] and the people, by and large, with a few little scattered incidents that didn't amount to much, remained nonviolent. And it was not only that violence was used against the Negro; it was that the Negro, by and large, absorbed that violence. Even after three children were murdered, [Negroes] did not take to the streets and raise hell. They said, "We're still going to be nonviolent." This deeply touched the hearts of the American people. Wherever social change is involved, some violence is inevitable, usually on the part of those who have, rather than those who have not. To the degree that the have-nots can remain nonviolent, they therefore reduce the inevitable violence to its irreducible minimum. To the degree that they retaliate with violence, to that degree do they bring more violence into the situation and thus multiply it. But Gandhi used to say, "Be courageous and accept in a great movement, death, as you would accept your pillow at night, but do not resort to violence yourself." And I think that this is true. There will be injury. The purpose of our movement is to reduce that injury to the least possible.

RPW: Yes, but some people would maintain that the nonviolence succeeds only because there's a threat of violence at the same time, that the nonviolence succeeds because of the threat of a Harlem riot or the threat of a riot in Jackson, Mississippi. It didn't come off but the threat was there. This is a built-in paradox. Does that make any sense to you?

BR: Yes, it does. But I'd like to state it another way. It seems to me that people who speak in this manner see what I call the open violence, but they do not see the covert violence. For example, I think the violence of our society, of keeping people in ghettoes, is a much more extreme form of violence because it touches the entire personality and warps it. It's more than Negroes throwing stones and Molotov cocktails during a so-called Harlem riot. In injustice there is violence, hidden and unseen. What one does in a nonviolent project is to not create violence, but to bring it to the surface so that, like a sore, it can get light and air and be cured. This is, as you say, a part of the—what was the word you used?

RPW: A built-in paradox.

BR: This is a built-in paradox. It's there, and somehow or other what you have to do is get it up to the surface where it can be dealt with. I'll give you one illustration of a simple thing, but it impressed me deeply. Some years ago I was at a university in the Midwest. A girl was supposed to have lunch with me. She was from the Deep South. [Another] woman said, "This dear girl can't do it. To have to sit with you at lunch is going to make her terribly sick."

I said, "I think you ought to encourage her to come."

The girl came, and in the midst of the meal she threw up all over the place and ran out crying. Now, I was accused by some people of creating a violent situation. I feel that nothing is better than if she faced this, and this was a kind of psychological violence I was encouraging. But I am good friends with that girl now. And she's working for the national YWCA. The paradox is there.

I am sure a man who owns a store who is being boycotted feels that people are behaving violently toward him, but it is a fact that until his pocketbook has been touched, he is not made to face the reality of the situation and to become a human being himself. It's a tedious process, and love is not all soft. Love has a very hard side, and that is making people face themselves. If I went into a boycott because I wanted to put the man out of business, then I was not behaving nonviolently. And if a man were put out of business and really changed his mind, I would be the first one to go to the Negro community and say let's take up a collection and put him back in business.

RPW: Let me go back to the time of the demonstration again just for a moment. Back in Nashville, two or three years now, there have been demonstrations with pretty clear-cut targets. And they've been fairly successful. Last spring, there were demonstrations that seemed to have no formidable targets, no formidable objectives. One of the spokesmen, a clergyman, said these demonstrations are not against anything except against being a Negro in America. That seemed to me to indicate that a demonstration with no target is an expression. Now, what do you make of that distinction?

BR: I think this is an excellent distinction and one that I constantly try to make. A demonstration should have an immediately achievable target. Now, when a demonstration is just against being a black man in America, this is not a demonstration to me; it is a gimmick. This is not real. And sooner or later even one's own group will not tolerate this, because they have to have victories in order to stay in the movement. And those victories must be clearly interpreted to them, so that they know, truly, what they have won. There is nothing you can win by going out on a demonstration [just] because you're black.

RPW: I suppose the only asset that can be credited to something like that, if it's possible, is the threat element.

BR: To the degree that there is just a threat element, then I say you're in trouble. And that is one of the reasons I have been in favor of pray-ins. It's one thing for a white person to say, "I will not take communion with Negroes." It is another thing to refuse to take communion when a Negro is [actually] there. The Negro's objective in being there is not to embarrass or to disturb the service but, by his own attitude of simplicity and gentleness, to get people to see that he is a human being like they are.

RPW: You know the line that Dr. Kenneth Clark takes about the whole nonviolent movement.

BR: No, I'm not sure I do.

RPW: Well, I haven't the quotes handy. He says to ask the Negro to love his oppressor is to impose an intolerable psychological burden.

BR: Well, you see I do not use the word "love" very often, although I am, as a Quaker, profoundly impressed with what I think it means. Let me put it this way: to love [Mississippi] Senator [James] Eastland is, essentially, to take from him that which makes love for him impossible—privileged power. Sometimes people have to give it up or have it taken from them, in a situation which they consider to be extremely unpleasant for them, before they can be stripped enough to be real. Jesus was not talking to the whole world when he said, to a particular young man, your problem is money, and until you give it away you will find no peace. Take all thou hast, give it to the poor, and find your humanity again. He was telling him, get rid of power as you have exercised it because it stands in the way of your being a human being. Therefore, to create a political situation where Mr. Eastland's power is limited is to love him, because you are making it possible for him to see himself as a human being. Now, any Negro or any white, no matter what his condition, who is not prepared to do those things which help to make other people human beings is himself not a human being. And, in this sense, love is the cement which holds the bricks of society together. A mother loves her child when she calls him in and scolds him for stealing. She's saving him. He doesn't like it, he feels he'd rather be anywhere than in the kitchen being scolded by her. But she loves him, and she can't let him stay in that condition.

Furthermore, what weapons does a minority group like the Negroes have for winning over other people? Are we going to force nine-tenths of the population to accept us? We have the economic power to make them accept us? We can create enough violence to frighten them to death? No. We have to win them.

RPW: Now, some people would say that there is enough power—not power at gunpoint, but a combination of powers—to actually make the power stick.

BR: I don't believe it. Negroes—one-tenth of the population—have no social, economic, or political power to force anybody to do anything. What the Negro has is the power to behave in such a way that he will, out of his dynamism and his nonviolence, cause the church to move for the civil rights bill, cause the Negro movement to begin to move on economic questions. He will create an alliance of true power, made up of many segments of this society, who will then begin to look at the society.

RPW: Do you mean then, you'd be a catalyst, to use a previous word of yours, which will organize real, practical power in a new constellation, is that it?

BR: Exactly. Negro protests would never have gotten us the civil rights bill. What got us the civil rights bill is labor, and the churches going into the Middle West and certain parts of the upper South, and particularly in the Midwest, where we didn't have Negroes to do it, and putting extreme pressure on these congressmen to do the right thing, to stand up and to break that alliance between Southern Democrats and Northern Republicans, which made cloture possible. We never had the power to do it alone. You cannot get the Negro power to put Negroes back to work. You've got to get all kinds of segments of this society to come out for full employment.

Warren asks Rustin about the contradictory impulses he's observed in some black people who appeal to Washington for help in combating racial discrimination, but who also say "to hell with the white liberal or moderate" in Washington who might be an ally.

BR: I think that this is another one of the sicknesses which spring from intense frustration. But I want to put this in a broader context. When, ten years ago, the 1954 Supreme Court decision came down, Negroes interpreted this, rightly or wrongly, as the beginning of a new era. Many people were writing at the time that this was an across-the-board decision in principle and that things were going to jump. Now, ten years after that, there are actually—and discrimination is not the whole reason for it—but there are literally more Negro children going to segregated classrooms now than before. There are more Negroes out of work. There are more Negroes in slums. Many young Negroes, then, say three things. If things are this bad in '64, there's something wrong with the major leadership; they've taken us down the wrong road. There's something wrong with nonviolence, and therefore let's start really asking how we can get something going [through] violence. And third, there's something wrong with these whites who pretend to be our friends. They haven't made things better in the last ten years. We depended on them.

Now, this is the result of, again, this kind of frustration where people, instead of being analytical, tend to react emotionally to a series of circumstances, and they are frightfully inconsistent. The other aspect of this is that many young Negroes say, "I've been to jail; other Negroes have been to jail." And you become valuable in terms of how many times you have been to jail, or how many times you've prepared to bare your chest. And what I'm trying to say is, not only in the white community but Negroes also are judged wrongly. Have you been to jail? How many times have you been on the picket line? As if that's all. And therefore this attack on the white liberal is in part an attack [that] ought to be directed toward the objective situation, which is a difficult one for everybody.

Warren asks Rustin about the idea that racial discrimination may be easier to defeat in the South than in the North.

BR: This is one of the reasons that I hope that we find some means of keeping a number of Negro [farmers] on the land if we can. The potential voting power of the Negro, disgraced as he is in the South, is conducive to a settlement. I think that if the government is to put people back to work, it is going to have to do infinitely more, economically, for the South. And I am convinced that is more important than anything else. Because what is generally called the racial attitude of the South, I believe, is in large part an economic attitude. When you have as many poor whites and poor Negroes side by side [as in the South], this is a part of the problem. In a situation where, economically, they are both being uplifted, a great deal of this thing we call prejudice is going to disappear. And my experience is that when people in the South finally see the light, they are often infinitely more consistent than a number of people in the North, who never have been through the traumatic experience of change. People who have had to go through a traumatic experience often come out with much more insight, and that is my hope for the South.

Warren asks Rustin to explain his thinking about the identity crisis afflicting some black people.

BR: I think the identity crisis, on the part of a number of Negro writers and thinkers today, has attempted to turn the Negro toward a separate state—nationalism or a return to Africa—or to a rejection of whites. It's calling for the emergence of a Negro expression. Many of them talk about Negroes as being the soul people. And they feel that from this a great new thing is going to spring. I happen to believe that the Negro does have a very peculiar mission, that he is, as it were, the chosen people. By that I do not mean superior, or that he's any better, or that he's any more noble or any more depraved. It means that he has an identity which is a part of the national struggle in this country for the extension of democracy. Like many who are at the bottom of the barrel, if he shakes, the barrel shakes. And I believe that we are chosen—nonviolently—to eradicate from this country the last vestiges of privilege and racism. This is our destiny.

To the degree that a Negro goes into the streets, or into courts, or into restaurants, theaters, hotels, into the legislative halls or marches before them, he will find his true identity. Which is to say that, out of his absence of privilege, he moves beautifully and nonviolently, and in the process brings a great deal of beauty to his country. Therefore, you will not find those who are deeply involved in the struggle concerned with the problem of identity to the degree that you will find those who stand outside the struggle doing nothing about it, debating who they are. A man finds out who he is existentially.

I'd like to give you a few illustrations. For many years, they have been telling us we have an inferior school system in this country. I think it was not until Negroes moved to get quality, integrated education that the whole nation was forced to debate the school question. President Kennedy promised the Negro and white leaders who marched on Washington—when they went in to see him the night of the March for Jobs and Freedom—he promised them he would do something about it. His answer was inadequate but a good start: a war on poverty. This was not because the white poor were moving, but because the Negroes had to move. Therefore, we gave something to the whole nation.

When one considers the situation in Congress, where the Congress seems to be designed so that social legislation is difficult to get, it is the movement of the Negroes trying to get the white to vote which will remove from Congress many reactionary Southerners, who keep all of our grandparents from getting medical care, because they block it. Now, our identity is to put content, total content, into the Declaration of Independence, into the Constitution of the United States, which from the beginning institutionalized slavery. Our destiny is to clarify this and to make a great contribution to all people. That is to say, number one, our destiny is here, not in Africa. It is in cooperating with white people, not separating ourselves from them and thinking we're different. It is in working with them, and being the catalyst for basic social change in this country. And that's what I think our true identity is—struggle—and not a lot of foolishness about culture and the like.

RPW: That leads to another question. This, like all questions in the future, is bound to be an open question, but what do you envisage as the meaning of integration? How do you think of it?

BR: Every individual, regardless of his color, will have both rights and obligations, which are implied in the Constitution. This means that children will go to school together. It means that color will have no place in jobs, that before the law all men are equal. In other words, you do not change attitudes first. Attitudes are gravely shaped by the institutional way of life we live. Therefore, I do not expect every white person in the country to like me, given our history, any more than I cannot have some bitterness, at times, toward

white people. We are both victims of having been trapped for three
hundred years, and it wasn't your grandfather's nor my grandfather's
fault, really. And if it was, what difference does it make? We're here,
now, sitting together. And if I have to deal with you and you are ill-
mannered, I do not have time to look into a psychological history
to find out why. I should deal with the situation the way it is. And
I think the same thing has to be true of our social behavior. And,
therefore, some Negroes will be rejected just because they are not
nice people. What's wrong is when they are rejected *because* they're
Negroes, even if they are nice people.

*Warren asks Rustin about the notion that the civil rights movement
should encourage economic self-improvement and a greater sense of social responsibility among black people.*

BR: I am very unimpressed with this kind of thinking, because
I look at how other groups in our society, who had many of the
characteristics—or were supposed to have had—that the Negroes
are now accused of. Let us take all the ugly things they said about
shanty Irish, all the things they said about the Italians being gang-
ster types and Jews being money crazy, all these things. As I look on
how other minority groups got out of the ghetto and joined American society fully, I discover that there were objective factors there,
and not the notion of self-improvement. Self-improvement follows
those factors. For example, many minority groups got out because
land was free. Others got out in times of economic expansion. Others got out in a time of building of our cities and industrialization.
Others got out as the trade union movement was being built. Others got out because of objective circumstances.

This is the reason I came forth with the economic program I
have outlined to you. I do not mean that we should not teach our

children to be honest and to be moral and not to use dope, and all these things. But the economic self-improvement that's so often talked about is ridiculous. I say the best way for the Negro to really improve himself is to become a part of the struggle. Illustration: in Montgomery, when Dr. King was [leading the bus boycott], crime amongst Negroes fell almost to nothing because they had a sense of dignity.

RPW: Yes, I remember.

BR: Certainly we should live up to all the standards, strive for all the standards of society. This gives me an opportunity to say something about Malcolm X here. Malcolm X and the Muslims claim that they have cured prostitutes and dope addicts, and perhaps they have. I know one fellow who was a dope addict that they cured. What they fail to see is that they do not work to destroy ghettoes. They do not work to get real jobs that are obtainable for people. They do not work to get real education for the Negroes. Their mind is off on Arabic somewhere. So the ghetto gets bigger and conditions get worse. For every prostitute or dope addict that they, by some religious mysticism, bring out of it—and I'm more happy for their doing it—the ghetto itself makes ten more. Therefore I think one must keep one's eyes on removing the objective situation that makes for ghetto life.

RPW: There is a good deal of debate in the Negro leadership about the future of demonstrations, about the kind of demonstrations that are possible in the next phase. What's your line of thought on that?

BR: I have two things to say. We are in a period, now, where the fundamental problems can be solved through assistance from the federal government. We're going to need millions and billions of dollars for tearing down slums, for public works, and putting everybody back to work. That's a political job, and you have to work at it politically. Therefore, we must go into that job more deeply. Secondly, I think that demonstrations must still be called upon because demonstrations have two objectives, not one. A demonstration, first of all, calls attention to an evil and simultaneously pricks the conscience of men. This will have to be done in the future at many levels. The problem is that in public accommodations it was possible to do the first and the second simultaneously, and the second is to cure the evil. You can go in front of a restaurant and demonstrate and prick the conscience, and integrate it, in the same act.

Today in the North, however, where you are attempting to deal with jobs, schools, and housing, you cannot simultaneously prick the conscience and solve it. You have to go to the legislature to solve it because you have to have billions of dollars. Many people don't understand this need. But the demonstration is still valuable for the first aspect.

A third fact about demonstrations is that instead of demonstrations, now, attempting to be fundamentally Negroes parading, we must gear these demonstrations so that more and more of the white dispossessed feel comfortable in them. That is to say, what we should be marching for, the Negro and white together, is saying we will not fight [each other] in the streets over jobs. We know that full employment has to be had. Give us work. We want no more relief. So I think there needs to be something new brought into it.

RPW: What do you take as the gains in Mississippi this summer—the summer [voting registration] campaign?

BR: The major gain of the Mississippi project this summer was that there were a thousand youngsters from all over the North who carried back home an experience that, if translated back home, can be very helpful. Most of these youngsters are going to college campuses where they will interpret to other students on the campus what life really is like in Mississippi: the terror, the dread, the fear on the part of whites and blacks, because everybody is trapped.

Acknowledgments

The authors are grateful to Robert Penn Warren's children, Rosanna Warren and Gabriel Warren, for their support of this book. We are also grateful to Warren's literary executor, Professor John D. Burt, for his help with the project. We wish to thank Mona Frederick, executive director of the Robert Penn Warren Center for the Humanities at Vanderbilt University, who spearheaded the creation of the rich and valuable *Who Speaks for the Negro?* digital archive at Vanderbilt, and who generously shared her expertise. We also thank our editor at The New Press, Marc Favreau, and the stellar crew that makes up TNP.

Selected Bibliography

Als, Hilton. "The Enemy Within: The Making and Unmaking of James Baldwin." *New Yorker,* February 16, 1998.

_____. "On the Mountain: The Complicated Legacy of James Baldwin." *New Yorker,* April 28, 2014.

Angelou, Maya. "James Baldwin: His Voice Remembered; A Brother's Love." *New York Times,* December 20, 1987.

Arsenault, Raymond. *Freedom Riders: 1961 and the Struggle for Racial Justice.* New York: Oxford University Press, 2006.

Baldwin, James. *The Fire Next Time.* New York: Vintage International, 1993 (1963).

_____. "The Art of Fiction No. 78." Interview by Jordan Elgrably. *Paris Review,* no. 91 (Spring 1984). https://www.theparisreview.org/interviews/2994/james-baldwin-the-art-of-fiction-no-78-james-baldwin.

Blight, David W. Introduction to *Who Speaks for the Negro?* by Robert Penn Warren, revised edition. New Haven: Yale University Press, 2014.

Botsch, Carol Sears. "Septima Poinsette Clark." Last modified August 3, 2000. http://polisci.usca.edu/aasc/Clark.htm.

Branch, Taylor. *Parting the Waters: America in the King Years, 1954–63.* New York: Simon & Schuster, 1988.

——. *Pillar of Fire: America in the King Years, 1963–65.* New York: Simon & Schuster, 1998.

Carson, Clayborne. *In Struggle: SNCC and the Black Awakening of the 1960s.* Cambridge, MA: Harvard University Press, 1981.

Clark, Kenneth B., and Marnie Phipps Clark. "The Development of Consciousness of Self in Negro Preschool Children," *Journal of Experimental Education,* 1938.

Clark, Kenneth B. "Deconstructing Brown." *New York Times,* May 18, 1982.

——. Interview conducted by Blackside, Inc., on November 4, 1985, for *Eyes on the Prize: America's Civil Rights Years (1954-1965).* Washington University Libraries, Film and Media Archive, Henry Hampton Collection. http://repository.wustl.edu/concern/videos/v405sc20j.

—— and Michael Meyers. "Separate Is Never Equal." *New York Times,* April 1, 1995.

Cleaver, Eldridge. *Soul on Ice.* New York: Random House, 1968.

Coates, Ta-Nehisi. "The Legacy of Malcolm X: Why His Vision Lives on in Barack Obama." *Atlantic,* May 2011.

Cole, Teju. "Black Body: Rereading James Baldwin's 'Stranger in the Village.' " *New Yorker,* August 19, 2014.

Daniels, Lee A. "James Baldwin, Eloquent Writer in Behalf of Civil Rights, Is Dead." *New York Times,* December 2, 1987.

Davis, David A. "Climbing out of 'The Briar Patch': Robert Penn

Warren and the Divided Conscience of Segregation." *Southern Quarterly*, no. 40.1 (Fall 2001).

Dittmer, John. *Local People: The Struggle for Civil Rights in Mississippi*. Champaign, IL: University of Illinois Press, 1995.

Dreier, Peter. "A Totally Moral Man: The Life of Nonviolent Organizer Rev. James Lawson." *Truthout*, August 15, 2012. https://truthout.org/articles/a-totally-moral-man-the-life-of-nonviolent-organizer-rev-james-lawson.

Du Bois, W.E.B. *The Souls of Black Folk*. Dover Thrift Edition, 1994 (1903).

Ellison, Ralph. *Invisible Man*. New York: Random House, 1980 (1952).

_____. "The Art of Fiction No. 8." Interview by Alfred Chester and Vilma Howard. *Paris Review*, no. 8 (Spring 1955). https://www.theparisreview.org/interviews/5053/ralph-ellison-the-art-of-fiction-no-8-ralph-ellison.

Emery, Theo. "Activist Ousted from Vanderbilt Is Back, as a Teacher." *New York Times*, October 4, 2006.

Erskine, Albert. Letter to Robert Penn Warren, July 26, 1965. https://whospeaks.library.vanderbilt.edu/media/erskine-rpw-letter-72765.

Garrow, David J. *Bearing the Cross: Martin Luther King Jr. and the Southern Christian Leadership Conference*. New York: William Morrow, 1986.

Greif, Mark. "Black and White Life." *London Review of Books*, November 1, 2007.

Haley, Alex. Interview conducted by Blackside, Inc., on October 24, 1988, for *Eyes on the Prize II: America at the Racial Crossroads 1965 to 1985*. Washington University Libraries, Film and Media Archive, Henry Hampton Collection. http://digital.wustl.edu/cgi/t/text/text-idx?c=eop;cc=eop;rgn=main;view=text;idno=hal5427.0088.062.

Harvey, Clarie Collins. Interview by John Dittmer and John Jones for the Mississippi Department of Archives and History. April 21, 1981.

Hayden, Tom. "Bob Moses." *Nation*, July 21, 2003.

Hentoff, Nat. "The Integrationist." *New Yorker*, August 23, 1982.

Honey, Michael K. *Going Down Jericho Road: The Memphis Strike, Martin Luther King's Last Campaign.* New York: Norton, 2007.

Krebs, Alben. "Roy Wilkins, 50-Year Veteran of Civil Rights Fight, Is Dead." *New York Times,* September 9, 1981.

Kreyling, Michael. *The South That Wasn't There: Postsouthern Memory and History.* Baton Rouge: Louisiana State University Press, 2010.

Lawson, James. Interview conducted by Blackside, Inc., on December 2, 1985, for *Eyes on the Prize: America's Civil Rights Years (1954–1965).* Washington University Libraries, Film and Media Archive, Henry Hampton Collection. http://repository.wustl.edu/concern/videos/mp48sf472.

Marable, Manning. *Malcolm X: A Life of Reinvention.* New York: Viking, 2011.

Meier, August. "The Question Is not Answered." *Dissent* (Autumn, 1965).

Morrison, Toni. "James Baldwin: His Voice Remembered; Life in His Language." *New York Times,* December 20, 1987.

Murray, Albert. "Who Speaks for the Negro?" *New Leader*, June 21, 1965.

Olson, Lynn. *Freedom's Daughters: The Unsung Heroines of the Civil Rights Movement from 1830 to 1970.* New York: Simon & Schuster, 2001.

Payne, Charles. *I've Got the Light of Freedom: The Organizing*

Tradition and the Mississippi Freedom Struggle. Berkeley: University of California Press, 1995.

Perot, Ruth Turner. Conference Proceedings, Robert Penn Warren Center for the Humanities at Vanderbilt University. 2016.

Pierpont, Claudia Roth. "Another Country: James Baldwin's Flight from America," *New Yorker*, February 9, 2009.

Pinckney, Darryl. "On James Baldwin." *New York Review of Books*, April 4, 2013.

Ralph, James R., Jr. "Roy Wilkins: The Quiet Revolutionary and the NAACP." *The Historian*, Summer 2016.

Remnick, David. "Visible Man." *New Yorker*, March 14, 1994.

_____. "This American Life: The Making and Remaking of Malcolm X." *New Yorker*, April 25, 2011.

Severo, Richard. "Kenneth Clark, Who Helped End Segregation, Dies." *New York Times*, May 2, 2005.

Sewell, George A., and Margaret L. Dwight. "Clarie Collins Harvey: Mortuary Entrepreneur," in *Mississippi Black History Makers*. Jackson: University Press of Mississippi, 2012.

Styron, William. "James Baldwin: His Voice Remembered; Jimmy in the House," *New York Times*, December 20, 1987.

Walker, Wyatt Tee. Interview conducted by Blackside, Inc., on October 11, 1985, for *Eyes on the Prize: America's Civil Rights Years (1954–1965)*. Washington University Libraries, Film and Media Archive, Henry Hampton Collection. http://repository.wustl.edu/concern/videos/ht24wm403.

Warren, Robert Penn. "Briar Pitch," in *I'll Take My Stand: The South and the Agrarian Tradition*. New York: Peter Smith, 1951.

———. *Segregation: The Inner Conflict in the South*. New York: Random House, 1956.

———. "The Negro Now." *Look*, March 23, 1965.

————. *Who Speaks for the Negro?* New York: Random House, 1965.

————. *Who Speaks for the Negro?* Revised edition. New Haven: Yale University Press, 2014.

Young, Andrew. Interview conducted by Blackside, Inc., on October 11, 1985, for *Eyes on the Prize: America's Civil Rights Years (1954–1965)*. Washington University Libraries, Film and Media Archive, Henry Hampton Colection. http://repository.wustl.edu /concern/videos/sf268667q.

————. *An Easy Burden: The Civil Rights Movement and the Transformation of America*. New York: HarperCollins, 1996.

Young, Whitney M., Jr. Interview by Tom Buckley. *New York Times,* September 20, 1970.

About the Editors

Stephen Drury Smith is the executive editor and host of APM Reports®, the acclaimed documentary unit of American Public Media. He is a co-editor (with Catherine Ellis) of *Say It Plain: A Century of Great African American Speeches* and *Say It Loud: Great Speeches on Civil Rights and African American Identity* and (with Mary Marshall Clark, Peter Bearman, and Catherine Ellis) of *After the Fall: New Yorkers Remember September 2001 and the Years That Followed*, all published by The New Press. He lives in St. Paul, Minnesota.

Catherine Ellis is a broadcast and podcast journalist, and the founder of Audio Memoir. She is a co-editor of *Say It Plain: A Century of Great African American Speeches*, *Say It Loud: Great Speeches on Civil Rights and African American Identity*, and *After the Fall: New Yorkers Remember September 2001 and the Years That Followed*, all published by The New Press. Ellis holds a PhD in anthropology from Columbia University, where her dissertation compared the way whites and African Americans in Louisiana remember the Jim Crow era. She lives in Boston, Massachusetts.

Publishing in the Public Interest

Thank you for reading this book published by The New Press. The New Press is a nonprofit, public interest publisher. New Press books and authors play a crucial role in sparking conversations about the key political and social issues of our day.

We hope you enjoyed this book and that you will stay in touch with The New Press. Here are a few ways to stay up to date with our books, events, and the issues we cover:

- Sign up at www.thenewpress.com/subscribe to receive updates on New Press authors and issues and to be notified about local events
- Like us on Facebook: www.facebook.com/newpressbooks
- Follow us on Twitter: www.twitter.com/thenewpress

Please consider buying New Press books for yourself; for friends and family; or to donate to schools, libraries, community centers, prison libraries, and other organizations involved with the issues our authors write about.

The New Press is a 501(c)(3) nonprofit organization. You can also support our work with a tax-deductible gift by visiting www.thenewpress.com/donate.